Fork It Over

Fork It Over

The Intrepid Adventures of a Professional Eater

ALAN RICHMAN

HarperCollins*Publishers*

HarperCollins books may be purchased for educational, business, or sales promotional use. For information, please write: Special Markets Department, HarperCollins Publishers Inc., 10 East 53rd Street, New York, NY 10022.

The majority of these selections appeared, in slightly altered form, in GQ.

FIRST EDITION

Designed by Laura Lindgren

Printed on acid-free paper

Library of Congress Cataloging-in-Publication Data is available upon request.

ISBN 0-06-058629-X

04 05 06 07 08 ❖/RRD 10 9 8 7 6 5 4 3 2 1

For my wife, Lettie Teague,
and the man we both loved, Art Cooper

Contents

Fork It Over

AMUSE-BOUCHE

THE EATING LIFE

I am a restaurant critic. I eat for a living.

Chefs complain about people like me. They argue that we are not qualified to do our jobs because we do not know how to cook. I tell them I'm not entirely pleased with the way they do their jobs, either, because they do not know how to eat. I have visited most of the best restaurants of the world, and they have not. I believe I know how to eat as well as any man alive.

I dine out constantly, but there is a great deal I do in restaurants that people who eat purely for pleasure would not consider part of a normal meal. You would not enjoy having dinner with me.

I lie—make a reservation under a false name. I steal—the menu, not the silverware. I wander. I am always getting up from my table in order to check out my surroundings. I drift around, and the meandering invariably ends when a well-meaning captain taps me on the shoulder and points me in the direction of the men's room, wrongly assuming that is where I wish to go. I rarely talk to the people dining with me, but I love to chat with waiters and busboys. They know the secrets lurking behind the swinging kitchen doors.

Friends who accompany me to meals are bored by the absence of conversation. They are unhappy with the dishes I choose for them— they have their hearts set on a lovely salad of poached Maine lobster and become cranky when I tell them they must sample the seared calf's brain. The warm mandarin soufflé they've been anticipating all evening is finally set before them, and I stick my spoon in it before they have a taste.

Yet everybody envies what I do. They think it's the gastronomic counterpart of test-driving Mercedes sports coupes or helping Las Vegas chorus girls dress. They believe it involves little more than eating unceasingly and being reimbursed for the privilege. There's some truth to that, but sometimes I am obligated to eat three full meals a day, day after day, which is not always easy, even on an expense account. I generally receive little sympathy when I make that point.

A critic has to understand when food is correct, which is to be admired, and when it is inspired, which we would call a miracle. The job is part analysis (Is this good?), part self-analysis (It's good, but am I the only person who likes it?), and part gluttony (Have I tried everything on the menu?).

I've never been a victim of culinary fatigue, because I can reverse direction and concentrate on the humble whenever I weary of the haute. A natural-casing hot dog off the grill can be as thrilling as Charlie Trotter's terrine of asparagus with goat cheese, beet juice, and hundred-year-old balsamic vinegar.

I often make that point when it's my turn to pay.

I knew I had found my calling one day in the mid-fifties when I was having lunch with my mother at the Chuckwagon, in our little Philadelphia suburb of Elkins Park. She told me I should have the pastrami instead of corned beef.

My streak was over. For years, my standard lunch had been hot corned beef on seeded rye with a cream soda. This was before animal fats were considered fattening. (The milkman usually dropped off "extra rich" milk at our house.) I so liked corned beef that I hadn't come up with a compelling reason to gamble on anything else. I considered myself set for life.

I expected nothing to come of this unsolicited pastrami sandwich, but the first bite was so profound I recall the moment the way others would remember a first date—years away in my case. I see myself at one of the Chuckwagon's lacquered tables, my mother seated to my left and intensely alert. She was like a mother robin watching her young swallowing worms. All was still. When I tasted the fatty-smoky-tender meatiness, I realized that I would never again have to accept the mundane.

All else was forgotten, even the unobtainable Olivia Biggs, a pigtailed skinny blonde I worshiped, aware that she accepted me as an occasional partner at Friday-night dances only because I came with a Pez dispenser and shamelessly doled out all the candy she desired.

The pastrami taught me to understand life's infinite possibilities. Eating was no longer a mildly pleasurable undertaking that peaked with a five-cent box of nonpareils or a six-cent cherry Coke. Although I would not embrace eating as a profession for decades (and never touched Olivia Biggs), I sensed that food offered delights that could not be equaled, not even by the attractions found in the pages of the *Playboy* magazines I accidentally flipped open while perusing comic books at the drugstore.

Despite its seminal gastronomic importance in my life, I was never that enchanted by the Chuckwagon, only by the pastrami. My first meaningful restaurant experience occurred a few months later, on a family trip across the country. As we drove through downtown Chicago, my father pointed to a sign and said, "We'll eat there."

I remember the lure, a steak dinner for $1.09, spelled out in neon. The restaurant was Tad's, the brand-new flagship of a future national chain. There I learned that dining out represented an entirely different experience from dinner at home. My mother's consistently excellent recipes offered whatever a guest at her table might desire, except for the unexpected. She could cook, but she could not surprise.

I had eaten full-course dinners in restaurants before, but my parents tended to take my sister and me to places that mimicked my mother's cooking, whereas Tad's offered mysterious forms of nourishment—fatty steaks reeking with charred goodness, baked potatoes as big as footballs, an unhealthy breadstuff of indescribable appeal. We were there because it was inexpensive and, I'm sure, because we had come to stockyards territory and my parents believed my sister and I would benefit from sampling the local bounty. They practiced straight-forward parenting and intended to teach us that the beef in Chicago was tops because there was so much of it around. (For a similar reason, my mother joined the Catholics in broiling fish on Friday nights.)

Tad's had a cafeteria line, the better to save on tips. The steak was thin and tough, but it had a quality I can best describe as not-my-mother's-cooking, the flavor of an open fire in an untamed land. It was black and gritty and delicious, the piquancy of an unfamiliar culture. I believe I shivered at the unfamiliarity of Tad's greasy sirloin—the basic steak that was the centerpiece of the $1.09 special. My family didn't do upgrades.

I subsequently learned that the charcoal fire wasn't real. It was made with tiles painted to resemble glowing embers, a breakthrough by the Tad's scientific staff. I couldn't have been more convinced it was charcoal had I carried in the Kingsford myself. The overly thick slice of bread, painted with an oily product and laid grease-side down on the grill, provided a mouthwatering succulence I would later find duplicated only in seared foie gras. Finally, there was the potato. Such tubers were unavailable at the A&P where I often shopped with my mother. The potatoes we ate at home were tiny and immaterial, but the Tad's spud was buttery and vaguely nutty, a combination I don't recall encountering again, even on one of my infrequent visits to Idaho. We carried our trays to a back room done up in some sort of bawdy red velveteen that I figured had to cost a million dollars. I felt like Marshal Matt Dillon, sitting loose and ready in the Long Branch Saloon, waiting for Miss Kitty to sashay in.

Years passed, but my taste in food remained the same. When it came time for college, I stayed close to home, attending the University of Pennsylvania, where I traded in my mother's healthful cooking for Pop's, a one-man campus dump owned and operated by a gnomish reprobate with black fingernails, a fat cigar stub in his mouth, and a filthy meat-slicing machine. His fifty-cent, five-inch-thick delicatessen sandwiches were so savory I frequently cut chemistry lab to get to the front of the line, which might have led to my taking an incomplete in the course. When I wasn't at Pop's, I'd generally dine on broasted chicken, a newly invented method of poultry cooking that combined, as the name implies, broiling and roasting. The chicken pieces that emerged from the broaster were simultaneously crunchy and soggy.

Philadelphia in the sixties was still a decade away from the dining revolution that would make it, all too briefly, the most creative restaurant city in America. The only remaining reliable food was the renowned cheese steak, best when consumed at three A.M. Cheese steaks possess minimal nutritional value, but they are useful as a remedy for hangovers, particularly those that blossom following a long night quaffing Philadelphia's very own Schmidt's beer.

College was followed, as was relatively routine in the pre-protest sixties, by the army. I realize that the youth of today view time in the military and time in a penitentiary as essentially the same experience, but the only aspect of the military I found as dreadful as commonly believed was mess-hall food. I also learned, during my overseas assignments, that the excellence of a country's cuisine tends to vary in inverse proportion to the number of uniformed men stationed there. In other words, I did not eat excellently in either of the countries I invaded, the Dominican Republic and, later, Vietnam.

I committed, to my knowledge, only one war crime. That occurred near San Isidro Airfield, outside Santo Domingo. I was a willing participant in the theft, slaughter, and roasting of a goat that had strayed from its home. Several of us, crazed from months of military rations, constructed a great pyre and blistered the innocent beast. We did not escape justice, because all of us who consumed the meat became deathly sick. Even today, when I am in a restaurant and the waiter proudly announces that the special is goat, I am visited by queasy flashbacks to the bonfire of shame in the field behind the macadam-paved strip where the Dominican Republic Air Force parked its World War II–era P-51 Mustangs.

I ate badly in Vietnam, too, although I did gain considerable weight from the huge bowls of strawberry ice cream I'd plunder from the mess hall every afternoon. It was so hot the ice cream boiled in the bowl as it passed from a solid to a gaseous state without ever becoming a liquid, a phenomenon I was able to identify as sublimation from my ineffectual tenure as a chemistry major.

I had come home from Vietnam and was working on the *Philadelphia Evening Bulletin* when a colleague taught me an invaluable lesson: how to lunch in style. She was Leslie Bennetts, then a feature writer for the paper and now a contributing editor to *Vanity Fair*. When I was leaving to take a job as the sports columnist for the *Montreal Star,* Leslie invited me to a good-bye lunch, a gesture of generosity she appeared to regret when I recently reminded her of it. I phoned to tell her the meal had meant a great deal to me, and she replied, "I treated you to lunch? Why did I do that? Are you sure this is true?" Then she laughed, rather unkindly.

She went on to explain how little she liked me in those years, because I was alleged to have referred to her as stuck-up when she arrived in Philadelphia from New York. It was probably true, because we Philadelphians assumed all New Yorkers were that way. Leslie seemed to confirm this assessment when she said, "Certainly I was more sophisticated than you. I came from New York and went out with older men."

I recall the restaurant as small and extremely French. I ordered chicken tarragon, new to me. I drank white wine with it, and though this wasn't my first drink, I'd never sipped wine in broad daylight sitting alongside a tall blonde of overweening New York sophistication. I perspired heavily throughout the meal, but that might have had less to do with Leslie's attractiveness than with the all-rayon shirt under my all-polyester blazer, a Stanley Blacker double-knit in chocolate brown with gold buttons.

Leslie, who claimed to have remembered nothing about our lunch, added, unnecessarily, "I never let men pay for me, but I don't know why I would have paid for you." She said what she remembered of my dining habits is that occasionally my mother would stop by the *Bulletin* offices to drop off brown-bag lunches. "And one rainy day," she cruelly noted, "she brought galoshes in for you."

. . .

I didn't become a full-time restaurant critic until the start of the nineties. I dabbled in reviewing before then, treating it more like a hobby than a calling. While I was a sportswriter in Boston, the *Globe* sent me off to find the best Peking duck in the city, and I managed to turn that into a sideline lasting nearly a year. While I was the sports columnist for the *Montreal Star*, I was made the co-restaurant critic under a pseudonym. That part-time position provided me with dinners for more than a year. My motivation for doing both assignments was simple: the glorious prospect of free food. I was paid hardly anything extra, which is where I got the idea that I couldn't actually make a living being a restaurant critic. Critics got fat, I thought, but they didn't get rich.

I was hired by *Gentlemen's Quarterly* in 1989 to do profiles, but I still dabbled in comestibles. I was writing a monthly wine column for *GQ* when the editor-in-chief, Art Cooper, asked me if I wouldn't mind turning it into a food column. That was my big break: becoming a food writer who was paid like a profile writer. I had the best job in the entire field of criticism: restaurant reviewer. With all due respect to art, film, and theater critics, I've always believed their work was less fundamental than mine. Food is life. The rest is parsley.

I was well-prepared for the job. I'd eaten my way through all the important American food trends. The majority of them occurred from 1975 into the early nineties, exactly when I was traveling around the country the most. I got to forty-four states, a pretty extensive overview. I even ate at the Safari Grill in Manhattan, where the cooks wore pith helmets. I didn't miss a lot.

Much that I've experienced has come and gone, but a few trends have gripped our culture and cannot be shaken loose—Perrier water, domestic goat cheese, comfort food, celebrity chefs, free-range chicken, farm-raised game, baby vegetables, microbreweries, recitations of specials, vertical presentations, tapas, raw fish, olive oil, arugula, cilantro, white truffles, molten chocolate cakes, reconfirming reservations, wild greens, power breakfasts, *menus dégustations*, fresh ground pepper, sun-dried tomatoes, and undercooking. I remember telling Fabio Picchi, chef-owner of Cibrèo in Florence, that Americans were demanding their food barely warmed, and he replied, "Yes, I know this problem."

Not all food trends stuck. Basically gone are oat-bran bagels, edible flowers, white eggplant, mesquite grilling, cold pasta (or maybe that's just wishful thinking on my part), dry beer, blue-corn chips, cuttlefish ink, wine coolers, blackened fish, mung beans, and nouvelle cuisine. Southwestern cuisine has almost disappeared (except in the Southwest), whereas French bistros come and go.

Great chefs do not. To me, the most consequential chef working in an American kitchen in the past quarter-century was not James Beard, André Soltner, Alice Waters, Wolfgang Puck, Charlie Trotter, Daniel Boulud, Jean-Georges Vongerichten, David Bouley, Nobu Matsuhisa, or even the late Jean-Louis Palladin, who prepared classic French food in this country better than anybody else. (Julia Child was certainly monumental, but she wasn't a chef.) Rather, I favor the late Gilbert Le Coze, whom I met in the eighties, when he and his sister, Maguy, opened their French seafood restaurant Le Bernardin in New York. Much of what we know about serving fish in fine restaurants we learned from Le Coze. Had he not arrived, we might still be eating frozen scrod.

Le Coze loved working in America, except for one peculiarity. He would stand by the front door of his restaurant, immaculate in chef's whites, greeting customers as they arrived, and they would respond to his welcome by asking, "Where's the bathroom?" It drove him to distraction. He could not understand why Americans needed to go to the bathroom the moment they arrived at a restaurant, because the French were taught as children to go before they went out.

The fish at a dazzling restaurant like Le Bernardin was irreproachable, but I remember being just as excited by the seafood at Margaret Tayar, little more than a ruin of a bar located behind a beachfront parking lot in Tel Aviv. The experiences I've had eating unlikely food in distant spots are among my most vivid memories.

Margaret Tayar, the owner, made a fish burger so profound I cannot help but banish those made with beef to afterthoughts. It was prepared from *loup de mer* and grilled very rare. She told me all her fish was caught by a man of about seventy who had fished since he was ten but had not learned to swim. Six times he had fallen into the sea and six times the sea had carried him ashore, but ultimately, he told her, it would not.

In the Republic of Djibouti, an African country so hot that food practically cooks itself, I ate a memorable lunch at the commando training center for French Foreign Legion troops. The meal began with a seven-pound lobster harvested by a Schwarzenegger-sized soldier with a terrible scar on his left arm that looked as though it had been inflicted in close combat. He swore it was a burn scar from when he was eighteen months old. Five of us ate the lobster cold, in chunks, dipped in mayonnaise from a jar. The entree was a spicy, gorgeously rich veal stew with tiny macaroni prepared by a native Djiboutian cook who wore a souvenir Philadelphia T-shirt. On that visit, I learned how to construct a homemade mine out of plastique and a dinner plate, making me potentially the most deadly food writer of all time.

I don't cook, but I never cease thinking about kitchens. To me the home kitchen is a place of sweetness and sentiment, of a mother's apron scented with onions and powdered with flour. The restaurant kitchen is even more magical. There stands the great chef, wearing his dress whites, as majestic as a naval commander on the quarterdeck of his ship-of-war. As much as I admire kitchens, I spend as little time as possible in them. I have been known to stand in front of my microwave, reheating coffee, wondering why it takes so long.

Once, and only once, have I triumphed in the kitchen. I cooked dinner for Claudette Colbert, Academy Award winner for Best Actress in 1935. I haven't done much in my life a lot better than that.

She was in her eighties. I was in my forties. I had been sent by a magazine to Perth, Australia, to interview her while she was appearing in a play with Rex Harrison. Colbert did not invite him to dine with us, and I got the impression that however charming Harrison appeared onstage, he was not so appealing after hours.

Colbert was staying in a hotel suite, and her maid (and cook) was in an adjoining suite equipped with a small kitchen. Each morning Colbert went shopping for groceries, usually fish and vegetables, the two items I prepare the most inadequately when I am forced by circumstances to make food. As we were leaving the market one day, she smiled in her mischievous way—if you've seen her films, you know that look—and announced I would be manning the stove that night. I really dislike standing in front of stoves. I find them uncomfortably hot.

Her maid, thank goodness, had cookbooks, and she watched skeptically as I desperately scoured them, seeking a recipe easy enough for the likes of me. Luckily, I came upon *bonne femme*, whose literal translation is "good wife" but means "in a simple manner." I believe the recipe included mushrooms, wine, and butter, three unintimidating ingredients. We sat side by side in her suite and ate my fish, and she kept telling me how delicious the food was, even if it was not.

I'll say this about early-twentieth-century movie stars: they sure understood men.

After eating about fifty thousand hot breakfasts, lunches, and dinners (my mother never served a cold meal at home), I stand firm on certain issues. I believe boiled lobster is a great mistake. Remember, I'm from Philadelphia, home of the broiled lobster. It is my belief that boiling is an inferior technique popularized by New England seafood shanties too lazy to cook lobster the correct way.

I believe in American beef, but I'm convinced French chefs cook steak better than Americans. I am certain the finest food book is *Larousse Gastronomique*, an encyclopedia of (mostly) French food that I skim on quiet nights, the way some men peruse baseball record books. I think side dishes are the most overlooked aspect of cuisine, and the most skilled practitioner of that art is Vongerichten, whose chickpea fries and beet tartare should be celebrated as his signature side dishes. I am thankful for muffins, because their acceptance has made it permissible for us to eat cake for breakfast.

I have also never been able to resist the classics. When Eric Ripert, the current owner and chef of Le Bernardin, prepared sole almondine using fish from Brittany and fresh almonds, I declared it one of his greatest triumphs and announced that the item had to go on his menu. He replied, "You're crazy if you think I will put a dish two hundred years old on my menu and go out of business."

I love the hopelessly outdated dessert cart at Le Bec-Fin in Philadelphia. Georges Perrier's pastries include buttercream *dacquoise*, opera cake, and even a slice of all-but-forgotten *marjolaine*, an ancient cream cake. I cannot resist cheese steaks, regardless of how little I respect them, because all Philadelphians are drawn to them. I don't admire Sunday buffets; the steamship round of beef is invariably tough. I don't enjoy eating outdoors, although folks in Manhattan make a habit of it, inhaling the bracing scent of buses passing by. I despise menus with heart symbols alongside the low-fat items, which only goes to remind me that the food I've ordered amounts to suicide. I refuse to dine out more than once with anybody who orders a Cognac when the rest of us are finished and ready to go home. I miss tableside preparations, even though they were typically done by captains who couldn't cook.

I also have a dream menu. My perfect meal would start with an assortment of *amuse-gueules* from the French Laundry in Napa Valley, supplemented by lobster-and-black-truffle beggar's purses from March in Manhattan. The first course would be *carne cruda* (raw chopped veal) with white truffles from Trattoria della Posta in Monforte d'Alba, and if truffles weren't in season, I'd happily switch to the red-curry steak tartare from Lumiere in West Newton, outside Boston.

Then soup—I have stronger feelings about soup than the average man. No soup surpasses the artichoke puree with black truffles and Parmigiano Reggiano from Guy Savoy in Paris, but I equally love the steamed pork-and-crab soup buns topped with fresh ginger and black vinegar sauce from Shanghai Tide in Queens.

I'd slip in something Tuscan about now. First the ricotta-and-potato flan with ragu from Cibrèo, followed by tagliatelle made from chestnut flour and topped with fresh ricotta cheese and toasted pine nuts from

Da Delfina in Artimino, outside Florence. My fish course would be rum-and-pepper-painted grouper from Norman's in Coral Gables, Florida. I'd also want a shrimp-and-roasted-garlic tamale from Mesa Grill in New York. I'm a little ashamed to admit that this is my favorite Mexican dish, because it almost certainly isn't authentically Mexican.

If some kindly wine collector would supply a 1978 Bruno Giacosa Santa Stefano Riserva Barbaresco, the meat course would be a buffalo filet with porcini mushrooms from the Four Seasons restaurant in New York. You can't count on those wine collectors, though, so I'll happily accept the cured, poached, braised, and glazed pork breast from Restaurant Daniel in Manhattan. It is so soft and savory I think of it as Kobe pork.

The cheese: Vacherin, perfectly ripe, or Epoisses, almost over the hill. The wines: white and red Burgundies from the list at restaurant Montrachet in Manhattan, even though I can't afford any bottle labeled Le Montrachet.

For dessert I'd have Pavlova the way it's done at JoJo in New York: soft meringue, passion fruit sorbet, whipped cream, and passion fruit seeds. The Pavlova is light, though, and I might also require a small crème brûlée, most profoundly prepared at Manhattan's Le Cirque 2000.

I want to have this fantasy meal at Le Cirque, at my favorite table. It's down the corridor from the entrance, halfway to the bar, up a few steps, out of the way. From there I can see everybody and everything without being noticed. I'm certain I'm the only patron who would consider this an ideal table, but, after all, I am a restaurant critic.

— *Alan Richman*
June 2004

APPETIZERS

A MOTHER'S KNISHES

When my mother was a younger woman, scarcely into her eighties, she required surgery. The procedure did not go well, which surprised me, because she is so resilient I'd expected her to check into the hospital before dawn and be out in time for an Early Bird.

I immediately flew to southern Florida, both to comfort her and to take my father out for a meal. The nurses on her floor had alerted me that he wasn't eating, which they blamed on anxiety. I had a different interpretation. Anybody who had dined at my mother's table for nearly a half-century would find it depressing to eat at anybody else's.

My mother rallied long enough to brief me on the contents of her freezer, should we wish to stop home for a bite, and my father and I left for lunch. We drove to Sam's, in the nearby town of Margate, an informal kosher spot he would grudgingly patronize on the occasions when my mother refused to cook. That occurred rarely, and only after she decided she was being exploited because the other Jewish women in her building had negotiated freedom from the culinary arts as part of their retirement packages. Within twenty-four hours, my mother would be back at the stove, drawn like a blintz to sour cream.

My father tolerated Sam's because the food seemed Jewish and a complete lunch went for $5.99. Since nothing was going to rival what he got at home, he thought it wasteful to allow the price of a restaurant meal to creep into double figures.

I made him finish everything, from the chicken soup to the noodle pudding. We lingered, never imagining that we were needed back at the hospital. Minutes after our departure, the surgeon who had performed the first operation on my mother decided she needed a second one without delay.

He ordered her strapped to a gurney, then stood by, awaiting my father's signature on a release form. As we walked through the front door, an alert guard spotted us and rushed us upstairs. Immediately, orderlies started pushing my mother through the hallway with me half-walking and half-running by her side. A sense of peril overwhelmed me. I was certain this was the last time I would see her alive.

As they turned to enter a waiting elevator, my mother grabbed my arm and weakly spoke my name. I nearly burst out sobbing, for I knew these would be the last words I would hear from her.

I leaned close.

"How was the soup?" she asked.

My mother is ninety-four and doing all right, although not as well as my sister and I would like. Ida and Norman still live in their Florida retirement community, which permits no dogs, no kids, and no striplings under fifty-five. I talk a lot with my sister, Lynn, about how long they can hold out. They have help, women who are hired to work twelve hours a day but who stay overnight on the difficult days, when the anguish of being elderly becomes an impossible burden. The women who watch after them were not born in this country and are candidates for beatification, which should clarify my position on this nation's immigration policy.

Pretty much to the exclusion of all else, my mother spent her adult life cooking for her family. (To be honest, she cleaned incessantly, too.) I understand that all Jewish mothers are expected to be kitchen enthusiasts, but my mother was defined by her cooking. She was admired for those skills, and even today, when she can't do much, the people in her building greet her warmly, the sort of recognition André Soltner must get when he walks down Fiftieth Street near Lutèce. Indra Chattoo, who has commanded the team overseeing my parents for the past three years, says my mother remains a luminary among residents, acclaimed for her brisket of beef and her rolled cabbage. Chattoo told me, "The people remember the taste of her food, and they still talk about it."

Cooking gave my mother stature in the world outside her kitchen. Long before the advent of celebrity chefs, she was the celebrity cook of our neighborhood, no matter where we lived. Her cooking was ritualistic, because she would prepare the same recipes over and over, but she was no different from the conductors of symphony orchestras, who have personal repertoires.

Food was her means of expressing love. Some might argue that a few hugs would have been more beneficial to a growing child, but I tried to understand. She wasn't tremendously confident, and bestowing food was a wonderful way of making a fuss without chancing rejection. Even people who don't want to be squeezed enjoy being fed.

I try to cook exactly as my mother did, even though she stubbornly resisted my efforts to learn from her. Her rolled cabbage stuffed with rice and ground beef, which she would not teach me to make, was the finest the world has known. Its secret is lost. By hanging around I picked up enough about her cheese blintzes and her brisket that I now do a credible job of imitating the former and am on the verge of a breakthrough with the latter.

One afternoon, to my disbelief, she prepared her poor-man's soup before my eyes. It's a blend of Manischewitz split-pea soup mix, beef-marrow bones, chopped onions, and grated carrots. I made a pot of it for my father a few months ago, to see if I'd gotten it right, and he reacted as though his only son had translated the Dead Sea Scrolls. This man, who in his later years laughs hesitantly and smiles infrequently, beamed with such pleasure he reminded me of the young fellow I'd heard stories about—the captain of his college baseball team, a nimble and hard-hitting second baseman who tried out for the Cincinnati Reds in the 1930s but was denied an opportunity to play in the major leagues for the same reason as so many other Jews: he was remarkably slow afoot.

Because I grew up eating only my mother's cooking, I find it unsatisfactory to work from recipe books, prepare food devised by people I've never met. I believe I love restaurants so much because I ate in so few of them as a child that they seem the greatest of luxuries. When my mother and father went out for dinner, which wasn't often, they seldom took my sister and me with them. When they did, my mother never failed to reinforce her dessert credo, which I adhere to even today: "You can't go wrong with ice cream."

My mother still cooks, sort of. She sits in the kitchen with the saintly women who care for her and instructs them in modified kosher cuisine. She has taught them the difference between *milchedig* (dairy-based) and *flayshedig* (meat-based) meals. They made gefilte fish (Jewish quenelles) for the religious holidays. The recipe, as practiced by a ninety-four-year-old woman: Purchase one can of Rokeach gefilte fish. Remove fish and place in a pot. Add the goo from the can, sliced carrots, chopped onions, salt, pepper, sugar, and a bay leaf. Boil. Cool. Serve. It isn't her real recipe, but there is something of my mother in it, and that's pretty good.

When I asked my father what he missed most about my mother these days, he said, predictably, "Her cooking, very much." I asked him what he thought about when he saw her in the kitchen, and he said, "She's not able to do anything anymore. She is sitting there, watching somebody else peel the potatoes, and I can only think she must be terribly hurt inside."

Not long ago, I drove to Somerville, New Jersey. I was born there, in the house where my mother grew up. In the forties and fifties it was the nicest home on the block, but now most of the original dark-brown shingles are gone, replaced by shingles painted three or four different colors and some not painted at all. Quite a few aren't even shingles, just scraps of wood hammered over holes.

Both my parents were born on New York's Lower East Side, and they carried out their courtship in Somerville, over a table in the back of my grandmother's store. They met in the thirties, the time of the Great

Depression. Although the people of that era are now extravagantly referred to as the Greatest Generation, I think of my mother and father as members of the Quietest Generation. They and their parents had endured too much poverty, death, and hunger for their lives to be colorfully anecdotal. They were children of the oppressed, of parents who lived in the meager shtetls of Europe, the Jewish ghettos famous for all manner of deficiencies, among them food. A few years back, I managed to coerce my parents into providing an outline of their lives, a few stark facts.

My father told me he grew up so poor he and his brothers got jobs in food markets in order to bring home groceries, never mind asking for cash. My mother said, "We weren't poor," which she certainly wasn't in comparison to my father.

"My mother had a store," she said, "and we took things off the shelf to eat. She had a kitchen in the back, and we ate in the store."

I asked my father, jokingly, if he married my mother for her food, and he said, "It's no joke. After I graduated from Montclair State, I got my first job, and I was still kosher. My father, who was in wholesale dry goods, had two or three customers in Somerville who kept kosher, and he solicited them to see if he could find somewhere for me to eat. One agreed, for fifty cents a dinner. After two years, they threw me out because I didn't pay enough attention to their daughter. Then, where did I turn to get a kosher meal? Ida's mother."

At the time, he was living in a boardinghouse run by a kindly Irish lady, Mrs. Flaherty, who tried unsuccessfully to get him to eat bacon for breakfast. Dinner at the Flaherty's was not an option. He and my mother worked at the same school, and he asked her if he could eat with her family for the same fifty cents. The money, my mother proudly told me, went into a little can used by Jewish families to collect contributions for the poor. Every home had one of them, a *pushke*, a can with a slot in the top for coins. When I was a child, ours seemed sacred to me. I might once or twice have lifted a nickel from my sister's piggy bank, driven by an addiction to Raisinets, but on my life I would not have stolen from that holy tin can.

I asked my father if he enjoyed my grandmother's food, and he replied diplomatically, "It was very good." Actually, she wasn't much of a cook, but she was a lovely grandmother who had a habit of bringing me a football whenever she visited.

"I was happy to find somewhere to eat," my father added.

"And I was happy to find a boyfriend," said my mother. "There was nobody in Somerville, and then he came along, a Jewish boy." He was quite a catch, a young man who had a master's degree, played baseball, kept kosher, and said his morning prayers.

My sister and I grew up outside Philadelphia in a sprawling, low-rise, postwar apartment complex. She's a few years older, and my first food memory is of crying uncontrollably when she came home from first grade and announced that hot dogs had been served in the cafeteria. I haven't felt so cheated since. Her favorite food was the fried clams at Howard Johnson's, the highway restaurant chain whose business would ultimately be usurped by McDonald's, which prevailed, in my opinion, by staying out of the clam business. I was bewitched by the hamburgers seared on a flat metal grill at the Drexelbrook Swimming Club, which we didn't belong to but I could look down upon from the yard behind our building. I was never fortunate enough to eat one of those burgers, but when the winds drifted upward, carrying their bouquet, my craving was nearly unbearable.

I remember that Dick Clark, not yet a national phenomenon, lived in our apartment complex, a factoid I've dined out on for decades. My father recently informed me that I was wrong and that the celebrity was Ed McMahon. Possibly neither of us is correct, for the memories of young boys and old men are equally unreliable. I vividly recall a childhood craving for another savory foodstuff denied me, the Taylor Pork Roll sandwich sold on the boardwalk in Atlantic City. My father may have tolerated non-kosher, but he never moderated his prohibition against pig.

He was an executive with Gimbel Brothers, and on Wednesdays, when the Philadelphia department stores remained open late, he didn't come home for dinner. On those nights, my mother would often broil a ham steak with pineapple and brown sugar, a treat beyond imagining, although I seem to recall her overcooking it from fear of trichinosis, a dread disease of the 1950s that deviant Jewish pork-eaters dared not ignore. Fridays we ate broiled flounder, the rationale being that the fish had to be fresh for the Catholics. My sister reminded me that Fridays were the only nights my mother served bread with our meals; it was on hand to rescue us in the event a bone became caught in our throats. None did, so I never learned exactly how white bread saves lives.

For more than twenty years, I've been visiting my parents at Wynmoor Village, a gated community with walls so low I assume they were constructed not to keep cat burglars out but to keep the less nimble occupants in. Their apartment is on the second floor of a four-story pink-and-white building. I remember when they stopped using the stairs and started using the elevator. I remember when I did, too.

When my parents left Philadelphia for Florida in the late seventies, my mother continued preparing meals much as before. Leaving the single-family, split-level house where she and my father had lived since the late fifties meant adjusting to a much smaller kitchen, which she managed effortlessly. Unlike the other great cooks of the late twentieth century, she was no prima donna who demanded state-of-the-art equipment before she would broil a veal chop. Nor was she dismayed by Florida's heat and humidity. She was as tough as a steel-worker, having spent her life standing over a stove.

My sister and I each visit four or five times a year, mostly because very few others do. My father's brothers and sisters, all of them still in New Jersey, have difficulty traveling. All three of my father's golf partners, Larry, Irving, and Sidney, passed away. I enjoyed their company a lot, because they were sweethearts and I could outdrive them.

When I asked my father if he had seen my mother's oldest friend, a woman from Somerville, he replied, "At some point, she forgot about us." The last time I went down to see them, I learned that my mother's closest friend from the building, a widow, had died, but she hadn't been around for the previous five years. She'd been in a nursing home all that time. When I hear something like that, I do the math: five years in a nursing home equals 1,825 days at $185 a day, about a third of a million dollars. I asked my father to tell me what he knew of the life she led in the home. "She just lay there," he said.

I always feel pain when I think about my mother. She can hardly use the telephone, and the television disturbs her. Because her legs are so weak, she can no longer stand outside the apartment on the terrace, watching over the parking area, hoping to see me drive up when she knows I'm coming for a visit. I'm not always sure she remembers when I'm coming for a visit. Having parents as old as mine is about knots in your stomach. People who have aging parents might think they understand, but a slightly dotty mother who forgets where she puts the car keys is different from parents who have reached their late eighties or nineties. I cannot think of a single advantage to being my mother's age except one. She is now so old that her doctor has lifted all dietary restrictions and she is allowed to eat whatever she wants.

I don't believe I missed a meal in my life. My mother cooked, day and night. "It used to drive me crazy," said my sister, "hot food three times a day and meat and potatoes at lunch." I'm sure I developed my contempt for salads and my need to toast or grill sandwiches from this childhood taboo on cold food.

The only time my father prepared food was when we had a barbecue—that's what we northerners call food burned in our backyards. I would gather twigs, and he would twist newspapers, and we would finally get the briquettes to glow. For a long time, I found it impossible to understand how my father got permission to cook. It wasn't like my mother to relinquish control of a meal. Only recently, when I spoke to my Aunt Dorothy, did I obtain an explanation that made sense. She told me that while my father was making burgers and hot dogs outside, my mother was in the kitchen readying brisket and chicken as a backup.

I didn't resent my mother's refusal to teach me to cook. I come from an era when parents did what they did and kids did what they did and the borders weren't crossed. I played outside a lot, read a lot, and hated piano lessons more than any kid alive, which means I was a pretty standard fifties-era child, unexceptional in every way. Because I never knew hunger, my mother always found clothing for me in the "husky" section of the children's departments, and when I finally confronted her on that, she said, "You weren't fat. *Plump*." I know school counselors of today think this is a recent trend, kids desperately wanting to be thin, but I have firsthand knowledge that it wasn't unheard of when I was growing up.

My mother represented what she had come from: industrious, Eastern European, rising-middle-class stock. I know she regretted not going to college, but she had no idea how to express such a lofty ambition and was held back by timidity. My sister, who went to graduate school, claims that my father had no desire to send her to college and that without my mother's insistence it would not have been possible.

My mother was a housewife, as were most of her friends. A few helped out in their husbands' businesses, but that meant not being home to make dinner, which would have been unimaginable. She wasn't beautiful, but I believe she might have been described as handsome had she not been short and a little portly. I always thought she looked nice, and that skinny women such as Twiggy and Audrey Hepburn were more to be pitied than admired. I remember her on her knees a lot, scrubbing floors, and I remember that she often smelled of onions, or at least her apron did. I wasn't much of an eater until I was five or six, and so my mother spoke often about the starving children of Europe and how grateful they would be for the food I refused. I always thought of them as Nazis and didn't care.

Most of all, my mother was upright. That was vital to American Jews of her peer group, because they were the last generation of Jews to be intimidated by an ironfisted lesson of history: Jews never got away with much, and even when they weren't trying to get away with anything, somebody powerful thought they were. She went to synagogue, put coins in the *pushke*, made her son wear itchy wool suits on the High Holidays, stayed on a first-name basis with butchers, and cleaned the house before the housecleaner arrived to make certain no inappropriate impressions were formed. We may have been colorless, but we played it straight. I don't remember missing much that other kids had, except for the Taylor Pork Roll sandwich.

My parents weren't formal people, but I don't recall them slouching. My father's posture was perfect when he watched baseball on our black-and-white TV. I wasn't privy to my parents' thoughts, because they discussed nothing in front of my sister and me. Whenever my wife accuses me of not having an "inner life," I know where I didn't get it from. My parents were never rumpled. Even today, when we go out to eat, I tell them how nice they look compared to me. This is not flattery; it's a fact. I do not know of divorce or incest or cruelty or illegitimacy in our family tree. Perhaps ugly truths about my relatives are hidden in an attic in some otherwise placid New Jersey town, but I would be shocked to learn of them. When it comes to exemplary behavior, I would put my parents and their sisters and brothers up against the Mennonites or the Quakers any day.

My mother is sweeter than ever. She's lost weight, which looks good on her. She's stopped dying her hair, so now she appears angelic, surrounded by a halo of white. She holds my father's hand and kisses him often. If she did that in the old days, I wasn't around to see it.

Whenever something is done for her, she's grateful, which isn't the mother I knew. These days she complains so infrequently my father says he longs for the days when she was difficult. "I miss her disappointments," he says. She communicates mostly by touching, in a way that says more than she did back when she talked a lot. Because she says so little and forgets so much, I tend to underrate her mentality. She recently lost track of how many children she had, and I said to her, "Maybe you should have had more." She replied, impeccably, "Not at my age." And when I confronted her on the ham-steak issue, demanding to know if those Wednesday pork nights reflected a rebellious streak we didn't know she had, she replied, "Don't tell everybody."

When I travel down to Florida these days, I always spend time visiting nursing homes, reassuring my father that it's not for now but for emergencies. My father is opposed to a nursing home for my mother because he believes it means permanent separation and it will hasten her death. He is correct on both counts. The nursing homes I've seen have lots of services that none of the patients are in any shape to appreciate. I can't say how many times I've gone into a cheerfully painted room to find the wheelchairs lined up in a semicircle and the occupants sitting motionless, heads lolling to the side, while activity directors jump up and down clapping their hands.

When I see a piano in a nursing-home dining room, I wonder how frequently anybody is hired to play. When I see a nicely furnished private room designed for family dining, I wonder how often families come to eat.

My mother talks about death all the time. She might not understand actuarial tables, but she knows how long she has lived and how long she has left. The last time I asked her what she thinks about, she replied, "Dying," so I dropped the subject. I asked her if she had learned anything about life after so many years, and she said, "It was fast."

I'm ready for the day I'll have to set off on the mission I've dreaded for so long, the day the fragile life-support system my sister and I put in place becomes inadequate and my mother will be wheeled into a nursing home. I won't feel guilty, because we've done everything possible to postpone it, but I believe that someday history will judge this country harshly for placing our elderly in such facilities, no matter how nicely decorated they are. I hate thinking of my mother in a nursing home, her head lolling, but even worse is that once she's in such a place, nobody will ask her for a recipe or for advice on how to cook. She will never step into a kitchen again.

GQ, DECEMBER 2001

WHAT A DIVE!

Seldom praised and often shunned, joints are the most misunderstood of American restaurants. If they only had been labeled bistros, which they resemble in countless ways, they would be beloved.

Joints are ignored by foodies and critics and are treasured only by the people who regularly eat in them. Joints are creatures of neighborhoods, not restaurant guides. Those who dismiss them lose out on bare-knuckled food, good-hearted (if rarely good-natured) service, and a rambunctious ambiance impossible to capture in the pages of an architectural magazine. A joint brings joy to the heart. Depending on whether or not the cook is having a good day, heartburn is also a possibility.

Unquestionably, joints have sunk perilously close to the bottom of the restaurant caste system, so low that upon occasion they are misidentified as dumps. This is because the food lacks a certain . . . what's the right word? . . . *elegance.* So much about dining today concerns appearances—the comely chef, the artful cuisine, the gleaming kitchen, the designer walls. A plate overflowing with a very large portion of very decent food is seldom admired. Still, the good joints quietly linger on, surviving every intimidating food trend, every urban renewal project that threatens to close them down. Were they more chichi, they'd be classified as cafés, and eager tourists would storm their doors.

I recently asked David Rockwell, the eminent restaurant designer, if he could express in technical terms the difference between a joint and a dump. He explained, "A dump is a place on the way down; it probably didn't start out being a dump. A joint is and always has been a joint."

A joint has no high concept. It just is. It is a safe haven in a culinary world that swirls with inconsistencies. It is a respite from fast food, small food, tall food, and fancy food. Nothing is flambéed in a joint—except accidentally, should there be a grease fire. While the food in a joint is usually native-born American, the people who work in them are more likely to have been naturalized. English is always spoken, but not necessarily by the employee assigned the job of answering the telephone.

My two favorite joints are Big Nick's in New York City and The Pantry in Los Angeles. What they both have that I particularly admire are (1) long hours: The Pantry never closes and Big Nick's shuts down its pizza operation for an hour each day, and (2) one-pound hamburgers. Joints have a lot of leeway where menus are concerned, but a great hamburger is pretty much a prerequisite.

I paid a visit to Big Nick's (technically, Big Nick's Burger and Pizza Joint) on Broadway near Seventy-seventh Street recently, squeezing into a booth for four that would be tight for two, knowing that I would order the same food I always order. My only dilemma: Did I want to go for the small (quarter-pound), the medium (half-pound), or the Sumo (full-pound) burger? When I opted for the $6.50 Sumo, which is what the owner, Demetrios Nicholas Imirziades, calls his magnificent mound of freshly ground chuck and sirloin cooked on an indoor charcoal grill, the waitress looked skeptically at me.

"It's big," she said.

"Fine," I replied.

"It's big and gross," she added.

"Just the way I like it," I replied.

Grudgingly, she wrote down my order. As she turned, she looked back over her shoulder and said, "It's big."

Undaunted, I replied, "Fine."

I didn't show it, but my feelings were hurt. The guy one table over had just ordered a Swiss cheese and onion omelette with hash browns, Italian sausage, and a Bud Light, and she hadn't doubted his capabilities. Just to show her, I ate every bite. Well, almost every bite.

I have to confess that I haven't been to The Pantry (technically, The Original Pantry Cafe), located at Ninth and Figueroa in downtown L.A. in three or four years. I was a regular there in the seventies, when I was a much-traveled sportswriter. In recent years, after becoming a food writer, I started neglecting it in favor of lesser restaurants with better public relations departments.

The place has globe lights, heavy crockery, cheap flatware, and a dull patina. What I particularly love about The Pantry is the rumor that all the employees are ex-convicts, which I refuse to check out because I don't want to find out it's untrue. The last time I was there, a counterman who served me a bowl of clam chowder while I was waiting for a friend to join me for lunch sure looked as though he'd received a pardon from the governor. He was an old guy with a buzz cut who never smiled.

"Doesn't seem to like me," I said to the big guy on the next stool.

"It started long before you got here," he replied.

I telephoned a friend living in Los Angeles, a retired sportswriter named George Kiseda, who had introduced me to the place. I asked him to eat there and report back to me. He said he'd be happy to do so since he was obligated to take his brother and sister-in-law out to dinner, and this way he'd have to spend only seven dollars apiece on their meal.

When he got back to me, he said his brother, no denizen of joints, was astonished by the brusqueness of their waiter. Instead of chatting endlessly, as L.A. waiters usually do, this fellow was uncomfortably precise.

"What comes with this?" asked the brother, referring to the $6.65 hamburger steak meal. (I believe the absence of a bun is what makes this hamburger a steak in the opinion of management.)

"Vegetables," was the reply.

"Do I have a choice?"

"No."

Kiseda then presented his comprehensive report: "I figured out why it's a joint. No maître d'. No menu. No tablecloth. No chandeliers. No froufrou of any kind. No reservations. No power table. No waiter named Tab or Sean or Daryl just passing through on the way to an Oscar. No credit cards. Just food."

I asked him what he had for dinner, and he said he had what he always had, the hamburger steak laced with chopped onions and accompanied with a few complimentary servings of coleslaw. "I don't like coleslaw. But they have great coleslaw," Kiseda said.

Lest it seem that Big Nick's and The Pantry are exactly alike, I should point out a few significant differences: Big Nick's has a menu so large, so comprehensive, and so badly arranged that it is virtually impossible to understand. This is one reason why I stick to the burgers. The Pantry has no menu, just a few dozen items printed on the wall plus specials of the day scrawled on a blackboard in handwriting that's nearly impossible to read.

The walls of The Pantry are basically bare. Big Nick's walls are blanketed with all manner of stuff, primarily celebrity photos of people you've never heard of. My favorite is a glamour shot of Madonna—a gal named Madonna Chavez, that is. The tables at The Pantry are Formica and the chairs wood. The booths at Big Nick's are constructed of plywood.

All this is pretty wonderful, but it has occurred to me that the people who run The Pantry and Big Nick's might feel otherwise, harbor some long-repressed desire that their establishments be considered on a par with the restaurant elite. This seems not to be the case.

Big Nick, of course, named his place Big Nick's Burger Joint when he opened it twenty-eight years ago, and he says, "How can it be anything else? There's writing on the wall, crazy people are inside screaming, it's narrow and not comfortable to have a meal, you see the smoke when you come in the door—excuse me, but we are making hamburgers up there, you cannot a hundred percent hide the smoke and the grease." David Hixon, one of the waiters at The Pantry, though not for all of its seventy-one years, says, "It is a joint. I think a joint has a feeling of old-timeness, and a broad cross section of a clientele." The phrase "broad cross section" rang an alarm with me, and he conceded that the customers who wander in aren't always the most desirable, being that The Pantry is located "in the bowels of downtown L.A."

Indeed, joints do have a few drawbacks, but at a time when Americans claim to be coveting value, quality, and unpretentiousness, a joint fills every expectation, meets every requirement. Joints are exactly what we want, and they are exactly what they always were. To me, a good place to grab a meal need rise no higher than that.

Food & Wine, OCTOBER 1995

HUNGRY IN THE HAMPTONS

At 5:30 P.M. on a Friday in early May, I am seated at a table under the stiff blue awning that shades the deck of Bostwick's Seafood Grill. I order the "sun-dried" pizza, anticipating that it will, at the very least, be fresh. I am this restaurant's first customer. The first ever.

Before me, bobbing fetchingly in the Maidstone Marina, are six-figure sailboats owned by mariners who think "Land ho!" is something you cry out while closing a real estate deal. To the side, the Stars and Stripes snaps smartly in the cool, offshore breeze. My waitress, who could not be lovelier in shorts, T-shirt, and turquoise earrings, tells me she has just arrived in East Hampton, a village a hundred miles east of Manhattan, to begin a new life. It is something she has in common with Bostwick's, which has had many other lives, many other names. The manager stops by to ask if everything is all right.

"Perfect," I reply, not exaggerating a bit.

And yet . . .

Somewhere, just over the horizon, economic thunderclouds gather. This is no fault of Bostwick's. On the contrary. In my travels through the Hamptons over the course of two long weekends, there aren't many meals I enjoy more than this sun-dried tomato, pesto, and goat-cheese pizza served beside a harbor on a delightful spring day.

What darkens the promise of this and every other restaurant in the area is the location. The Hamptons, so sublimely beautiful in the summer, so beloved by those possessing exquisite taste and excessive money, are a restaurant graveyard.

Last year, Bostwick's was the Little Rock Yacht Club. Before that, it was the Sea Wolf and before that the Silver Sea Horse. Just outside the village of East Hampton is Jackstraw's Cafe, which is preparing for its grand opening. It is situated in a lovely old shingled house that once was the Spring Close House (for fine family dining) and then the Beach Plum (for downscale beach fare) and then the Ballpark (for "people with fishhooks in their cheeks," I'm told), and then Violet's (for elegant evenings out). Now, as Jackstraw's Cafe, it will feature Southwestern cuisine. The decor is sort of New Mexican Gothic, a combination of old gilded art left over from Violet's and new serapes brought in for Jackstraw's. It's how Dracula would decorate if he moved to Sante Fe.

When winter arrives in the Hamptons, eating establishments vanish like beach umbrellas in a hurricane. "In the off-season, business stops like a heart attack," says Robert Durkin, chef and co-owner of Karen Lee's, in Bridgehampton.

Despite that, the Hamptons have become one of the hottest restaurant regions in the country. Restaurateurs, many with successful establishments in Manhattan, are flocking here, so many that they deserve group rates on the Hampton Jitney. They are encouraged by a prevailing sense of economic optimism and a belief that their best customers— wealthy Manhattanites with summer homes—are eagerly awaiting the arrival of the same kind of food they've been eating all winter. Nearly thirty-five years ago, Henri Soule, the owner of Le Pavillon, pioneered this concept when he came to the Hamptons and opened one of the first great resort restaurants, the Hedges. Craig Claiborne, the legendary *New York Times* food editor and critic, now retired to East Hampton, says, "In those days, almost all the well-known restaurants in Manhattan closed their doors in the summer months. Soule thought all the fancy international crowd would follow him if he moved to the Hamptons, and he was right."

Claiborne recalls Soule's establishment in the Hamptons as being "very fancy, very elegant." That is not the prevailing style today. For the most part, the new places are either of the Cal-Ital genre (sconces, uncluttered walls, blond-wood tables, terra-cotta floors) or of the storefront genre (smaller, darker, homier). The Honest Diner, operated by Jeff Salaway and Toni Ross—she being the daughter of the late Steve Ross, chairman of Time Warner—is much talked about, and the toughest table to get on a Saturday night is at The Palm steak house. Battling for top honors as the place to be seen are: Sapore di Mare, owned by Pino Luongo of Manhattan's Coco Pazzo; Della Femina and East Hampton Point, both owned by advertising icon Jerry Della Femina and operated by Drew Nieporent of Manhattan's Montrachet; and Nick & Toni's, also owned by Salaway and Ross.

Rivalries, however fierce, are usually friendly—Nick & Toni's sent flowers to Della Femina on opening night. The exception to this amiability is Luongo, who picks more fights than a sailor on shore leave. Earlier this year, he ran an ad across four columns of the *East Hampton Star* warning potential customers to beware of restaurants run by competitors with Italian-sounding last names who didn't offer a "real Italian dining experience."

The challenge facing all restaurateurs is simple and obvious: Who's going to be eating out in January and February? The village of East Hampton, which has a permanent population of only 1,500, has at least ten upscale restaurants. During July and August, it's a certainty that every one will be filled on Saturday night. Fred Price, a manager of the 400-seat East Hampton Point, says, "There'll be a Saturday night in the summer, I'm sure, when we'll serve a thousand. And then we're going to have to take the chef to the hospital." The only year-round sure thing in the Hamptons is the patronage of one remarkable customer: Billy Joel. He is to dining in the Hamptons what George Washington was to sleeping in Bucks County. They can all boast, Billy Joel Ate Here.

For my purposes, I define the Hamptons as beginning at Basilico, a restaurant in Southampton, and ending fifteen miles east, at the Honest Diner in Amagansett. I did not include Westhampton in my survey because it doesn't feel like a Hamptons town to me. I did include Sag

Harbor, which is located five miles north of Route 27, the main artery of the Hamptons. Sag Harbor is too cute to leave out. The village by which all others are measured is East Hampton, one of the most bucolic spots in America. No, you do not have enough money to buy there.

In two trips to the area, one in late April and the other in early May, I tried more than a dozen restaurants. A few times I ate only an appetizer. I spotted Eli Wallach (I think) at the Laundry, sat two tables from Princess Yasmin Khan (I was told) at The Palm, and saw Ralph Lauren (I'm certain) at Della Femina. Although I missed the grand opening of East Hampton Point, Billy Joel was there.

"I'll have the pepper steak," I tell Big Al Cavagnaro, the owner, chef, and bartender of Cavagnaro's Bar & Grill in East Hampton. To find the place, you drive around East Hampton until you see a neon-lit restaurant that doesn't look like it belongs in East Hampton. That's Cavagnaro's, which has been around far longer than all the places that look as though they do belong. Al's father opened for business in 1933, and Al, who lives in back, took over in 1951. Inside, regulars are drinking shots poured from a bottle of Imperial whiskey as big as a harbor buoy.

A sign on the door says: TRY OUR LUNCH. Offered are hamburgers, corned beef, roast beef, and more. The special of the day is pepper steak.

Al, a big old guy pushing eighty, looks at me suspiciously with his one good eye when I ask for the pepper steak.

"Had that the day before yesterday," he says.

"So why's the sign still there?" I ask.

"Too lazy to take it down."

"I'll take the hamburger."

"Didn't grind any meat today."

"I'll take anything you got."

"I got the spaghetti and meatballs I made yesterday."

I change my mind.

Al tells me to come back the next day, he'll have something for me to eat.

.   .   .

My first meal is at Southampton's Basilico, attractive in a formulaic way: awning over the door, bottle of olive oil on every table. I order an appetizer that comes with fried onions and fried basil. The greasiness drives me out the door. I try another appetizer at the just-opened 95 School Street in Bridgehampton. The place is comfortable and low-key, offering newspapers and magazines in the bar area. I order tuna carpaccio topped with grilled shrimp, an unusual combination of unlike seafoods. The silky tuna nicely compliments the crispy shrimp, although the dish is flawed by an excess of lemon juice. It turns the raw tuna into tuna ceviche.

I complete my three-village, three-restaurant dinner at the Laundry, in East Hampton. I'm stunned when I walk in. I expect to see Hef and his Bunnies lounging on the black-vinyl boomerang-shaped couch wrapped around a freestanding brick fireplace. This place is such a seventies period piece it should be in the Smithsonian. Dinner is pretty good, but everything I order turns out to be either sweet or creamy; sweet vinaigrette on salad greens, mint-and-garlic sauce on very good snapper filets, raspberry puree on the strawberry shortcake.

The Laundry, which has been around since 1980, qualifies as one of the Old Guard places to eat and be seen. This category is led by Bobby Van's, in Bridgehampton, where Truman Capote went to drink and be seen. Also edging into the Old Guard division, although only around since 1989, is Karen Lee's, which fulfills my expectations of what a neighborhood spot should be. Warm and inviting, dark and clubby, with an astonishingly large menu, it suffers only from the undue richness of its food. Worth the sacrifice is the meltingly tender Long Island duckling in blackberry sauce and the chocolate sorbet, richer than some hot fudge I've come across.

Also well established, yet remaining one of the hot spots, is Luongo's Sapore de Mare, located in the practically nonexistent hamlet of Wainscott. The restaurant has been around for six seasons and has earned a solid reputation for good food and surly service. I order a house specialty, pasta with sausage, peas, tomatoes, parmesan, and heavy cream, after my waitress proudly informs me that customers come from all over to have it. Although it tastes as though it's from the Upper East Side, not Tuscany, it's generous and satisfying, far better than I expect from such an unlikely combination of ingredients.

The house sparkling wine, Foss Marai Prosecco, is very good. So is the bread. So is the olive oil for dipping the bread. Service is just fine. I wonder why everything is so pleasant, and then I notice Pino Luongo isn't around. That has to be it.

"You know," Big Al is saying a day later, "even in the old days we had a lot of good people out here: Andrew Mellon, Henry Ford, Jacqueline Onassis—she came in, had chicken and rice."

Sounds good, chicken and rice. At Big Al's, everything sounds good, but I can't get any of it. While Al's pouring shots for his midday clientele, I poke my head into the kitchen. There's a ten-burner Garland range in there, but nothing's on it. Al would rather talk than cook.

"Jackson Pollock used to come in with his girlfriend when his wife was in France," Al says. "He'd drink Old Grand-Dad on the rocks. I'll tell you, that girl was stacked."

Makes me think about pancakes, that story. Al says tomorrow, for sure, he'll have a hamburger for me. I've been in a lot of restaurants where you can only eat what the cook wants you to eat, but this is different. You can only eat *when* the cook wants you to eat.

The Honest Diner is supposed to represent the fifties. It does. The food could not be more bland. I have the luncheon special: an open-faced pot-roast sandwich with mashed potatoes and gravy. On my table are salt, pepper, mustard, ketchup, A-1, and Tabasco. I'm tempted to use them all. Unfortunately, no condiment can save the coconut custard pie.

Nick & Toni's in East Hampton has the same owners but a different chef. The place is practically whitewashed, it's so simple in design. I try two dishes, both made in a wood-burning pizza oven, and either one could qualify as the best food in the Hamptons. I must confess, however, that I walked in with Craig Claiborne, which is like walking into a casino with Frank Sinatra. Much attention is paid to us.

The first dish is a smoked-salmon pizza with mild red onions, a layer of mascarpone cheese, and a sprinkling of capers. Maybe this is what people eat on Sunday mornings on the Upper West Side of Rome. The second is a whole striped bass scored and quickly cooked in that 600-degree heat, then brushed with rosemary-scented olive oil. The skin crackles, the flesh is soft and moist. We drink Coulée de Serrant, the finest and longest-lived Chenin Blanc in the world, priced at $26.

The same wine costs $65 at the American Hotel, in Sag Harbor, which is often praised for its stupendous wine list. After seeing the prices, I'm not impressed. Any restaurant can list wine. I prefer restaurants that want to sell wine. The classic French cooking, however, is excellent. I have a sumptuous quail terrine infused with dabs of foie gras and succulent game hen crowned with a shortbread pastry crust, the sort of chicken potpie Escoffier's mother must have made.

The Maidstone Arms, in East Hampton, has much better wine prices, as well as wonderful luncheon specials. The prize is a 1961 Château Latour, priced at about one-half Manhattan prices. Were I celebrating a million-dollar advance on my novel or the sale of my record company, as everyone in East Hampton does sooner or later, this would be my splurge.

"Been married fifty-four years, I got a damn good wife," Al is saying while my long-awaited hamburger cooks on his indoor grill.

"She comes in, checks on me, makes sure the place is clean, I'm not raising too much hell."

Al is at his usual spot, the corner of the bar by the door. The burger is in back, unsupervised. I'm nervous. I don't want it to burn. I know there will be no second chance.

Al finally returns to the kitchen, yells out, "You want a hard roll?" I holler acceptance.

"Good thing," says one of the guys at the bar. "He's going to give you a hard roll anyway."

The burger is thick, lean, and fresh, nicely served on a poppy-seed kaiser roll. With or without cheese, with or without fries, it costs five bucks. "What am I going to do," Al says, "add ten cents for this, four cents for that? Nobody wants that crap."

I take out my money, but Al says it's on the house.

I tell him I prefer to pay. That way I can protest the slow service by not leaving a tip.

Service has always been problematic in the Hamptons. At least with Al, you get a lopsided grin while you're waiting three days for your burger. On weekends in July and August, customers are routinely treated so rudely throughout the Hamptons that one veteran maître d' says to me, "To my worst enemy I wouldn't advise going out to eat on a Saturday night in the summer."

On my first Saturday night, I visit the place most recommended to me by food critics: the Old Stove Pub. Run by a Greek family, this venerable steak house is located in a tired old home on farmland between Bridgehampton and East Hampton. The sign out front says: WHEN YOU'RE FED UP WITH THE CHIC, COME TO THE GREEK. I'm told by three food writers that (1) "It's the best steak I ever had, a real down-home place, but you'll see Demi Moore there." (2) "It serves the best lamb chop in America." (3) "It has the best steak in the world." I notice that the *Zagat Tri-State Restaurant Survey* gives the Old Stove Pub a mediocre rating.

Based on a dinner for three, here are my Zagat-style impressions of the place. Food: terrible. Decor: worse. Service: unfathomable. Cost: high. The food brings to mind something Wolfgang Puck told me years ago, when he was reminiscing about his days as the grill cook at Maxim's, in Paris. Puck said that the Greek shipping tycoon Aristotle Onassis "used to eat a big fillet with a lot of fat, like eating barbecued grease." The steaks here are thick, horrendously trimmed, gristly, and charred deep-black.

On my second Saturday night, I go to The Palm, which is so popular that one restaurateur has said to me, "The maître d' there is the richest man in the Hamptons." The steak is a thick, tender, beautifully trimmed sirloin. The lamb chops are even better. Compared to "the Greek," this is the Parthenon.

When I ask the maître d', Tomas Romano, if tips from guests desperate for tables have made him the richest man in the Hamptons, he replies, "I think I am the most hated man in the Hamptons. On a Saturday night, after three hundred people are seated, there are another three hundred left out. Can you imagine how much they like me, these people who cannot get in?"

He tells me of the many famous people who come every weekend but inexplicably leaves out Billy Joel. I ask him why he is the only maître d' in the Hamptons not to boast of his patronage.

"I do not have to say it," he says. "He is here all the time, anyway."

A day later, I stop in at Cyril's Fish House, located six miles east of my arbitrary Hamptons borderline, but worth a trip for its deep-fried fresh flounder coated with oregano-garlic breadcrumbs. Cyril says, "He comes here a lot, Billy Joel. His secretary called an hour ago, looking for him."

I'm sure that Christie Brinkley is a wonderful wife and mother, but I'm starting to suspect she's not such a great cook.

A STATEMENT FROM BILLY JOEL

"I am a year-rounder, and I like to sample all the local places. I'm afraid to praise one over another because they've all treated me so nicely. In truth, every restaurant I've been to has something unique and delicious to offer, from the lowest diner to the fanciest Tuscan restaurant. I am particularly partial to those places that remain open during the cold-weather months."

Jerry Della Femina might be the most important man in the Hamptons. He has the most tables and chairs.

He is also vying for Joel's loyalty. He opened Della Femina last August and kept it operating all winter. He opened East Hampton Point this past May with the intention of keeping it operating year-round. He is assured of stunning short-term success.

Della Femina immediately moved up alongside Nick & Toni's in the race for maximum celebrity saturation. East Hampton Point, located in a slightly out-of-the-way spot overlooking Joel's yacht, was only in business for a few days when I stopped by. Its desserts were already polished works of art, particularly the fruit tart and the chocolate truffle cake.

I can imagine nothing more blissful than sitting at one of the six window tables in the main dining room, eating dessert at sunset. I can think of nothing more awesome than the clout one will require to get one of those tables on a Saturday night.

One last place.

In the center of Amagansett is the Stephen Talkhouse bar, renowned for attracting rock stars of magnitude, the kind who fill football stadiums.

For years, Elwood of Elwood and Ettie's Dixie Smoked Barbecue labored on a deck behind the bar. When I stop by, I'm told that Elwood will not be returning. He will be missed, of course, and I have no way of knowing whether his replacement will cook as well, but I am confident I can recommend the Stephen Talkhouse bar.

Billy Joel plays there.

GQ, AUGUST 1993

THE SAUCIER'S APPRENTICE

Posing as a hapless student cook—an effortless subterfuge on my part—I have infiltrated the French culinary establishment. I am enrolled at Paul Bocuse's École des Arts Culinaires et de l'Hôtellerie, a school dedicated to the advancement of the cuisine of Lyons, a city widely admired as the gastronomic capital of France.

Here, a simple lunch might include a veal hoof, a slice of extra-thick tripe, and a sausage made from pork innards. Add a soupçon of butter, a gravy boat of cream, and, voilà, simple home cooking is transformed into some of the world's fanciest food. We Americans might find such cuisine unthinkable, to say nothing of unaffordable, but to most of the world this is the epitome of sophistication. If the awe one feels while consuming such profound creations is occasionally intermingled with indigestion, well, that's the price one must pay for eating too well.

No other country has a table the equal of France's, and no chef in France is as acclaimed as Bocuse. Here, at his own school, unbeknownst to his staff, I plan to investigate the mysteries of French food. I will peel away the veils of secrecy much as Bocuse peels away the layers of an *oignon*.

I will try to discover why the French are so different from us, why they are concerned only with pleasure, never with nourishment. Why is it, I have been wondering, that people in other countries gather together whatever meager provisions they can find in order to feed their families, whereas the French gather up their families in order to feed them at restaurants?

I will endeavor to learn how the French manage to eat so well in times of war or natural disaster—although I've heard that during famines they skip the petits fours. Why do Americans require Hamburger Helper to get by, while every Frenchman is entitled to a daily helping of steak tartare? I will attempt to find out why the French are guiltless where food is concerned. They believe eating veal is immoral only when it is tough.

I have five days to learn all of this, five days in a course called "Cuisine and Culture for French Food Lovers," something I definitely was until my last trip to Paris, when none of my meals was any good. The course costs about $1,000, and consists of cooking lessons and demonstrations that start a 9:00 A.M. each day and go on until 4:30 or 5:00 P.M.

We are promised a chance to work on more than a dozen recipes in kitchens that gleam like Napoleon's cavalry. We will observe top-notch professionals preparing classics, the kinds of dishes once reserved for noblemen in velvet pants. For an additional $250, we can even sleep on campus, although those lured to the school by photos of the headquarters, a lush nineteenth-century château, should be forewarned: the residence hall has aqua walls and yellow doors and looks as though it belongs on the campus of a cash-starved Sunbelt junior college. My class numbers about a dozen, all but one of us American, and includes an oboe player, a housewife, and a honeymooning couple who have taken advantage of the housing offer and are sleeping in twin beds.

My classmates and I are issued lab coats and funny little paper chef's hats that must be stapled together before they are worn. The school's hats look like galvanized stovepipes and denote status within the food community: the taller the hat, the more important the chef. Our instructor, Chef Antoine Fremont, is a Big Hat. His assistant, Hélène Rebourseau, a first-year student in a two-year course, wears a hat only half as big.

Our first recipe is salmon medallions in a Beaujolais sauce with bone marrow and grapes. As you can tell, we have already crossed the line that separates what the Lyonnaise consider good eatin' from what everybody else considers good eatin'. Chef Antoine asks if anyone has any questions before we begin. One student asks if he could have another staple in his hat. Chef Antoine does not look pleased.

Lesson number one is how to blanch onions. Lesson number two is how to blanch salt pork. Already my mission is a success, for I have learned about this odd French addiction to blanching, a cooking technique that consists of plunging the ingredient in question into boiling water while exclaiming, "Voilà!"

When they are not blanching, the French seem always to be deglazing. This is a fancy word for removing the cruddy stuff that sticks to the bottom of a roasting pan. Voilà! The cruddy stuff is the basis for all those rich sauces Americans pay so much for in restaurants, not realizing what they are made from. The French so admire the cruddy stuff that they even have a name for it, "*le suc.*" I'm not saying that American chefs don't deglaze, but you've got to admit that giving the cruddy stuff its very own name demonstrates an unnatural degree of affection.

As we proceed with the salmon recipe, I learn all of the following: how to remove pits from whole grapes using a paper clip (a process not much different from removing wax from your ear using a paper clip), how to pop near-frozen marrow from a bone so it comes out in one conical piece (a really disgusting procedure you don't want to know about), and how to make *lardons*. This last is an eye-opener. When Americans dine at cute little French bistros, they often order salads with *lardons*, thinking they're getting something moderately healthy, a bunch of frizzy greens with a few chunks of bacon tossed in. Those chunks of bacon are lardons, cubes of pork fried in butter. The French really like fatty food fried in butter, especially if the fatty food is blanched first.

For our next dish, Chef Antoine instructs us in the preparation of salmon cutlets wrapped in smoked bacon. I raise my hand and ask Chef Antoine if the French feel cheated if they do not have pork with their fish. Chef Antoine does not look pleased. He tells us how to wrap a cutlet: encircle the salmon with a strip of bacon (much as a filet mignon is wrapped in American restaurants I try to avoid). Should the bacon be too large and require trimming, cut away the meaty parts. Real French chefs never waste pork fat.

Our salmon cutlets wrapped in the fattiest possible smoked bacon are to be served with broccoli butter, which causes some of my veggy-loving classmates to sigh with happiness. They have no idea. Should you wish to prepare broccoli butter, here is the recipe: Blanch a little broc-coli. Place in a blender with lemon, salt, and pepper. Jam in a massive amount of butter, as though you were stuffing a sausage casing. Blend. What comes out looks like green cookie dough but is far, far richer. To turn this faux cookie dough into a delicious vegetable sauce for the salmon, merely add a little cream.

Chef Antoine then shows us how to make jus, which is a light sauce of natural juices. He places a tomato peel in the jus, explaining that the acidity in the peel will clarify the jus. I studied chemistry once, and I find this fascinating.

"Why is that?" I ask.

"Because," he replies.

Chef Antoine already seems to be tiring of me, and it is only our first day.

At lunchtime I chat with Patrick Huriet, the *directeur général* of the school. He tells me that many French students who secure cooking internships in the United States hope to return there to work after grad-uation because they are treated so well in American kitchens. "In France everybody is yelling. It is our way of showing strong authority," he explains. "Part of our culture is to bully." Actually, I already knew this. I am hoping that Chef Antoine will teach me to curse like a real French chef.

Our lunch each day consists of what we prepare each day with our own French Food Lovers' hands. Today it's those two salmon-and-pork preparations, which settle on my stomach like a combo platter at a bar-becue joint. Students not in our course are enjoying the school lunch of the day: brochettes of sausage and smoked pork fried in oil accom-panied by stuffed baked potatoes. Their dessert is floating island—meringue in a custard sauce.

Also savoring the school lunch, even though it is much lighter than what they normally have at home, is a contingent of German students. They have all won a day at the school as prizes in a recipe contest.

I ask one of the Germans for her winning recipe, for it is not often that the French find virtue in German cooking. She says she merely had to answer a question on a postcard, and while she doesn't recall the question, she clearly remembers her prizewinning answer: "Putten a turkey from France."

I am no linguist, so I want to make certain I have not misunderstood.

"Putten a turkey from France?" I repeat.

"Yes," she says, flapping her arms like a turkey. "Turkey, turkey."

"*Nein*," I say. "What means 'putten'?"

"'Putten' means 'putten,'" she says.

I ask Chef Antoine if he will be teaching us this prizewinning recipe. He just rolls his eyes. As you might have guessed, Chef Antoine is a pretty patient guy for a French chef.

A highlight of our stay at the school is a personal appearance by Bocuse himself, who drives up in his Mercedes and parks it in an unauthorized spot, the only person who dares to take such liberties. Bocuse is a combination of Julia Child, Charles de Gaulle, and Ronald McDonald—celebrity chef, Gallic symbol, promotional figure. He is the president of the school, as well as the proprietor of a three-star restaurant on the outskirts of Lyons.

Bocuse shows us how to make coq au vin, the first and only dish we are taught that I might possibly attempt at home. The catch is that his recipe calls for fresh chicken blood, which is pretty difficult to get in America unless you're a Santeria priest. Blood aside, Bocuse's coq au vin isn't much different from what you find in French cookbooks, but the first step is a standout: cut off the chicken's feet and blanch them.

We have one other memorable cooking session, a demonstration of how to assemble fillet of lamb in a pastry crust. Actually, that's an oversimplification. It's lamb encased in lamb mousse, wrapped in cabbage, and enrobed in a filigreed pastry crust. Three Big Hat chefs work for nearly three hours constructing the monumental work of meat, and they are able to finish that quickly only because the pastry dough was prepared in advance. I calculate that it would take me, working alone and starting from scratch, twenty-four hours straight to duplicate their efforts. Remember when you were a child and your mother said to you, as mothers always do, "Don't eat so fast, that took me all day to make!" You never believed her, but now you know the dish she was talking about.

The week concludes with two days of pastry and dessert classes taught by Chef Alain Berne, who wears the red-white-and-blue collar of *a Meilleur Ouvrier de France,* which means he is about as good as it gets. Chef Alain can chop a half of a canned peach into perfect one-eighth-inch-thick slices in four seconds, make a trout out of sugar, and a violin out of ice. I can make Toll House cookies using the recipe on the back of the bag. Chef Alain's classes are a little over my head.

The world of the pastry chef is alien to me. It is a place where French meringue and Italian meringue and Swiss meringue are all different, where a *biscuit* is not a biscuit, and where ice-cold cream poured into caramelized sugar will explode. Every preparation requires enormous amounts of time, effort, and meringue. And yet the pastry chef suffers like no other man. His delicacies are either thoughtlessly popped in the mouth, as though they were Chiclets, or refused by overstuffed diners who have gorged on a tasting menu and decided to skip dessert. My final pastry humiliation occurs when Chef Alain fires up a blowtorch and prepares to caramelize something. I failed shop when I was in junior high school and cannot imagine such a weapon in my hands.

My week at the school, I must say, has been as rich and filling as the lunchroom's *croquettes de pommes de terre*—potatoes mashed with egg yolks and butter, then breaded and deep-fried. While I have not learned as much as I had hoped, Chef Antoine has taught me lessons about French cooking and culture that I will never forget:

1. Never lose control of your shallots. I have no idea what this means, but Chef Antoine warned us about this during classes and I pass it

on. Losing control of your shallots is not to be confused with sweating your carrots, which is a good thing.

2. Washing your mushrooms is perfectly fine. I can't tell you how happy I am about this. I never serve mushrooms when friends come over, because one of them will invariably launch into a diatribe when I wash my mushrooms instead of brushing each one with a dry cloth. Chef Antoine says wiping mushrooms is ridiculous. "You have time in the United States for things like that," he says.

3. My final lesson comes from the cultural side of the curriculum. Chef Antoine says that a French chef never lies. When I ask him if he ever put frozen fish on his menu and sold it as fresh, he explains, "Yes, but that is business."

GQ, JUNE 1995

BOCUSE MUST GO

Paul Bocuse has done more to glorify French cuisine than any other living restaurateur, and for this he has been suitably honored. He was named "chef of the century" by the Gault Millau restaurant guide and has been immortalized in statuary at the Musée Grevin in Paris. He created a prize, the Bocuse d'Or, that is coveted by cooks simply because his name is on it, and he is so cherished throughout his homeland that he has been known to drag massive cuts of well-marbled American beef through French customs while inspectors shrug and look the other way.

Now, as he approaches eighty years of age, he need perform only one more gracious act to preserve his reputation. He must close his restaurant.

The restaurant Paul Bocuse, which he named for himself before such a vain (if logical) act was commonplace, can be found just outside Lyons, a city long considered (except by me) to be the gastronomic capital of the nation. Paul Bocuse retains a score of three stars, the highest awarded by the Michelin guide. Such a rating denotes exceptional cuisine "worth a special journey."

The experience of dining at Bocuse cannot be duplicated at any other Michelin three-star establishment. It is uniquely disturbing. At a visit this past January, I spent most of the dinner shaking my head in disappointment, although at moments I was bent over with laughter (during the cheese course) or sitting bolt upright in outrage (throughout a musical performance by a black employee dressed as an organ-grinder's monkey). This is not how I would choose to remember the greatest *cuisinier* since the fabled Auguste Escoffier, but I have no choice, because I will never enter that establishment again.

While ostentatious and somewhat dated, the building that houses the restaurant does not detract from the pleasure of a meal. Inside, the restaurant is too bright and too warm and the tables are too close together, but the copper pots gleam, the shelves appear to be dusted regularly, and the napery is luxurious. The place isn't Versailles, but it's more than respectable.

I've been there twice. During the first visit, in the mid-nineties, the room was almost empty and the meal was acceptable, if forgettable. A day later, I couldn't remember much of what I'd eaten except for the famous black-truffle soup with its puff-pastry dome, as good as its reputation. This past January, I returned with four friends. We each ate a fixed-price meal that cost approximately $190, tax and tip (but not wine) included. On the set menu was the same signature soup, pan-fried scallops with *sauce Perigueux,* a *granité* prepared with Beaujolais wine, chicken with black truffles cooked in a pig's bladder, cheeses, and a selection of desserts.

The truffle-scented soup, which exhales an ambrosial cloud of pungent vapor when its crust is pierced, was again the only noteworthy dish. The flavor of the Gamay grape was captured by the *granité,* so I suppose that was also to be admired. Wine service was nonchalant, wineglasses too small, cheeses a joke, and many of the desserts inedible. Even the bread—two kinds of rolls relentlessly offered with every course—was the stuff of a neighborhood *boulangerie.*

Most depressing were the disastrous main courses, because they supposedly epitomize the cuisine of Bocuse. The pan-fried scallops came in an overly sweet, shockingly rustic, dull brown interpretation of *sauce Perigueux,* which is made with Madeira wine, foie gras, and chopped black truffles. Only if I had been dining in a farmhouse would I have sent my compliments to the cook.

Chicken cooked *en vessie,* which means in a swollen pig's bladder, is intended to be an exercise in culinary showmanship. The dish dates from the days when French furniture and French food had much in common—they were both about ornamentation, not pleasure.

The presentation was delightful, but then we were obliged to eat. Steaming a chicken in a bladder might seal in flavor, but it turns nearly everything inside either tough and rubbery (the skin) or mushy and overcooked (the vegetables). By scraping aside most of what was on my plate (bloated rice, soggy greens, revolting skin) and concentrating on the edible bits, I was able to cobble together a few nice bites of chicken with morels in cream sauce—tolerable bistro cuisine.

What made the main courses particularly distressing is that Bocuse was around throughout the dinner service, presumably to assure that every dish leaving the kitchen was up to three-star standards. In reality, he strode through the dining room looking both majestic and remote, once or twice stopping for a photograph with a favored customer. He has become the Flying Dutchman of French cuisine, sailing aimlessly through his premises.

The cheese cart was unquestionably the worst I've come upon in a Michelin-starred restaurant, and the only one I've seen presented without pride. The theme: unripe cheeses with hard rolls. My knife literally bounced off an elasticized Camembert. There was an impressive quantity of cheeses on the cart, but only because of mindless repetition—a long line of tiny pyramids of goat cheese, disc after disc of the same St.-Marcellin. I studied the selections carefully, looking for signs of ripeness, and when I noticed a single promising St.-Marcellin, I eagerly pointed to it. The indifferent captain ignored my request, stuck his knife into an already cut half-disc close to him, and dropped it on my plate. That's when we all burst out laughing.

The first dessert, intended as a prelude, was a small crème brûlée. As I was praising mine on the grounds of acceptability, which was all we could hope for by now, a friend sitting next to me pointed to his. There was a runny residue under the brittle caramelized sugar.

For my principal dessert, I selected *baba au rhum*, which is rum-soaked sponge cake, a favorite of mine. The texture was of a cake soaked days earlier. The flavor was decidedly off, as though the rum were corked, like a spoiled wine. I tasted a friend's apple tart, which consisted of mushy apples over a good, crunchy crust topped with flavorless vanilla ice cream.

Couldn't get worse?

It did, because Paul Bocuse manages to set back cuisine and endorse cultural stereotypes at one sitting.

The person who had opened the restaurant door for us when we arrived was a small black man wearing a short, tight jacket and a flat, round cap. Outfits like those are generally seen on bellhops in 1930s Hollywood films and on the monkeys that dance to barrel organs. While we were having dessert, this man was called on to provide entertainment. He operated some sort of upright musical instrument that imitated an organ-grinder's music. I would suggest to Bocuse, if he so enjoys offensive gestures, another way of entertaining his guests: hire a clueless French film critic to lecture on the greatness of Jerry Lewis. The fun could go on and on.

I can tell you exactly what organization is to blame for all of this: the Michelin guide. Supposedly incorruptible, it has lowered its standards in the case of Bocuse, not for payoffs or for advertising but for sentiment. It has refused to do what is essential, something it has done countless times before: declare by means of lower ratings that a chef's time is done. The guide has been appropriately ruthless with chefs as accomplished (but not as revered) as Bocuse, including Roger Verge of Moulin de Mougins and Marc Meneau of L'Espérance. Even Alain Ducasse, the preeminent French restaurateur of this generation, has seen stars come and go and come back again.

One of my friends at the dinner said he thought it might be possible to enjoy the cuisine of Bocuse, although nowhere near Lyons. He claimed to have had a very satisfactory meal of escargots, fish, and crème brûlée at the Epcot Center in Florida, where Bocuse lends his name to the dining pavilion called Chefs de France. He said Bocuse as interpreted by Disney was preferable to Bocuse left on his own.

GQ, JUNE 2003

A ROOM OF ONE'S OWN

I believe I am the only man alive who loves an empty restaurant.

I am speaking of an establishment that nobody else has decided to patronize, at least on the night when I'm there. I feel blessed, not desperate, when I look around and see every table vacant except the one that I (and my fortunate guest) occupy. I don't ask myself why I didn't stay home and eat in my bathrobe, thus avoiding the humiliation of dining in virtual quarantine. I sense opportunity, not catastrophe.

I understand that a restaurant meal is meant to be an experience in communal rhapsody, you and others of equivalent economic standing joining together in appreciation of a chef's talent, or, at the very least, a joint's popularity. Young people today are never more comfortable than when they are prowling society in boisterous groups, and this is especially true in Manhattan, where top restaurants are rarely without packs of supplicants pleading for admission.

Perhaps I am an outdated fellow, but I believe that being alone with a beloved companion has certain advantages over being crammed in the culinary equivalent of the bleachers. To me, empty restaurants are romantic in a way that ones filled with roses are not.

I also love empty restaurants because I like bargains, and I appreciate that the proprietor has spent thousands of dollars on rent, salaries, and flowers just for my enjoyment. I know I should decorate my dining room at home and hire a maidservant and butler for the evening if I like that style of treatment so much, but I shudder at the expense.

A while ago, when I was visiting Madrid with my wife, I had numerous chances to hone my dining-alone skills. In Spain, restaurants open at nine P.M., and woe to the early bird who actually arrives at that hour. The stove is barely warm, and the waiters are still in shirtsleeves, fiddling with their ties. My wife and I believe entrees are tastiest before the sun goes down, and so we were inevitably at the door of whatever restaurant we had chosen promptly at the opening bell, knocking loudly and demanding admittance. I felt like one of those ladies who line up outside department stories on sale days to try on half-price shifts.

One Sunday night, we chose the restaurant of our hotel, the Orfila, a small, lavish, entirely admirable nineteenth-century palace. We were the first to be seated, and then I realized we were also the last to be seated. The restaurant is not unpopular. In fact, we had been unable to obtain a table on a Friday or a Saturday evening, and it was nearly full for Sunday lunch.

On the night we were there, the restaurant had only two other bookings, and neither of the couples showed up or called to cancel. In America, staff and management would have been outraged at such discourteous behavior, but our waiter, whose name was Santiago, said, "Is normal in Spain."

That left three of us allied for the evening: my wife, Santiago, and me.

She wasn't pleased. "I don't like it so empty that I'm self-conscious," she said. Under more advantageous conditions—for example, had I been with a woman other than my spouse—I could have entertained her with delightful bons mots, but after years of marriage no man sounds witty to his wife. She added, "I like a minimum of three tables to be occupied. That gives the waiter two extra things to focus on but not enough to detract from the service. I don't like just one other table. I get competitive. I ask myself if the waiter likes the people at the other table better than he likes us." Whenever Santiago and the second waiter on duty stood whispering to each other, she was certain they were talking about us.

Santiago was every bit as uncomfortable. He compensated by trying too hard. He rushed over with bread, and then, concerned that he hadn't done enough, he brought dishes of bar snacks—potato chips and salted almonds. The quiet was overwhelming. We could hear the ice in our wine bucket melting and shifting, the swinging door to the kitchen creaking open and whumping closed. *Creak. Whump. Creak. Whump.*

I realized I had to take charge of this floundering dinner party before my wife (as well as Santiago) fled, victims of the unbearable pressure. I am not making reference to the cuisine of the hotel when I say I felt as though I were in command on Pork Chop Hill and my unit was pinned down.

First, I took my wife for a stroll through the restaurant, impossible when others are present. We admired the walls, because they were fabulous, some covered with trompe l'oeil marble-patterned wallpaper, others with yellow-striped wallpaper of woven cloth. Then we looked over the artwork, still lifes that appeared to her to be moving faster than this meal. When the excursion was over and we had started to eat, I recognized that my next task was to make Santiago understand that we were in this together and even if the room echoed with loneliness, we would have the time of our lives.

Luckily for all of us, I dropped a forkful of fish. It didn't seem fortunate at the moment, because the staff would certainly know the identity of the dolt who had dropped his cod on the carpet. (It would not have been chivalrous to point to my wife and shake my head reproachfully, although I was tempted.) The word would spread through the hotel: "The guy in room 32 can't hold his cod." So I bend down to pick up the fish at the precise moment when Santiago arrived with a plate and a napkin to save me from the demeaning task. Our heads banged under the table. A bond of friendship and international goodwill was forged.

The rest of the evening passed without incident or discomfort. The food was easily the best I experienced during my three days in Madrid. The *bacalao*, or dried cod, was superb, the skin crisp and the flesh soft, the flavor enhanced with bits of sausage and a few scattered olives and tomatoes. The pigeon breast was rare, sliced and arranged around a well-cooked leg atop a layer of artichoke bottoms, and the breast of duck came in a light, yellow-tinted sauce made with carrots and ginger that looked Indian but tasted Asian.

Afterward, I concluded that I had behaved so exquisitely, head butting notwithstanding, that it had become my duty to prepare a brief guide to dining in an empty restaurant. As a public service I offer this advice:

1. If the restaurant has a piano player, tip him immediately. These guys are morose enough without having to play to a single table of uninterested patrons. If there's a piano and nobody's playing it, you must. Learn a song if you don't know one. Mine is "The Little Shoemaker," a ditty I perfected when I was nine years old.

2. Reign over the restaurant. Do not cower in a corner. Insist on a table in the center of the room. Overflow with benevolence. Lavish praise and attention on the staff so at the end of the evening they will remember you forever, grateful for having had the opportunity to serve you, a baron of the dining arts.

3. Treat your consort as though she were a queen. Remember that alcohol and excess are your allies in getting through a potentially awkward evening. Order champagne as quickly as possible.

4. Do not whisper, although you will be tempted to do so. Speak more forcefully than usual, as though you were in the banquet room of your château. Certainly the waiters will overhear you, but your conversation will be so well-bred they will be awed.

5. Never order an abbreviated dinner. If there is a cheese course, have it. Let the world know—not that the world is watching—that you are fully at ease in a situation that would overwhelm a less confident person.

6. Leave at least a 25 percent tip. An entire restaurant has existed merely to please you. Your magnificent presence has brightened what could have been a miserable evening for the staff, so don't ruin everything by leaving 12 percent, the way you usually do.

After the meal, I rather hoped my wife would compliment me on my performance, but of course she did not. (See previous reference to matrimonial behavior.) She said that despite my antics, the restaurant still felt empty to her. I told her she was mistaken, because I had demonstrated that my ego was large enough to fill any room.

GQ, APRIL 2003

Ten Commandments for Diners

1. Don't Give Them Your Credit Card Until After Dessert

Restaurants have started asking customers to guarantee reservations with credit cards. Don't do it. Assure them you'll show up. Promise them you'll call to reconfirm—thoughtful restaurants will even provide special numbers for this service. Frankly, if restaurants want to start acting like airlines, they should offer similar perks, such as frequent-diner upgrades (*"Ma'am, your pork loin tonight will now be prime rib—at no extra cost to you . . ."*).

2. Pay No Attention When the Waiter Suggests a "Favorite Dish"

I sympathize with waiters, I really do. They're hardworking, starving actors barely surviving on one meal a day—but I never listen when they recommend their so-called favorite dish, the warm fricassee of roasted root vegetables with black truffle *jus*. The only *jus* they've ever tasted is canned gravy. It was a sad day in American dining when waiters decided their job was to give orders, not take them.

3. Insist on a Glass of Fresh, Tasty Ice Water

Restaurants are not selling bottled water to keep you hydrated. They sell it because it costs them seventy-five cents and they can charge nine dollars and seventy-five cents. Unless the civil defense agency of the state where you are dining has declared a water-rationing emergency, restaurants should place tap water on every table. Tap water is your friend.

4. Don't Order Steak at a Seafood Restaurant

However, seafood at a steakhouse is never bad.

5. Pass on the Omelette Station

You're on vacation, ready to splurge. That means the hotel's $39.95 Sunday buffet brunch. There's salmon, sushi, crab claws, shrimp, and eggs Benedict. You head straight for the omelette station, where a guy in a Hawaiian shirt who has never been to cooking school is making fluffy four-egg omelets with scallions, peppers, Bac'Os, and a grated cheese product. Nice going. You've just filled up on an egg dish that costs $3.99 at Denny's.

6. Stand Up for the Coat-Check Girl

Many restaurants have decided to profit from the decades of good will and affection that (male) customers have for coat-check girls. They do this by paying her a (meager) salary and keeping the tips for themselves. Shades of Oliver Twist, that buck or two that you press into her delicate palm is immediately snatched away. So I always ask the coat-check girl if she's permitted to keep her tips. If she tells me she isn't, I don't leave one. What I do is complain to the manager.

7. Demand to See the Chef

If dinner for two is costing $200, you have every right to expect the chef to be at work. Restaurants where the famous celebrity chef has taken the night off (or, more likely, is making a few thousand bucks cooking at a corporate event) should post a notice, similar to the ones seen in Broadway theaters: "The role of our highly publicized head chef will be played tonight by sous-chef Willie Norkin, who took one semester of home economics at Scarsdale High School and can't cook worth a damn."

8. Never Order the House Wine

Anything is better: lager brewed from the toxic waters of America's Great Lakes. Flat tonic water from the bartender's soda gun. No matter what beverage you request, it's going to be better than the house wine, which often comes from a box. If there are two of you having dinner, order the cheapest bottle on the list, even if you know you won't be able to finish it. And, please, whatever you do, don't sniff the cork—you'll learn nothing and only smudge your nose.

9. Never Eat a Dish Credited to the Chef's Mother
Honestly, do you really think Mom is back there at the stove? Maybe, just *maybe*, if you're driving through Italy and stop for lunch in The Piemonte region you might find a sweet old lady chained to a chair in the kitchen, forced to make a few thousand *agnolotti* before lunch. This doesn't happen in America. Any restaurant dish called "Mama's" was cooked up by some ungrateful son who probably hasn't called home in two and a half years.

10. Even Worse Is a Dish Invented by the Chef's Father
Because dads can't cook.

TOO MUCH IS NEVER ENOUGH

I came to Monte Carlo to eat, and to do so in a manner so ambitious that all who learned of my plan labeled me insane, except for the few who thought me blessed. My itinerary: book a room for five days at the Hôtel de Paris, home of Alain Ducasse's restaurant Le Louis XV, and while in residence eat all my meals in the hotel dining room. I thought it elegant and traditional, to say nothing of convenient, inasmuch as the hotel has a garage and on-street parking has always been problematic along the Mediterranean.

The reason for the intemperate reaction to my dining plan was that Le Louis XV is no ordinary hotel restaurant. It has three Michelin stars, and no restaurants are more illustrious—or more dedicated to over-indulgence—than those. They epitomize the glories of French dining, the pinnacle of culture in a country obsessed with good taste. While many persons, myself included, are horrified at the cost of three-star dining—to pay less than $150 per person is a boon, to pay more than $300 per person commonplace—the financial price of eating in these gastronomic temples is not as daunting as the physiological one. After one such meal—*amuse-bouche*, appetizer, fish course, meat course, dessert, and petits fours, unless the diner selects a tasting menu, which entails much more—the process of digestion is inadequate. What is required is decompression. And I was planning on ten meals in five days.

Others have attempted similar feats of gourmandise, generally fool-hardy travelers who make their way across France wolfing down prodigious repasts in as many three-star establishments as they can reach in as short a period of time as possible, lurching from meal to meal in the same béarnaise-flecked tie and Burgundy-stained suit, setting records for the most courses eaten without doing laundry. I wished no part of such buffoonery.

Before I set off for Monte Carlo, the business and tourism center of the principality of Monaco, I announced my intentions to Ducasse. I let him know that something was amiss about three-star dining if a man couldn't get off the elevator in his hotel lobby and get a little something to eat without a subsequent visit to a gastroenterologist.

He nodded, for that is his tight-lipped way, and I took that for agreement. His only stipulation was that I stop at his restaurant, Alain Ducasse, in Paris, on the way home. He wished me to compare the two styles of three-star cuisine. It was not the most odious of provisos, although not many people who eat ten three-star meals in a row are lining up for number eleven.

I set off believing all that was required of me upon arrival in Monte Carlo was a good appetite. Thus I was fortunate to have business beforehand in Milan, for this northern Italian city offers only two significant dishes, one of them veal Milanese, which is bland meat flattened, fried, and served with nothing to detract from its essential bleakness, and the other osso buco, which is the bony part of the veal that remains after most of the meat has been flattened and fried. Having quickly tired of those dishes, I was ravenous when I boarded the Milan-to-Monaco train, a local that proceeded halfway south in a conventional manner, then pulled into a small Alpine village station where it had no choice but to back out. Once the backing up began, it never ceased. We continued in this unsettling manner for hours, until the train finally backed into the station at Monte Carlo. It was a good reason to travel on an empty stomach.

I checked into the Hôtel de Paris, one of those imperial sanctuaries that deserves to stand on a square dominated by a statue of some long-forgotten grand marshal of the army of the emperor. Here, in deference to the needs and tastes of guests, the square outside the hotel is given over to Lamborghinis, Ferraris, and Bentleys. The microwheeled vehicle I arrived in, constructed from the same materials as lawn furniture, was snatched from sight so quickly I was nearly dragged away before I could release the handle of the door.

I had requested the kind of room that we Americans call, with some hilarity, a junior suite, as though it were proportioned for undersized executives. I cared only that the room had something other than a bed to rest upon, and such suites always have couches perfect for napping between meals. In the bathroom, I was distressed to note, was a scale, which I vowed never to step on, even though it was thoughtfully accessorized with a doily that averted an untoward situation, bare feet touching cold metal. I knew what would come to pass were I to place my weight upon the scale, the needle jiggling and trembling and finally settling on the wrong number, in much the same way the steel ball of a roulette wheel always comes deliciously close to dropping into my number before leaping away at the last moment. Monte Carlo has a famous casino that I had no intention of patronizing, for casinos and scales are much the same to me. With neither do I have luck.

What I had not told Ducasse, and I don't believe anybody in his right mind would have made this admission, was that the primary reason I wanted to spend my five days in Monte Carlo and not at his three-star Paris restaurant, is that I wished to evaluate the Mediterranean cuisine served at Le Louis XV. Ducasse is always referring to the food cooked in his Paris place as "northern cuisine," so much so that I have at times imagined him dishing up a Scandinavian smorgasbord, whereas it is actually the food we commonly associate with France, food lavished with butter and cream, exactly what I love.

Mediterranean food has always displeased me, but that might be because the only place I have eaten it regularly is the United States. Restaurants that specialize in American-style Mediterranean cuisine tend to feature out-of-season tomatoes, relentless quantities of zucchini and red peppers, and an alarming eagerness to bond tapenade, the anchovy-caper-olive paste, to anything to which it will stick. I also find that whenever I dine in the Mediterranean restaurants of New

York, I am always calling over waiters and complaining that I have found olives in my bread.

While my primary challenge to Ducasse was to determine if three-star dining could be an exercise in civility rather than gluttony, I also hoped to learn something that would diminish the apprehension I feel whenever I enter a restaurant offering Mediterranean cuisine.

Le Louis XV, for all its fame and pedigree, is a room of modest dimensions, except vertically. The ceiling is so high that if all the soufflés ever cooked in France were stacked one atop the other, they would barely reach the naked ladies gamboling in the fresco up there. Closer to earth are fifteen tables set with gold-rimmed Limoges china and gold-tone silver flatware, a marble grandfather clock that might be a hand-me-down from Versailles, busts of haughty French women (are there other kinds?), and all the accoutrements of a lavish eighteenth-century lifestyle: gilded and beveled mirrors, heavy draperies with tasseled tiebacks, looming chandeliers.

The waiters, dressed in a variety of formal wear representing a service hierarchy too complex for a visitor not of royal blood to comprehend, weave among the tables like a corps de ballet. They are mostly tall young men with black hair and fabulous dispositions. I induced polite chuckles from them whenever they began their routine of resetting the table for dessert, at which time I would threaten to go upstairs and change my shirt and tie. A regular Jerry Lewis, that's me.

My first meal, planned and executed by Ducasse's chef de cuisine, Franck Cerutti, was a culinary triumph that left me apprehensive. The *amuse-bouche* was a luscious curlicue of pure white Italian lard, not a product that has entered the mainstream of three-star dining but admirable for its agrarian ancestry. From there I proceeded to lentil-and-pheasant bouillon topped with ricotta-cheese gnocchi so light they failed to break the surface tension of the soup, sea scallops slathered with black truffles, and bass roasted to unparalleled richness. The truffles were a bonus I hadn't anticipated. I had forgotten that during black-truffle season, December through March, three-star restaurants employ them much as midwestern housewives use Shake 'n Bake.

Dessert was *baba au rhum*, the rum-soaked, cream-topped sponge cake I have always considered the French equivalent of our cream-filled Twinkies. Both are mass-produced sweets that satisfy innate societal cravings, ours for calories and theirs for alcohol. The *baba au rhum* at Le Louis XV brought enlightenment. The cake was fresh, conveyed to the table in a highly polished brass dish that cast back the golden highlights in the cake while twinkling a merry pastry greeting all its own. Offered a choice of five rums to be poured over the top, I selected the dark 1984 vintage Rhum JM from Martinique. Then the waiter held aloft a gigantic dollop of whipped cream and asked if I wished it or not. When my delighted laugh rose to a near-cackle, he said, "It was only a question."

Following the dessert course came the petits fours, pastries, and candies. There were thirty-five. I ate ten or twelve, hoping my inadequate consumption would not be perceived by the kitchen staff as an insult. I shoved a few of the wrapped caramels in my pocket to eat later.

I have never been certain what purpose petits fours serve, for at this point in the meal no further nutrition is required. In fact, the presentation of these tiny sweets depresses me, because I feel I must consume every one of them or be responsible for havoc in the notoriously demanding French kitchen—some junior member of the pastry brigade de-toqued and banished to a bakery in the Massif Central to make cupcakes for the rest of his life.

Petits fours have yet another drawback. Although they are ostensibly complimentary, they increase the cost of a three-star meal, because serving them calls for an enormous investment in trays, bowls, baskets, jars, urns, tureens, and pots for transporting all the chocolates, caramels, marshmallows, madeleines, macaroons, and bonbons. I am certain the price of eighteenth-century sterling silver has been driven up by three-star chefs bidding against one another at auction houses just so hard-candy can be brought to the table with proper ceremony.

After the meal, I informed Cerutti that he had not lived up to

Ducasse's promise to feed me prudently. He replied that he considered the meal light, for he had given me only a small portion of the fish and one dessert instead of two. He used my selfless petit four consumption against me, claiming they were the reason I felt so full. He shook his finger at me and said from then on I could have only a single petit four with every meal, and he ignored my reasonable protest that a chef who wished a customer to have only one petit four would not serve thirty-five of them.

With dinner only four hours away, I returned to my room to nap, which I find the only civilized restoration between meals. I do not understand people who walk after eating, which is not all that different from swimming, which is considered suicidal. Anyway, why walk at a time when you have no interest in peering into the windows of charcuteries and patisseries?

I fell asleep on my couch, but I had eaten too much to rest well. Were I French, I would have had no problems, for overeating comes naturally to them. They even have an imaginary ailment to blame whenever they feel uncomfortable after the courses have mounted up, an imaginary malady they call *une crise de foie*, a liver attack. Having denounced a perfectly innocent internal organ—*J'accuse*, as they like to say—the crisis is over and they move on to their next meal. Americans don't get away with overeating so easily. I tossed and turned, and my nightmare brought a prophecy that proved all too true: I dreamed I was gaining weight.

"So," said Ducasse, "which do you prefer, the sea bass from Chile or the black bass from America?"

Little did I know when I signed up for this trip that a pop quiz would be involved. Ducasse, who flies back and forth between his two restaurants each week, amassing Michelin stars and frequent flyer miles, invited me to eat with him in the tiny chef's room off the kitchen. It contains a table that seats four as well as six grainy TV monitors for watching the cooks at work.

This Saturday lunch was my fifth meal at Le Louis XV, and it was an opportunity to complain to Ducasse about portion sizes. I felt that Cerutti was airlifting in supplies so my meals would be large enough. When I spoke of this too openly to Ducasse, Cerutti took me aside and informed me that he would get even if I kept up the complaints to his boss, so I said no more. Our main course was a piece of lightly salted cod, the salt adding flavor and substance to what is essentially a bland fish with a slithery texture. I complained mildly about the *mille-feuille* that we were served for dessert, whether the layers of pastry were perhaps too dense and too buttery, and whether the pastry cream should be so preemptively rich, so overwhelming that it drove out all thoughts of petits fours. Ducasse tasted his, declared it "the epitome of vanilla and carmelization," and informed me of his dessert philosophy: "You shouldn't eat dessert. Dessert is a sin. So if you are going to sin, do it freely. Having one dessert is like having one mistress, ridiculous. You must have two or three, once you get started."

He does not cook while in residence at Le Louis XV, nor does the public require that he do so. Whereas famous chefs in American restaurants must occasionally pretend they adore standing in front of a stove in order to satisfy the demands of critics and customers, French chefs at Ducasse's level of eminence are permitted to be businessmen. He runs an organization that includes the two three-star restaurants, a well-regarded inn in Provence, and a national hotel association. He enjoys challenging those around him, and in my case he was checking out my level of discernment when he asked whether I preferred the Chilean or the American bass.

"The black bass from America," I said, which was the wrong answer. His eyes shifted almost imperceptibly as I went from promising gourmet to irreparable jingoist in his estimation.

One morning, Cerutti met me at the outdoor market of Nice. Both Monte Carlo and Nice remain celebrated Riviera destinations, but they have grown apart over the years. Monte Carlo has become a whitewashed tax shelter of gleaming hillside condominiums populated by wealthy Europeans who earn too much to want to part with any of it. Nice continues to exude Gallic conventionality.

For a while, we walked from stall to stall. He kissed all the pretty girls, insisting that he was merely saying good morning in the French manner. He wore jeans, a sweater, and a backpack, and he was very much the celebrity—not, he explained, because of Le Louis XV but because years earlier he had operated his own restaurant only a few blocks away. It was midwinter and so freezing cold that whenever possible I sneaked off and stood in front of an outdoor rotisserie, trying to steal some of the heat from the chickens on the spit.

Cerutti showed me vegetables grown locally in the winter months: tiny broccoli called *brocoletti romano* being sold by a farmer wearing layers of unwashed clothes; herbs from a pretty girl (kissed); tiny winter apples from a middle-aged woman in a cardigan (not kissed). It is contrary to my urban nature to believe anything can grow in this kind of cold except lichen. Where I see tundra, Cerutti sees farmland. He said the Mediterranean cuisine is at its least interesting during the summer months, "when there are the worst products, the red pepper and tomato and zucchini," but now there were the small artichokes with the sharp pointed leaves and soon would come morels and green peas and the best baby broad beans in the world.

I saw beautiful goat cheeses, and I asked him why there were none on the cart at Le Louis XV. He explained that at this time of year the milk from the goats was needed to feed the babies, and the farmers who made goat cheese killed the babies to have more of the milk. This was the most compassionate statement about food I had ever heard from a Frenchman, and when I expressed my admiration, he said the business about saving the baby goats was all very nice but the real reason he didn't serve the cheeses was that the goats were kept indoors this time of year. Thus they could not roam the mountains, eating the wild herbs that gave their milk a special taste.

By now I was shaking. I had dressed in a T-shirt and a light jacket, thinking I would be warm enough, a misconception I blame on American restaurants that serve the same warm-weather Mediterranean food throughout the year. I had packed for this trip convinced it was always tomato-growing season along the Mediterranean. Cerutti took me to a small café so deteriorated I would have thought it abandoned had there not been so many people in it. He bought me a huge bowl of café au lait and told me a little of his life.

He grew up on a farm a few miles inland from Nice, went off to hotel cooking school, and eventually began working in hotel kitchens, preparing those fraudulent French luxury dishes that sound more interesting than they ever taste—dishes with the surnames of courtesans, like lamb *pompadour;* dishes that take on the names of regions, like sole *normande;* dishes that have names meant to impress tourists, where the peas are Saint-Germain and the asparagus is Argenteuil. "I was getting bored," he said. "I felt that if this was what cooking was all about, I would change jobs."

Then he met, in succession, Jacques Maximin, of the Hotel Negresco in Nice, and the younger and even more brilliant Ducasse. Cerutti kept going back and forth between the two, working for one and then the other. Ducasse found the situation amusing but Maximin hated it, always saying to him, "I never want to see you again." He cooked in Florence, and he had that restaurant in Nice, and when Ducasse asked him to work in Monte Carlo, he accepted. Ducasse says of his second-in-command, the man who executes the recipes that have made him the most famous chef in the world, "Franck would be unable to cook the kind of food we have in Paris, but he is the best interpreter of Mediterranean food there is. There is a strong relationship between what he is and what he does. He is a Latin. He must touch the products before he cooks them. He has olive oil instead of blood."

Although Monaco has no noticeable native cuisine, one evening Cerutti sent out an *amuse-bouche* called a Barbajuan, a fried puff pastry filled with Swiss chard, ricotta cheese, and leeks. It is a specialty of the principality. Because it was served in this restaurant, I found it tasty, but I can see how it might remind me of a frozen pizza roll somewhere else. Monaco does not have much of a native population, either, most of the locals having fled to escape the income-tax refugees pouring over the border in their Rolls-Royces. That same evening, a true Monegasque and his wife entered the dining room, moving with the elegance and pride of an endangered species. They were both in their heavy-spending years.

They set their handbags on the tiny settee placed beside every cushioned armchair for that purpose. She wore the sort of jewels Harry Winston lends out to starlets who try not to return them. He wore a diamond-studded pin on his velvet jacket and a pinkie ring with a sapphire so large it caught my eye from two tables away. Everything about him sparkled, including his hair. He bent to read the wine list with the aid of a lorgnette, reading glasses that come on a stem. They seemed happy together. If he was one of those men who keep mistresses, he loved his wife as much as any of them. They had beluga caviar and Gosset Rosé Champagne, and then he ordered 1983 La Mission Haut-Brion, a very nice wine, not too showy, just right.

I was eating alone, as I often do, and their mutual devotion caused me a moment of melancholy. I got over it quickly. There were decisions to be made: Which Champagne-by-the-glass would I have to begin? Which of the seven breads would I select? Did I desire the salted butter from Normandy in the gold dish or the unsalted butter from Normandy in the cute little basket? (What a relief not to have to dip my bread in olive oil, mandatory in the Mediterranean restaurants of New York.) I find that the more culinary dilemmas I face in the course of a meal, the happier I am to be sitting by myself. Without conversation, there is nothing to get in the way of the food.

When I am dining alone, I do not take out a paperback novel. I find that restaurants provide all the visual entertainment I need. I find I must occasionally resist the impulse to engage sommeliers in tedious, one-sided discourses on the greatness of the wines I have had back home, a particular Pinot Noir from the Russian River Valley, for example. I know I have gone too far when the sommelier is shaking with impatience, desperate to break away.

To my knowledge, I did that only once at Le Louis XV, when the chief sommelier, Noel Bajor, served a 1988 Coulée de Serrant and I tried to express my gratitude with a heartfelt discourse on the superiority of French Chenin Blanc over California Chenin Blanc. While I was speaking, I believe several customers fell from their chairs, fatally parched.

Cerutti and I settled into an agreeable if quarrelsome pattern. I would inform him that he was giving me too much to eat, and he would dispute this, claiming that it was my fault for eating too fast or eating too much bread or eating too many petits fours. Occasionally he would waggle a finger at me and say, "No cheese!"

The maître d' of the restaurant was continually trying to brighten my mood, announcing cheerily, "Very light today, only two courses." Then out would come food on plates so large they appeared seaworthy. One of the "very light today" meals started with the signature dish of the restaurant: zucchini, turnips, fennel, carrots, and cabbage cooked with olive oil and black truffles. The baby vegetables in this assemblage were soft and impossibly succulent, bound up with the chopped truffles and olive oil. The dish was so savory I could imagine never needing meat again. It was also so oversize I could imagine never eating again.

Next came veal, and never before had I tasted veal this tender and yet this flavorful, slice after slice of delicately pink loin, so many slices this was no mere dish of veal. This was a vista of veal, veal that seemed to go on forever, fading into the horizon, and surrounding the veal were spinach-flecked potato gnocchi in a black truffle sauce. Cerutti came out and applied the coup de grâce, shaving black truffles over the dish. I ate every bite of the best vegetables I'd ever had in my life, and then I ate every bite of the best veal I'd ever had in my life, and then I stumbled into the kitchen, barely able to remain upright.

This was the showdown. With whatever formality I was able to muster, I informed Cerutti that he had let me down. Much to my surprise, he expressed his regret. He said the veal had to be cooked for two, and what else was he to do inasmuch as I was eating alone but give me both portions.

This did not prevent him from presenting me with dessert. Out came mascarpone sorbet with wild strawberries. I counted the strawberries, and there were forty-six of them. I let Cerutti know about this, too, and he walked away, shaking his head, muttering, "Forty-six, forty-six," as though I were the one who had lost his senses, not he. I ate every one of the barely warmed berries with the cooling sorbet. I did it to prove to Cerutti that he could not get the better of me.

What I did not want him to know, for it would have altered our quarrelsome relationship, was that never had I experienced food of such clarity prepared so exquisitely. There were no tomatoes, except a few that had been sun-dried, and barely any olives. I could have done with fewer artichokes, but Cerutti explained that I had come during the season of the wonderful Sardinian artichokes, and nobody could have too many of those.

He served Mediterranean fish soup at one meal. It smelled sweetly of the sea, and accompanying it was rouille, which is the traditional spicy, garlicky, reddish sauce. I was relieved when Cerutti told me I need not stir the rouille into the broth. All my life I have been ruining perfectly good fish soup out of an obligation to add ridiculous amounts of sauce to it, and now I don't ever have to do that again. I had turbot on a layer of crabmeat, and accompanying the fish were grilled endive and raw endive stuffed with crabmeat, an example of the reiteration of flavors that is characteristic of Ducasse's style. The simplest food served to me was spit-roasted leg of lamb, the best I've ever tasted. The most unexpected was the stomach of a codfish, prepared like tripe, a daring dish for a three-star restaurant. The only food I truly disliked were the marshmallows, a part of the petit four collection. They smelled like dried flowers in the drawing room of a widowed aunt. I told Cerutti they'd only please me if he built a campfire in the center of the dining room and allowed me to roast them on sticks.

I was right about the limitations of Mediterranean restaurants in America. Ducasse sided with me on this point, if on no other. He said Mediterranean food becomes less authentic the farther it moves from the

Mediterranean, which makes it "enormously difficult" to do in Paris and "a caricature" in the United States. I was surprised to discover that Le Louis XV is actually a regional restaurant—not a humble one, but a regional restaurant nonetheless. Eating the Mediterranean food there gave me the same good feeling I might have experienced had I stumbled upon an unknown bistro in Nice with a genius for a cook.

As for Cerutti, I owe him an apology. After leaving Monte Carlo, I flew to Paris for the promised dinner at Alain Ducasse, where the style of food is less homey but otherwise similar to that of Le Louis XV. Nothing seemed very different until the dishes were cleared away and it came time for the petits fours.

They did not arrive, as they did at Le Louis XV, on an assortment of splendid plates. They came on a polished cart the size of a resupply wagon. On this conveyance were vanilla ice cream, strawberry sorbet, roasted almonds dipped in chocolate powder, sugar tarts, Paris-Brest (an exquisite pastry honoring an old bicycle race), apricots dipped in sugar, raspberries dipped in sugar, preserved orange dipped in chocolate, chocolates with nuts and dried fruit, marshmallows, two kinds of macaroons, four kinds of bonbons, and warm madeleines.

I do not forgive Cerutti his indifference to portion control, but in the matter of petits fours, I realize that he is not such an unreasonable fellow after all.

GQ, MAY 1999

PLAY IT AGAIN, LAM

I'm going to be honest with you. Where war is concerned, few people are. I'm going to tell you a story about Vietnam unlike any you've read before.

Nobody dies in my story. I served in the Republic of South Vietnam a quarter-century ago as the executive officer of a U.S. Army boat company, and I don't know anybody who was killed in the war. Whenever I think that life hasn't given me a break, I remember that.

There's something else I should confess about my year in Vietnam: I gained weight while I was there.

I was a captain, a deskbound Transportation Corps officer assigned to the U.S. Army Harbor Craft Company (Provisional) in Saigon. At the time, it was the largest boat company in the army. Yes, the army has boats, lots of them: tugs, floating cranes, tankers, landing craft, barges, and more.

You hear a lot these days about "good" wars and "bad" wars, but I've always suspected mine was the third kind, an unexceptional war. When I went to the Washington National Records Center, in Maryland, to look for information about my unit, nobody could find any evidence in the 300,000 square feet of paper stored there that it had even existed. A clerk said to me, "The record-keeping over there was pathetic, at best. When somebody does a history of Vietnam based on what we have here, anything that is close to accurate will be purely accidental."

I was there, all right, and so was the harborcraft company, even if the government refuses to admit it. Almost every morning, one of our tug-boats would head up the Dong Nai River to Long Binh Post, making about two knots against the current, towing a barge wallowing under a massive load of fuel or ammunition. It was the ammunition, the tons of assorted explosives, that troubled those of us who rode along. The riverbanks were dense with foliage, plenty of cover for an overly ambi-tious Vietcong armed with an RPG launcher and willing to fire a round that would blow up the barge, the tug, and probably himself.

Most mornings, the tug left without me. That's because I was an REMF, the unofficial designation given to soldiers who never went into the field by the men who actually fought. I didn't ask to be an REMF, nor did I volunteer for more demanding duty when I became one. I took what the army gave me. REMF stands for "rear echelon motherfucker." There were a lot of us.

I didn't endure many hardships, except when the mess hall ran out of ice cream, my customary late-afternoon snack. I've heard that only about 15 percent of U.S. forces sent to Vietnam were actually in com-bat, which means that about 85 percent of all the soldiers, sailors, marines, and airmen (only members of the Salvation Army see less combat than the modern airman) were pretty much like me. Not long ago I called my former boss, who was the best officer I ever knew and is now retired in Phoenix. I asked him what he thought of me as a sol-dier. "I was always impressed by your cheerfulness," said Victor Largesse, then a major and the company commander. I figured that for a euphe-mism, and I was right. "I always thought you were on a lark, never took it seriously."

When people talk about the turning point of the Vietnam War, they always bring up the Tet Offensive of 1968, when the Vietcong achieved tremendous psychological victories, even capturing the U.S. Embassy in Saigon for a few hours. I always thought the turning point came in 1969. When I arrived early that year, Saigon still felt like a combat zone. By the time I left, my unit was marching in parades. The REMFs had taken control.

Once or twice a month, I got out of my swivel chair and went to war. I didn't have to, but I did. It was guilt, not patriotism or heroism, that inspired me. I was always ashamed that the only time I regularly went on the water was for dinner on our hundred-ton floating crane, the one with the recently naturalized cook who had mastered his Italian mother's recipes. To this day I don't recall many meals I enjoyed more than his lobster *fra diavalo,* made with pilfered lobster tails.

I would grab my helmet and flak jacket and jump on one of the tugs heading up the Dong Nai. Once I was aboard, my mission was not to get in the way. No shot was ever fired at a boat while I was on it, and while I like to think my steadfast presence behind a machine gun made a difference, I know it was luck. The trip took hours, and standing for that long with that much clothing on in the intense heat of a country that is almost always hot and wet builds a thirst.

By the time we docked, I'd be hungry and dehydrated, and I'd head for the Chinese restaurant on post for sweet-and-sour pork with three or four Cokes. I don't eat much sweet-and-sour pork anymore, but when I do, I recall those rides upriver and immediately need a Coke. You've heard about Vietnam flashbacks. That's mine.

"Where are you staying?" asked Tony Newman, chief of the Saigon office of the International Organization for Migration. Officially, Saigon is now Ho Chi Minh City, but only people who don't live there call it that.

"The Majestic," I replied.

"Which room?"

"Five-oh-one."

"I think Westmoreland stayed there."

In defense of William C. Westmoreland, commander of U.S. forces in Vietnam throughout most of the sixties, I would like to say this: he was an uninspiring general, but he had standards. He would not have found room 501 of the Majestic acceptable.

Don't get me wrong. When I returned to Saigon a few months ago, I made sure I stayed there. The Majestic once offered the grandest lodgings in a city once called "the Paris of the Orient," and the Saigon of decades past is what I hoped to find.

It wasn't difficult. Saigon doesn't look much like Paris anymore, but for that matter, it didn't look much like Paris back in 1969. The city does look remarkably like it did a quarter-century ago, which cannot be said of Bangkok, Singapore, Tokyo, and most of the other metropolitan centers of Asia. Credit for this time warp goes to the economic boycott imposed by the United States and to the less-than-innovative development strategies implemented by the Socialist Republic of Vietnam under the leadership of the former U.S.S.R. Saigon is a city that has stood still.

Camp Davies, where I was stationed, was an obscure chunk of dock space on the fringe of the city in 1969. The docks, warehouses, and even the Quonset hut where I slept are still there, looking more insignificant than ever, although nobody seems to remember it was an American military installation named Camp Davies.

Astonishingly, the monetary system remains almost exactly as it was during the war: back then the standard currencies were American dollars (or American military scrip) and Vietnam *piastres*. Today they are American dollars and Vietnamese *dong*.

The famous Bun Ho Hue soup, a thin scallion-flavored meat broth sold at stands everywhere for a few cents, is still sold at stands everywhere for a few cents. As it did then, it fills me with awe and respect for a people who relish hot soup in ninety-five-degree heat. One newfangled idea that has taken hold is the emergence of pizza delivery. I ordered a large pie from Annie's Pizza—"Annie is the long form of Ann, which is an Americanization of "Anh"—and it was delivered to my hotel in a cardboard box bearing the catchy slogan "When the taste of home beats ya, call for Annie's Pizza."

I didn't return to see Vietnam. I didn't see much of it during the war. I went back to see Saigon. Almost every night during my tour of duty, while most officers hung out at Camp Davies' sorry excuse for an officers' club and watched a movie projected on a bedsheet, I got in my jeep and went to town. I loved Saigon, especially the women, exquisitely dressed in the traditional flowing, high-necked *ao dai*. I ate out almost every night, and I learned to say "No *nuoc mam* [fermented fish sauce], please." I survived the heat, which was so intense I had difficulty writing home—the perspiration would pour down my arm and smear the ink.

This time, I made certain I had air-conditioning. The Majestic did, and that's all I needed to know. I wasn't concerned that it once had a reputation as "the CIA hotel," or that it served as a Japanese barracks during World War II. For $65 a night, single occupancy, I got a platform bed as hard as a tank turret, a couch covered in an oilcloth-like bright-yellow fabric, a telephone made of red-and-white Lucite, and red wall-to-wall carpeting accented with a lime-green throw rug. The TV received three stations, all providing the same in-depth coverage of foreign dignitaries arriving to discuss the industrial development of Vietnam. A warning sign posted on the inside of the door gave the rules: No cooking, ironing, weapons, toxics, explosives, inflammables, pets, or prostitutes. (I cheated and brought a travel iron.) The night attendant on my floor was a former UH-1B (Huey) helicopter pilot for our ally, the Republic of South Vietnam.

From my picture window overlooking the Saigon River, I could see the new Saigon Floating Hotel as well as the infamous My Canh floating restaurant, bombed by the Vietcong in 1968. That attack pointed out the difference between the futile strategy of Westmoreland and the successful strategy of the Vietcong. He went after their hearts and minds. They went after our stomachs.

From Tony Newman's description, I figured out that Westmoreland's room must have been 504, a top-of-the-line, $120-per-night suite down the hall. Gaudily decorated in chinoiserie, it has lacquered furniture, a Yamaha piano, and a sixties-era sunken tub. I could just picture Westy, immersed in bubbles, walkie-talkie to his ear, learning of the fall of Hue while an aide stood at attention, holding a fluffy towel. For the REMFs, Vietnam was that kind of war.

.   .   .

Newman drove over to the Majestic to pick me up. Traveling with me was Ron Wormser, a dentist and old friend. Ron thought I'd invited him along for companionship but he was wrong. You'd travel to Saigon with a dentist, too, if you'd had two impacted wisdom teeth chiseled out in a field hospital in 1969. I asked Newman to choose a restaurant I couldn't possibly have found on my own, and he headed toward Cholon, the Chinese section of the city, then turned into side streets. We ended up at Quan Bo Song, or "Riverside Tavern."

Seemingly tiny from the outside, the restaurant stretches far back, ending at the water. Its dimensions reminded me of churches I've visited in Venice. Newman recommended fried river crabs with tamarind sauce. After a few bites, I had an accurate premonition that crabs would become my favorite food of this visit. We sat at the tip of a pierlike extension jutting out into a tributary of the Saigon River, listening to the creaking of tired, unpainted fishing boats docked alongside. Newman talked about the fundamental changes that have occurred in Saigon since his arrival.

He said that four years ago, "this was a pretty paranoid, dark place. People were not ready to talk to you on the street, we were not allowed to visit a Vietnamese person's home, and they weren't allowed to visit us. All meetings took place in lobbies. I don't know how it happened, but suddenly it was no longer necessary."

His organization, acting something like a consulate, assists with the orderly departure of legal emigrants. Of the 350,000 émigrés helped in the past four years, about 30,000 were Amerasians, and tens of thousands of others were men and women who had spent years in the notorious reeducation camps.

The waiter brought us a two-pound river fish that he could not identify, even in Vietnamese. While it simmered in a light coconut-scented broth heated by Sterno, Newman pointed out some of the incongruities of Vietnam.

I asked him why the people of Saigon remain so friendly toward Americans, who abandoned them in 1975. He said, "They blame the Russians for all their problems. The Russians had no money." He said the government of Vietnam was trying to emulate Singapore, a one-party state that provides everything for citizens, notwithstanding the fact that Singapore is one of the most ardently anti-Communist states in the world. He said that while the opening up of Vietnam will allow more departures, he hears that some Vietnamese living in Southern California see it as an opportunity to come home. "People who left want to come back and die here. They're miserable in the United States. They can't contribute anything to the family, they can't understand their grandchildren, they miss the life here."

With our chopsticks we excavated chunks of fish, added mint and cucumber, wrapped the combination in lettuce, dipped it in vinegar sauce, and ate. Lunch for three, beer included, cost $13.

The seafood at this meal was the best I would eat in Saigon. Another search, for the finest Chinese food, turned out to be more difficult. At the well-regarded Phuong Hong, I immediately became discouraged by the menu, which included specialties such as sea ginseng on deer veins and the highly euphonious fried frogs in foil. (Any traveler desirous of epicurean extremes is advised to seek out restaurant Vinh Loi, where a signboard outside promises GREAT TASTE... GREAT VARIETY... GREAT SERVICE. SPECIAL DISHES: COBRA. TURTLE. BAT. EVERYONE WELCOME!)

While I was dispiritedly picking away at my Phuong Hong entree, fried rice with an egg on top, two young girls at a birthday celebration one table away started giggling uncontrollably. I believe they were wildly amused by my ineptness with chopsticks.

Well, this burned me up, so I did what any former American fighting man would do under the circumstances: I stuck a chopstick up each nostril. This incited such hilarity that I knew my presence would be missed at future gatherings of the family for years to come. My friend Ron and I were each given a slice of cake, included in a majority of birthday photos, and invited to dinner the following night.

That's how we came to be at Ha Ky, located on a block of Duong Ta Uyen Street lined with stands selling whole roasted chickens and pigs. The restaurant is tiny and un–air-conditioned, with four big round tables in the front room. Appropriately, the chicken was superb, easily the best I tasted in Saigon, and so were the large fried crabs, the kind that demand endless cracking to expose a few bites of incredibly sweet meat. A few days later we reassembled again at the Yellow Umbrella Cook Shop, a slightly more upscale storefront spot located on Mac Thi Buoi Street in the heart of what passes for Saigon's nightlife district. On the same street is the Hard Rock Cafe, no resemblance whatsoever to any establishment of the same name in capitalist society, and Apocalypse Now, the best known of the city's expat bars. It caters to European back-packers and middle-aged Americans in T-shirts. The recorded sixties and seventies rock is played so loud it could drown out an air strike.

Nobody shot at me during the war. I never thought anybody would. Because I had never fired an M16, the army's new combat rifle, I selected my own weapons: a .45-caliber pistol that I could use pretty well and an M79 grenade launcher that I had only the remotest idea how to operate. Then again, with a grenade I only had to come close.

One problem with being in my unit was that ammunition wasn't easily obtained. For administrative purposes we worked under a logis-tical command whose mission was to unload ships. This had advan-tages, since the soldiers who did the unloading were the very ones who stole the steaks and lobster tails I kept in the freezer compartment of the full-sized refrigerator in my quarters, but these guys had little use for ammunition. The only people likely to pull a gun on them were the captains of the American freighters they were plundering. The way we got most of our ammunition was to trade for it or to steal it.

Since we belonged to the unit that towed ammunition upriver, all that we required was within reach. What I most needed were the 40-mm grenades I enjoyed firing at the trees along the Dong Nai. (Officially, this was known as a reconnaissance-by-fire.) It didn't make sense to break into a pallet and steal a single box of grenades, because the theft would be noted and investigated. It was better to break into a pallet, take a single box of grenades, and throw the rest into the river. That way nobody would notice a thing. Now you know yet another reason why the Vietnam War cost so much.

I was reminded of our ammunition-procurement procedures when I browsed the gift shop of the Majestic Hotel and found souvenir cigarette lighters made from 40-mm grenades. Everywhere in Saigon I found war souvenirs for sale. At first glance it seems as though every bit of military equipment abandoned by American forces has been salvaged, cleaned, and put on the market. Certainly the legendary profligacy of the American soldier would tend to support this conclusion, as would the equally renowned resourcefulness of the Vietnamese people. In reality, almost all the goods are fake.

On my first morning in Saigon, I was walking down Dong Khoi Street, formerly Tu Do Street, in its day the Rodeo Drive of Southeast Asia. I gulped with nostalgia as I passed display cases filled with snap-top Zippo lighters engraved with the disheartening aphorisms of those who fought in Vietnam. "Live by chance . . . Love by choice . . . Kill by profession." Or: "If I had a farm in Vietnam and a home in hell, I'd sell my farm and go home." Later I realized they, too, were counterfeit. The so-called American Market is filled with all manner of ersatz war-surplus material, even helmet liners with yellowing instruction booklets inside. They're fakes. In all the dozens of booths and shops of the market I saw one item, a canteen, that might have been real. For friendly service and good prices on fake watches, I liked the War Time Souvenir Shop of the War Crimes Exhibition, which was known as the Museum of American War Crimes until diplomatic ties between Vietnam and the United States improved.

After strolling through a display of alleged American atrocities, Ron and I headed for a restaurant called Vietnam House, which has a cool, inviting, colonial-style piano bar. Play it again, Lam. The food was unexceptional, but we enjoyed eavesdropping on a young American businessman at the next table who was suggesting all kinds of exotic travel to his extremely young and beautiful Vietnamese companion.

Outside, we ran into the *mama-san* who had hired out the young and beautiful companion. She was pacing up and down, looking worried. She asked if we had seen the girl. We said that we had. She asked if the girl was being well treated. We assured her that as long as the child hadn't ordered the gummy fried rice served in a clay pot with nearly invisible bits of chicken, she was likely to survive.

Vietnamese women liked me, and Vietnam is a great place to be liked by women. This popularity with women wasn't noticeable before I arrived in Vietnam in 1969 and it has never recurred since. I've tried to understand. I think it was the fatigues.

I had great fatigues. I got them in the mid-sixties, when the United States invaded the Dominican Republic. Nobody remembers us invading the Dominican Republic, but we did. I was a second lieutenant then and quite nervous about joining the Inter-American Peace Force and going off to war, but everything worked out. My job was to load soldiers onto airplanes.

Back in those days, U.S. Army jungle fatigues looked like something you would buy at Banana Republic, except there was no Banana Republic back then. They had pockets and flaps all over. By the time I got to Vietnam, jungle fatigues had changed. They had been streamlined and didn't look good, but I had kept my old fatigues and wore them when I went out at night. Dressed in my multiflapped fatigues, adorned with captain's bars and the appropriate USFORDOMREP (United States Forces, Dominican Republic) right-shoulder combat patch, I looked great. Or at least I looked great until I started gaining weight from all that steak and lobster I kept in my freezer.

The most spectacular women I came upon worked at the South Vietnamese Air Force Officers' Club, located at Tan Son Nhut Air Base. The airport is still functioning, although now it has so many miles of excess runways and empty parking areas it looks forlorn. I couldn't find the old officers' club. It so exemplified imperial decadence, I suspect some government official ordered it destroyed.

As I recall, the ground-floor and upstairs function rooms were used for weddings, banquets, and other activities commonly associated with the social life of a military officer. Downstairs was the lewdest bar I've ever patronized. The front door opened onto a narrow, dark foyer lined with long benches packed with extremely tiny young women with extremely large breasts. Where they got them, I have no idea. As you walked this girlie gauntlet, they would reach out, clutch your arm in a death grip, and attempt to drag you through the bar into a nearly pitch-black back room.

I recall one memorable occasion when I declined to enter the back room and three girls desperate for business surrounded me and started pushing and pulling. Not willing to go but not wanting to hurt anyone, I stood perfectly still, rigid as a statue. Although I was wearing combat boots, they slid me along the floor like a piece of furniture.

Once in the back room, anything from fondling on up was available, providing drinks were purchased for the young lady. These drinks sold for two dollars and were called Saigon tea, which is what they were. In every bar in Saigon, the price was the same and the drink was the same. If you were in a discreet establishment where the women really were hostesses, you would be expected to buy a Saigon tea every fifteen or twenty minutes. In the back room of the South Vietnamese Air Force Officers' Club, they arrived every minute or two. I never sought the company of hostesses, rarely bought a Saigon tea, and refused to enter the back room of the officers club, at least not after my first, harrowing visit. I paid a price for my restraint. In my favorite bar, now gone, the women took note of my reluctance to purchase beverages. They nicknamed me "Captain Cheap."

Today, the solicitation is much more subtle. The woman who came up to Ron and me at a tranquil bar named Linda's Pub asked politely if she could sit with us, then said nothing at all until we offered to buy her a drink.

Shyly, she said, "I work here. Customer come here. He like me, he talk to me. Ask what me like drinking. I say okay."

"So," I said, "you'd like a drink."

No, she didn't want a drink.

Fine, she didn't have to have a drink.

Sadly, she replied, "But if you do not buy drink, boss he get angry with me."

"So," I said, clenching my teeth, "I'll buy you a drink."

No, I didn't have to if I didn't want to.

The old South Vietnamese regime might have been corrupt and pathetic, but at least the bars weren't so annoying.

I told her I insisted on buying her a drink.

She said in that case she'd have juice. She told us her name was Anh and she was sixteen years old. I took the same percentage off my age and told her I was thirty-four. She warned us to be careful if we were looking for women because "some are ladyboys, not true ladies." I told her I would have nothing to do with ladyboys, but I couldn't speak for Ron.

Economically, Saigon makes no sense. The average income is about two hundred dollars a month, but almost everybody seems to ride a two-thousand-dollar Honda. The standard of living is low, but shops teem with goods—at one stall, I counted twenty-one kinds of rice. If you compare the number of closed and shuttered storefronts in Saigon with those in Manhattan, you would assume it was America that was rising from the ashes of economic devastation.

With so many major Southeast Asian cities saturated, or at least running out of space for office towers, Saigon is a natural outlet for the economic energy of Asia. The price of property is already eight to ten times what it was two years ago. I heard stories of Vietnamese who hold long-term leases on property costing them forty dollars a month and charge three thousand a month in rent. The economic redevelopment of Vietnam is just about the only topic in the local news, and only a very few suggest that it isn't going to be as easy as generally believed.

Hoang Mgoc Nguyen, the managing editor of a semiofficial newspaper, the *Saigon Newsreader*, told me that an absence of skilled educators will curtail Vietnam's progress. "You cannot blame the Russian education in physics and chemistry, but it fails with economics and management," he said. "My staff is trained in the Soviet system. It has no idea how a free market operates. That is why I am cautious when I hear foreigners say, 'Your country will be a dragon in five years.' It is all rubbish to me."

Nguyen Ngoc Bich, a Harvard-trained lawyer and businessman who spent twelve years in reeducation camps and now practices commercial law in Saigon, believes the United States will not be a significant economic factor in Vietnam's reeducation. "If you analyze what America can give us—and what we can take from you—it is the leasing of oil and gas to American companies, telecommunications, and software." When Ron put in a plug for American medicine, Bich shook his head. "Too expensive. It must be a charity, not commercial."

The oil-and-gas industry, he said, will operate in remote areas and have limited impact. The software industry will back away as soon as it learns that Vietnam has no copyright law. And telecommunications is for the wealthy. He said that nothing America offers Vietnam is valuable enough to make the leaders of the country turn away from Communism, their lifelong philosophy. Not Kleenex, not computers, not Coke.

During the war, I often went to the roof of the Rex Hotel to eat dinner and listen to Filipino singers imitate Elvis Presley. They did a pretty good job, although the overall level of government-issued entertainment in Saigon wasn't that great. The guys actually fighting saw Bob Hope and Joey Heatherton. Those of us working in Saigon got the cruise-ship bands.

The Rex became a distasteful symbol of the Vietnam War, and rightfully so. The body counts and napalmed villages were the truly appalling images of the war, but the Rex was, in its own small way, loathsome. It was comfy quarters for coddled officers who paid Vietnamese attendants to spit-shine their boots. They were so removed from the war that even I felt contempt for them.

The roof of the Rex has become even more surrealistic since the war, which is hard to believe. Back then it offered slot machines, cheap steaks, and endless arrangements of "Heartbreak Hotel." Today it is a vista of outdoor tables amid a menagerie of cats (real), birds (real), fish (real), elephants (statuary), horses (statuary), tigers (statuary), and deer (topiary). It has every sort of imaginable outdoor ornamentation, as though the manager rented a station wagon and went shopping along U.S. 1 in Maine.

If the roof was a welcome sanctuary during the war, it is even more of one today. It is a place to escape the relentless begging on the streets. Walking along Dong Khoi and Le Loi, I came to recognize them all: the lady with the head-lolling drugged baby, the man with no face, the maimed kid who walked on his hands. Once I barely outran a footless man who dashed across the street to head me off. The rotten little-boy pickpockets are ruthless and the nasty little-girl postcard hawkers pinch if you don't buy. I learned to say, "No postcard, no stamp, no change money, no girl, no beer, no want nothing." Late in the afternoon, Ron and I would take the elevator to the roof for beer and an order of Imperial Rolls Saigon style. It became my favorite tourist food.

To the table would come a jack-o'-lantern carved from a pineapple. Stuck on toothpicks and protruding from the face were myriad crisp, two-bite-sized spring rolls. The normal accoutrements for wrapping— lettuce, mint, and a vinegar-based dipping sauce—were served alongside. On one occasion, when the hotel's usually overworked kitchen wasn't too busy, the presentation included the word *REX* and a crown, both carved from carrots. The cost: $2.34. Food prices tend to be low and not rounded off at government-sponsored restaurants.

The most famous hotel in Saigon, now and probably forever, is the Continental, constructed in the late nineteenth century and situated in splendor across from the Rex and the Municipal Theatre. I was never an admirer of the hotel's terrace, made famous by Graham Greene in *The Quiet American* and by Somerset Maugham in *The Gentleman in the Parlour*. To me, the place was too crowded with the kind of people who read Greene and Maugham. The hotel was taken over by the Socialist Republic in 1975, just after the fall of Saigon, and used as a government guest house until 1987, when it closed for two years of renovations. When it reopened, it was clear that the government felt the same way about the terrace that I did. It was no longer there.

Today the space is occupied by an oversize Italian restaurant called Chez Guido, which is the most dispirited eating establishment in the city. The room is high-ceilinged and filled with pillars and chandeliers, which makes it look more like a cavernous meeting hall than a restaurant. There's so much space between tables that the place feels empty even when it's full, and there's no music, just eerie silence. In a city of terrible service, Chez Guido offers some of the worst, inasmuch as the waiters tend to congregate in the back room and read magazines.

I started my meal with a carpaccio of fish the waiter claimed was tuna. It wasn't like any tuna I'd ever eaten, not in texture, taste, or appearance. It was pale, a ghost of seafood past. A risotto was gummy but the scaloppini "chez Guido" was absolutely first-rate. The noodles were fresh, the scallops of pork the best meat I ate in Saigon, and the tomato sauce not bad at all. I sniffed and skipped the grated cheese. Prewar, perhaps?

The Caravelle, the third in a lineup of top-notch hotels surrounding the theater building, was a favorite spot for American journalists during the war and is remembered as the home of the Caravelle Manifesto—in 1960, a few enlightened Vietnamese politicians met there to draw up a document calling for civil rights reforms. They were promptly jailed. During the war, I liked the restaurant on the top floor. My unit held farewell dinners there for officers about to return home.

Now there's a restaurant serving Japanese food on the tenth floor and one with a menu of French, Vietnamese, and Chinese dishes on the ninth. That's where Ron and I ate, mostly because I was taken with the decor: huge overhead fans that resembled propellers on WW II fighter planes; bizarre, spidery chandeliers; badly tended plants; and a brightly lit advertisement for Ken Y ice cream over the cashier's desk. Nothing on the menu cost more than three dollars, and while the food wasn't exceptional, it was worth the price.

The two most famous restaurants in Saigon are Maxim's, which has a cabaret downstairs and a girlie bar upstairs, and Madame Dai's Bibliothèque, where guests dine in the library of a beautiful home. At least the fortunate ones do. When Ron and I arrived, we were shown to a table in the garage, right next to Madame Dai's motorscooter.

We declined, to the surprise of Madame Dai, and moved on to

Maxim's, lured by the famous name. The downstairs cabaret and restaurant offer a lot for your money: an amateurish but enjoyable floor show, a bathroom attendant eager to shpritz customers with an evil-smelling cologne, and reasonably priced French and Chinese food. As soon as we sat down, we received complimentary snacks, including cashews in airline-type packets. We ordered Chinese mushrooms with shrimp stuffing, baked squab with rock salt, fried shrimp on toast, steamed fish with ginger, and braised spinach with crab meat. Every dish was bland. Our check, including the meal, the floor show, the tip, and two beers, was less than $35.

The entertainment highlight was a young woman in what looked like a prom dress—do Communists have proms?—holding a rose and singing "Unchained Melody." Men flushed with ardor jumped from their chairs to press carnations into her hands. As soon as she finished her performance, everybody got up and left. Everybody but us. Only Ron and I remained to applaud the tenacious young lady who performed a less-than-haunting "Ave Maria" on her cello.

For dessert, I ordered a mocha soufflé. Ron had crêpes Suzette. Extravagant? Perhaps, but where else in the world can you get two luxurious French desserts in a place called Maxim's for $1.44.

As I sat there on my final night in Saigon, eating my slightly collapsed soufflé, the seven-piece orchestra broke into a lush arrangement of "Smoke Gets in Your Eyes." I glanced up and realized that the eyes I was looking into were my dentist's. And you thought the Vietnam War ended badly.

GQ, SEPTEMBER 1994

MIAMI WEISS

Early Bird humor, overheard outside the Publix supermarket, Coconut Creek, Florida.

FIRST MAN: *I can prove Jesus wasn't Jewish.*

SECOND MAN: *How?*

FIRST MAN: *If he was Jewish, he wouldn't have been at the Last Supper. He'd have been at an Early Bird.*

I've come to south Florida to explore one of the nation's oddest food trends, the Early Bird Special. If you've never had an Early Bird, it means you are too rich, too thin, or too Christian. I've found my way to the city of Coconut Creek, which is ground zero for the Early Bird phenomenon—nearly a fifth of its population is both elderly and Jewish.

At the moment, I'm sitting in the kitchen of the world's absolute authority on the Early Bird. (The Formica, incidentally, is spotless.) The authority is a woman of more than seventy-five years who reacts to a few dollars off the price of a stuffed-flounder dinner the way others react to a winning Lotto ticket. The woman is my mother.

I know what you're thinking: pretty cushy work. Fly to Florida, see Mom, take a few notes, fly home with a slab of brisket packed in ice. You don't know my mother. Food she gives you. Editorial cooperation is something else. This is what happens when Norman, my father, suggests to Ida, my mother, that we begin our explorations at Love's, a legendary Fort Lauderdale Early Bird eatery.

IDA: Don't tell him to go there. Nobody goes there.

NORMAN: What do you mean, nobody goes there? It's been in business five years. When we went, there were lines. Everybody goes there.

IDA: When we went there, it was called something else.

NORMAN: It used to be called Belaire. You have to say, for the price it wasn't bad.

IDA: Anyplace where the meal is four dollars and fifty cents, what can they give you? A blintz is four-fifty. When I make a blintz, it costs more than that.

Debating my mother is slippery business. My father is more straightforward, but I'm afraid he orders too much bad veal parmigiana, the kind where the meat is chopped and the cheese solidified, to rate serious consideration as a food authority. However, he is something of a grassroots cultural anthropologist—that's a nice way of saying he gossips around the pool. I'm fascinated by the depth of his Early Bird lore.

He tells me the Early Bird is a meal served before peak dinner hours, one at which patrons are rewarded with discounts or with complimentary courses. It is good for retirees who like to get dinner finished early so they can take advantage of community activities. It is good for elderly persons who have difficulty driving at night, because they can return home before sundown. Mostly, it's a good deal. Early Bird devotees eat as much as they can, and then they take home everything left on the table. My father tells me they even clean out the bread basket, a suggestion that incenses my mother, who does not wish to be thought of as a character out of *Les Misérables*.

IDA: When have we ever taken bread home? Except at the Rascal House, of course.

NORMAN: Talk to Thelma. She's always taking bread home.

IDA: Oh, her. She takes everything home.

Thelma isn't her real name, by the way. Some journalists change names to protect the innocent. I've done it to protect the bridge club. Between having to assign an alias to "Thelma" and surviving the bread blowup, I realize that probing my mother and father for Early Bird inside information might not be such a good idea. I decide I will wait until I return to New York to seek an answer to the most delicate question of all: Why are there always so many Jews at Early Birds? I eventually ask this of comedian Jackie Mason, a leading authority on Jewish folkways.

"It's simple," he says. "Jews have one thing on their mind: food. At five o'clock, when gentiles are thinking, 'I want a drink,' Jews are thinking, 'I want to eat.' Gentiles go to a bar. Jews go to an Early Bird Special. It's the cocktail hour for Jews."

That's a neat explanation of why Jews eat early. I think I already know why Jews eat cheap. It has to do with a historic fear of being overcharged.

Take my mother. Sometimes I tell her about my favorite foods in New York, like the chicken with whipped potatoes and sweet garlic sauce at Montrachet. The price is $24. She's never had it, but according to her, you can find just as good in Florida for much less.

"We go to this kosher place, get a plate of soup, a half-chicken—that's *half a kosher chicken*—one vegetable, tea, four dollars and fifty cents."

I reply, "I thought you said nothing for four-fifty could be any good."

She looks at me scornfully. "This is lunch. I'm talking about lunch. Lunch is different."

What can I do but apologize?

At this point, I shut up and let her take charge. I say we'll go anywhere she wants to check out her Early Bird favorites, but lunches don't count. Lunches aren't Early Birds. I tell her that breakfast doesn't count, either, even if you can get two eggs, a bagel, and coffee for ninety-nine cents at Ann & Vince's Southgate Bagel & Deli, in North Lauderdale. By the way, you'd think this would constitute the ultimate breakfast experience for my mother, but she is not as predictable as that. She prefers Bageland of Margate, even though the breakfast specials there start at $1.39.

"At Bageland," she says, "I can send back the bagels to be toasted twice."

"So send them back twice at Southgate," I say.

"For ninety-nine cents, I haven't got the nerve."

I ask her if we could please stop with the bagels and get on with business, the Early Bird dinners. This gets her a little miffed. She informs me the food won't be fancy like I get at my big-shot New York restaurants. This is an important point. When you're talking Early Bird, you're not talking new wave Floribbean cuisine, the "seared citrus-crusted yellowfin tuna with a macedoine of papaya, mango and yellow pepper" we read about in *Time* magazine while I was down there. To be deprived of such dishes does not constitute a loss to my mother.

"I don't eat anything seared," she says.

The first stop on her restaurant itinerary is the Fifteenth Street Fisheries, in Fort Lauderdale, which offers an Early Bird from 5:00 P.M. to 5:15 P.M., a dangerously narrow window of opportunity. My father tells me that just before 5:00 P.M., everybody lines up outside. When the doors open, they race for the dining room, up on the second floor. It's sort of a Geriatric Olympics, everybody hitting the stairs like an Edwin Moses with varicose veins. Alas, we go on a slow night, so I do not witness this spectacle.

The Early Bird here is simple: $5 off any entrée except specials. My mother, who rates the place "pretty good," has harsh words for the salads, although I find them imaginative. "There isn't even a tomato," she says. "I wouldn't call that a salad, no tomato."

I praise the intermezzo, a tiny dish of tropical-fruit sorbet.

"Very classy," I say.

"My appetizer was one little piece of fish," she says. "After that I need an intermezzo?"

Also scoring high with me is Kelly, the bread girl. A girl that cute, I wouldn't take to an Early Bird. I don't ask an opinion of my mother. When the girl isn't Jewish, you don't bring her up.

Our next stop is a Margate seafood restaurant named Mr. G's. I'm told it's named for the owner, a fellow named Margolin. Naturally, I don't quite understand, so I ask for an explanation.

"It's for his first name," the waitress says. "It's Joe."

Service at most Early Bird establishments is friendly but not intellectual.

My mother declares that Mr. G's has the best Early Bird seafood in south Florida. She has the Canadian sea scallops casa, which I guess means casserole, since that's what it is. It comes with pasta, salad, coffee, and dessert, and it costs $10.95.

"Quite a bargain," I say.

"Eleven dollars isn't so cheap," Ida replies.

Our next stop is Raindancer, in Fort Lauderdale, her top-rated Early Bird establishment. I'm astonished by the portions, so huge I understand why retirees wear elasticized pants. The Early Bird includes entree, soup, salad bar, coffee, and "a choice of selected desserts" (that's a euphemism for "we're saving our best desserts for better-paying customers"). My mother is excited about the salad bar because it offers unlimited anchovies, the forbidden fruit of her low-salt diet. I warn her that her doctor is going to read about all the anchovy fillets on her plate. She says, "I don't ask my doctor what to eat."

By now, I'm feeling like a sport, having taken my parents out for three dinners. Perhaps you think otherwise, that I'm some sort of cheapskate son who won't spend more than eleven bucks on his mother. Let me tell you how generous I am. Because she is celebrating a birthday during this visit, I invite her to dinner at the Forge, a Miami Beach restaurant with more objets d'art than a Las Vegas shopping arcade. To me, the decor is excessive, but to my mother, who has always wanted to eat there, it is beautiful.

We go for the Early Bird, of course, although the Forge doesn't call it an Early Bird. It's Twilight Dining Service, three courses for $19.95.

Ida, tempted by the steak Rosanne, asks the captain for an explanation of the dish. He begins, "It's a ten-ounce steak, pounded—"

She interrupts.

"I don't eat anything pounded."

I ask for the free-range Wisconsin duck.

"Terrible," my mother says. "The last time I couldn't eat it. I should have sent it back. It was tough and stringy and—"

I stop her.

"I thought you said you'd never been here," I say.

"Oh," she says, "it wasn't here."

I have the duck. I give her a taste. "Now that's what I call duck," she says. She has the Forge special sirloin. Perfection. Dinner is accompanied by a bottle of slightly sweet Mosel wine, magnificently suited to the palate of a Jewish mother.

Service is exquisite, helped along by my father, who assists the busboy in piling up our plates. Coffee costs extra, which is known to cause food riots among Early Birders, but my mother so loves the Forge that she shrugs when I mention the extra $1.95 involved. "I got money," she says, implying that if a son won't buy a mother a cup of coffee, what good is he?

"You know," she says, transferring her affections, "I like the wine steward."

She decides to tip him. On the way out she slips him three bucks, quite proper for a twenty-one-dollar bottle of wine. The wine steward tells me it is the first time in his thirteen years at the Forge that a woman "of that age" ever tipped him.

"What age is that?" I innocently ask.

"Oh, sixty-five or seventy," he says.

I catch up with Ida and Norman outside. When I tell her the wine steward's estimate of her age, I expect her to simper with happiness.

Instead, she looks at me the way she did so many years ago, when I came home with a C on my report card.

"I gave him a tip," she says. "What do you think he's going to do, say I'm eighty?"

GQ, NOVEMBER 1991

THE LONG ALOHA

When I look back to my college days, what I remember most is my first dinner date and the Pub-Tiki's Sesame Chicken Aku-Aku. Let me tell you about this dish. Boneless white meat in a cream sauce as velvety as a warm tropical rain. Egg noodles as soft as twilight shadows. Sesame seeds, the most exotic seasoning I had ever tasted, sprinkled across the top. It was the very definition of alluring.

The woman was lovely, too. She was a raven-haired wordsmith who worked with me on the University of Pennsylvania student newspaper, and she always wore a formfitting, tightly belted black vinyl raincoat. I had no idea what I was doing out with a girl like her, a knockout even under deadline pressure, but for that matter, I had no idea what I was eating, either. All I knew about Polynesian food was that it deserved to be described in the words of the great philosophers. Now, thirty years later, I can no longer recall those words. For that matter, I seldom recalled them on exam days, either.

My status with this child-woman was somewhere between sycophant and manservant. Sometimes I ironed her hair before she went out with the older men she was used to dating, many of them twenty years old or more. I knew I had no chance with her, but I thought perhaps I could improve my station were I to escort her to the Pub-Tiki, the most sophisticated Polynesian restaurant in Philadelphia.

The main dining room featured eight-foot-tall wooden sculptures and a lava-rock fountain. The Outrigger Room had a genuine outrigger canoe hanging from the ceiling—outriggers have always been de rigueur in Polynesian restaurants. The Map Room dazzled with a hand-painted mural of Polynesia.

I could imagine how the date would go: when our modestly but fetchingly attired pseudo-Polynesian waitress came to take our order, I would take charge. For me, the sesame chicken. For her, the Shrimp Bongo-Bongo—red and green maraschino cherries electrified this dish. One bite of the succulent shrimp, deep-fried and immersed in a swooningly gooey sauce, would cause her to fall back into the depths of her wicker chair. It would be paradise by the tiki lights.

It's not easy explaining to people of today what Polynesian restaurants meant to those of us who came of age, culinarily, in the sixties. In those days, nobody had any idea where Polynesia actually was, or what Polynesians actually ate. As far as we knew, Elvis Presley's *Blue Hawaii* was a documentary. I suppose, if pressed, I might have said that Polynesians dressed in floral polyester shirts, listened to swaying Hawaiian music, and ate heavy-duty Chinese food.

Polynesian restaurants were nothing if not inauthentic, but they changed the way Americans dined out. Before they arrived, finding pleasure in restaurant food was something best left to the wealthy or the French. Restaurants like the Pub-Tiki transformed the dining culture of America, turned the unionized masses into a dinner crowd.

These places were also the precursor of food crazes to come. They had potted plants before anybody had ever heard of fern bars. They put ginger in food before the invention of Pacific Rim cuisine. They even made drinking a family sport. Perhaps those Polynesian concoctions— "island cocktails," according to Trader Vic's, the seminal Polynesian-restaurant chain—tasted a little too much like rum mixed with sugar and rubbing alcohol, but they were fun for Mom, Dad, and Junior, too.

The drinks came in whole pineapples or in coconut shells. Sometimes they came in ceramic bowls as big as wagon wheels, with flaming lavender gel and straws as long as canoe paddles. These cocktails were far greater than the sum of their rums. They carried you away to a rusted deck chair on a tramp steamer, or to a hemp hammock on a lost island. They were a state of mind, until you downed a few of them, and then they were a state of mindlessness.

Most important of all, the Polynesian palaces were America's first theme restaurants, and now they seem to be dying out, disappearing like thatched huts in a hurricane. My beloved Pub-Tiki closed in the early eighties. Trader Vic's, the General Motors of Polynesian restaurants, has six locations left in the United States, down from a peak of nine-teen in the early seventies. (The chain is doing better outside the U.S., where the concept is fresher.) Of the five great Polynesian restaurants that once thrived in Los Angeles—Trader Vic's, the Luau, the Islander, Kelbo's, and Don the Beachcomber—only the Trader Vic's in the Beverly Hilton Hotel remains a full-time restaurant. Kelbo's has been renamed Fantasy Island and operates as a "lingerie cabaret supper club," which apparently means its strippers stop short of removing all their clothing.

Polynesian restaurants are not only fading away, they seem to have been forgotten. A few months ago I read an article in USA Today that concluded: "Most restaurant experts agree the modern theme restau-rant era began in 1971, when Hard Rock Cafe opened in London." There was no mention whatsoever of Polynesian restaurants, no suggestion that the owners of today's theme restaurants should raise a mai tai in memory of the drink's creator, the late "Trader Vic" Bergeron.

It isn't hard to figure out why restaurants accenting Polynesia are no longer thriving. To start with, Polynesia seems to have lost its allure. Even though we know where it lies—between Hawaii and New Zealand, on this side of the International Date Line—we no longer care. Our travel fantasies have shifted to Italy. It could be argued that all the inauthentic Italian restaurants so popular in America today are really Italian theme restaurants, fulfilling the same fantasies that Polynesian restaurants once did.

Polynesian restaurants have fallen too far behind the times. Their cornstarch-based pseudo-Cantonese cuisine compares poorly with the creations of modern masters of the whimsical, like Wolfgang Puck, whose colorful, sweet, and creamy dishes are far tastier and infinitely

more refined. Even the classic Polynesian decor of spears, shields, water-
falls, footbridges, and tiki-people salt-and-pepper shakers seems hopelessly dated when contrasted with the interactive entertainment and
animated displays of modern theme restaurants.

Nevertheless, Polynesian restaurants were, and still are, something
that modern theme restaurants are not: in their own way, they are the
real thing. They are total packages of cuisine, attire, and decor, whereas
today's themeries are more in the entertainment-and-shopping business than in the food business.

With few exceptions, the menus in theme restaurants are hamburger-
and-pasta-based, their drinks are Polynesian-cocktail based, and their
waiters are out-of-work-actor based. They sell bomber jackets, glassware,
and sweatshirts, making anywhere from 25 to 50 percent of their prof-
its on merchandise. Robert Earl, the creator of Planet Hollywood, made
this remarkable statement: "I don't think of myself as a restaurateur;
I'm in the trademark business." Modern theme restaurants are perfectly
acceptable forms of family entertainment, but they are more amuse-
ment parks than restaurants.

Not long ago, I saw hope for a Polynesian resurgence in Gauguin,
which had replaced Trader Vic's at New York's Plaza Hotel. Unfortunately, before I had a chance to sample such new-style fantasies as wok-
seared lobster with black-bean butter sauce and flaming volcanic ice
cream island floating in a sea of blue curaçao, Gauguin closed down.
The Plaza's management called the place a "den of iniquity," incensed
not by the sarong-clad waitresses but by the male go-go dancers and "a
clientele with deviant sexual pleasures." That was the last true Polynesian stronghold in Manhattan. I searched, but the best I could come
up with was the Cantonese restaurant Tai Hong Lau on Mott Street in
Chinatown. I would not even have known it had Polynesian preten-
sions were it not for a basket of tiny umbrellas in one window.

I realized that if I was to find vestiges of this once-great dining tradition, I would have to head west, to California, the cradle of the Polynesian movement. I also understood that as a native Philadelphian, I
knew little about the once-flourishing West Coast Polynesian-restaurant

culture. Helpful contacts directed me to Max Baer, Jr., who played Jethro on *The Beverly Hillbillies*, and who retains a well-earned reputation as one of Hollywood's great Polynesian-restaurant regulars.

Baer once ate ribs with Elvis in a Polynesian restaurant—he thinks it was Kelbo's, although he isn't sure. Mostly he hung out at the Luau, on Rodeo Drive, with his friends from Warner Brothers, drinking Polynesian cocktails and eating whatever followed. "Let's face it," he says, "after three or four of those drinks, you could eat Alpo—you didn't know what they were feeding you."

As a Hollywood insider, Baer considered the Luau as much a clubhouse as a restaurant, a place where he'd meet up with Troy Donahue, Natalie Wood, Cesar Romero, and Broderick Crawford, among others. Crawford was the easiest to find. He'd be planted at the bar, drinking until he couldn't drink anymore. Not that Baer's self-discipline was much better. "I crawled out of the Luau more than once," he recalls. "Mostly I remember drinking mai tais and Scorpions. As far as I can tell, one was made with pineapple and one was not. I'd sit there getting shit-faced. Once, I remember, I was there with Lance Reventlow and Jill St. John, and I think Tony Curtis was there, too. The Luau had a walk with palms, and in the middle of the walk was a ship's steering wheel. I remember standing there one night at the helm, saying, 'I'll get this motherfucker to shore!'"

These days heavy drinking is considered untoward, but back then the fine-tuned alcoholic stupor validated a man's celebrity status (witness, for example, Dean Martin, Jackie Gleason, et al.). With cocktails at the core of every fine-dining experience, inebriation was a kind of Zen state, and the Polynesian cocktail was the most painless path to Nirvana.

Today's theme restaurants offer essentially the same kind of drinks, but they're no longer called the Zombie or the Suffering Bastard. The names are more obvious: the Die Harder, at Planet Hollywood; the Hot Pants, at Fashion Cafe; the Cannibal Concoction, at the Jekyll and Hyde Club; the 10W40, at the Harley-Davidson Cafe; and the Midnight Train to Georgia, at Motown Cafe. I'm certain that Trader Vic's endures because it has always done the cocktails better than anyplace else, particularly the communal cocktails for two or four that the restaurant chain calls "the ancient Polynesians' ceremonial luau drinks."

Bolstered by Baer's enthusiasm, I continued my search for Polynesian perfection at the Trader Vic's in Beverly Hills. When I walked in, the air smelled as smoky sweet as a Texas barbecue shack, and the bar was packed two deep. Young women were drinking from real pineapples, while young men were encouraging them to drink more. Except for the prices—$8.95 for one of those Pino Pepe pineapple jobs—I could have been in some sort of tiki time warp. I ordered a Scorpion, described on the illustrated drinks list as a "festive concoction of Rums, Fruit Juices and Brandy, with a whisper of Almond, and bedecked with a fragrant flower." I thought it tasted the way Annick Goutal perfume smells.

Besides pineapples, Trader Vic's serves drinks in ceramic coconuts (the Kamaaina), earthen bowls (the Tiki Bowl), and rum kegs (the Rum Keg). It has them in tall glasses and in small glasses, with long straws and with regular straws. They're garnished with sprigs and leaves and parrots and fruit and, of course, maraschino cherries. (The importance of maraschino cherries cannot be overemphasized—they are to Polynesian drinks what olives are to martinis.) They're made with light rum and dark rum and sometimes with a splash of 150-proof rum. They come, allegedly, from Montego Bay and Rangoon and Samoa and Barbados and Hawaii and Havana and Jamaica and Tahiti and Sibony—I don't remember anyplace called Sibony from the sixties, but I'm sure it was there even then. There's even a drink called the Chinese Itch—who knew that China was an exotic tropical isle?

Trader Vic's has everything anybody could want in a Polynesian drink, everything but undersized umbrellas. When one of my dinner guests requested any drink at all, as long as it came with a tiny parasol, our waiter replied, " Trader Vic's doesn't have umbrellas." I thought this was indeed a sign that the Polynesian apocalypse was upon us, but the waiter added, "Trader Vic's has never had umbrellas."

"Surely at one time . . ." I began.

"Never."

"How long have you been here?" I asked the upstart.

"Since 1972," he replied.

I guess Trader Vic's has never had umbrellas.

The drinks, even left unprotected from the elements, continued to please. Not so the cuisine. As much as I'd like to praise food that I once liked so much, I cannot. Not only did Trader Vic's food taste bad, it looked bad. In memory I see beautiful dishes. I see Shrimp Bongo-Bongo. At Trader Vic's, visually unappealing food was shoved together on the plate in such a manner that the half-empty dishes leaving the table in the hands of busboys looked pretty much the same as the full dishes that arrived in the hands of waiters. Only the coconut shrimp reminded me of classic Polynesian food—sweet, succulent, oily, and absurdly delightful.

Cuisine aside—and, admittedly, that's a big aside—the absolutely best spot to experience the nearly lost mysteries of Polynesia is the Tonga Restaurant & Hurricane Bar, located in San Francisco's Fairmont Hotel. The place has abandoned Polynesian cuisine in favor of the sort of indeterminate Chinese fare that's available on almost every corner in San Francisco, but the preparations are skillful and the prices extraordinarily low. Anyway, I didn't go to the Tonga room, as it's commonly called, for the Szechuan beef or the Canton prawns. I went for the atmosphere. In terms of sheer delight, the Tonga room is the Rainbow Room of Polynesia.

On weekdays from five P.M. to seven P.M., you can sit in the bar, listen to recorded Waikiki luau music, and quaff Polynesian drinks served by waitresses clad in red Susie Wong–style dresses. (Susie Wong was another mid-century icon.) I ordered the Bora Bora Horror, a blend of rum, banana liqueur, orange-flavored brandy, and pineapple juice. Do not repeat my mistake, for this was the worst Polynesian cocktail I've ever tasted. I liked the five-dollar all-you-can-eat happy-hour appetizer buffet, which included admirable miniature pork buns, tiny spareribs, and steamed shrimp dumplings.

I stayed on for dinner, happily paying the three-dollar entertainment charge. And what entertainment it was. A three-piece floating—

yes, *floating*—combo adrift in a large pool that is the centerpiece of the room played perky show tunes. But the real fun came at the breaks, when lightning crackled, thunder boomed, and rain—yes, real water—fell around the periphery of the pool. As I sat listening to the native rhythms pulse savagely and watching the lightning flicker wildly, I felt as though I was being swept away, as they used to say, to an island paradise.

It was supposed to be that way with her, all those decades ago. Our meal at the Pub-Tiki in Philadelphia was perfect, but she never looked at me the way she looked at older men. Not long afterward, we lost touch.

I called her a few months ago, just to see if she had any regrets. She told me she was divorced. I expressed my sympathies. Then she told me she was living with a man she had met in college when she was a sophomore and he was a senior. I tried not to laugh, but I couldn't help it. Nothing had changed.

I told her I had never forgotten our one dinner date. She told me she hadn't, either.

"Oh, yes," she said, "the steak came on an inch-and-a-half-thick wooden board, and there were mashed potatoes all around it—they looked like they had been put into a tube and somebody had squeezed them out like whipped cream."

I stopped her. She was speaking of Chateaubriand à la bouquetière, a thick cut of beef for two that was the epitome of romantic dining in the fifties and sixties. She was, of course, remembering dinner with another man. I told her how I recalled every detail of our dinner, too, especially how beautiful the Sesame Chicken Aku-Aku looked that night.

GQ, MARCH 1996

NOT MUCH OF A MAN IN HAVANA

On my first morning in Havana, this was my breakfast: six kinds of fruit juice, kielbasa, Vienna sausage, breakfast sausage, smoked bacon, unsmoked bacon, chickpeas, peas, cucumber slices, red peppers (mixed with corn), green peppers (sautéed), french fries, ratatouille, smoked salmon (after I elbowed my way past insatiable South Americans assembling overstuffed lox sandwiches, a habit they surely picked up at Wolfie's in Miami Beach), scrambled eggs, fried eggs, a cheese omelette (inexpertly made to order), a chicken wing, a jelly-filled crêpe, a sugared doughnut, a sugared roll, a chocolate-covered doughnut, a chocolate-covered roll, a raisin Danish, a cream-filled Danish, a cheese sandwich, a lunch-meat sandwich, a lunch-meat-and-cheese sandwich (these last three, all dreadful, out of my desire to be one with the Cuban people, who appear to eat little else), a banana, a chocolate-drizzled banana, grapefruit sections, orange sections, pineapple sections, melon sections, plain yogurt, orange-flavored yogurt, pears in syrup, four kinds of jam, two kinds of cellophane-wrapped cakes, *picadillo de res* (a sloppy joe–like hash so delicious I went back for seconds), eleven cereals (I was getting full so I didn't try them all), eleven kinds of cereal toppings (Special K with chocolate sauce is tastier than expected), sparkling water, mineral water, coffee, and tea.

A string trio played softly as I dined, slowly and with enormous resolve, finishing everything I took from my hotel's breakfast buffet except the omelette, the sandwiches, and the chocolate-drizzled banana.

In a country where almost everyone except tourists goes hungry, wasting food feels even more immoral than eating too much of it.

On that same morning, I visited a sixty-two-year-old Cuban woman named Nilsa. This is what she had for breakfast: a kind of powdered cereal commonly thought to be made from soy, to which she added water to make mush.

As patently offensive as the contrast in our fare appeared, I was almost as dismayed by the explanation behind her request that I not use her full name. In Cuba, the spoken word can be judged inappropriate by all manner of overseers, including the ever-watchful Committee for the Defense of the Revolution, a semi-vigilante, semi-volunteer organization made up of people who in most countries are referred to as neighbors. The members of the CDR are not gossips. They are for real. Even a Cuban as patriotic as Nilsa, a supporter of the revolution, a woman who went into the mountains during the literacy campaign of 1961 to teach reading to farmers, has to worry that her words will be harshly judged.

I spent two weeks in Havana, entering without a visa and violating all manner of Cuban and American restrictions—the American government forbids tourism to Cuba but readily allows journalists to go there, while Cuba welcomes American tourists but insists that journalists apply for authorization. By going in the way I did, with permission from nobody, I was able to spend my time without government supervision.

I met with no officials, took no specially arranged tours, and wandered wherever I wished. I did not enter the country to promote Cuban cigars, lobby for Cuban-American trade, or advocate the cause of some Cuban shortstop unfairly denied the right to earn $7 million a year in the Major Leagues. Traveling in this manner meant nobody was around to prevent me from asking impoverished Cubans how they felt about the glorious times tourists like me were having while they barely exist on rationed staples, no luxuries, and salaries averaging $10 a month.

I heard the same word over and over again. Whenever I asked for an explanation of the appalling inequities in their so-called workers' paradise, Cubans would offer a one-word explanation: "contradictions." It is the standard explanation for everything incomprehensible about Cuba. Why does Fidel Castro have a reported fifty-seven homes in a country with intolerable housing shortages? "Contradictions." Why does a country with more doctors per capita than anywhere else on earth have no aspirin? "Contradictions." Even highly educated professionals accept this excuse. Whenever the word is spoken, it is expressed with a shrug, much like a medieval peasant blaming a famine on "God's will." When everything in life is controlled by a supreme being—in Cuba, Castro is referred to as El Commandante—much forbearance is required of the populace.

Shabbily treated they may be, but no Cuban I met expressed unqualified admiration for the United States. I spoke to a professor, a teacher, an economist, and a researcher. Each one of them, at some time in our conversation, ceased being amiable long enough to protest the U.S. embargo of Cuba, which has been in effect for thirty-seven years and has accomplished little politically but caused incalculable damage economically. It is at least as responsible as Castro's inflexibility for the hardships that the Cuban people endure.

I arrived in Cuba expecting to find desperation. I came away awed by the patience and loyalty of an incredibly stressed populace. I thought Nilsa epitomized the stoicism of the typical Cuban. After I read her a list of everything I'd eaten from the breakfast buffet of the Melia Cohiba Hotel, she laughed without envy and said, "For me that is food for fifteen or twenty days." We talked about life in America. I told her that while she would have no difficulty eating well in America, her housing conditions would almost certainly decline were she to leave Havana for an apartment in New York or Miami. The small detached paint-peeling two-bedroom Spanish-style bungalow she owns was built in the 1950s in what was then a middle-class section of Havana. She has one semifunctional bathroom (fixing the toilet would cost about three dollars, which she does not have), a nonfunctional Russian TV, a megalithic Frigidaire she described as "bellisimo," cracks in the walls and ceilings, and a pump to deliver water from the street to her cistern.

Even though she considered my tales of less-than-commodious living in America far-fetched, she insisted that she is not one of those who think the streets are paved in gold. Nodding in the direction of a cousin who walked into her house without a greeting and started making telephone calls without asking, she said, "He is one of those who think when they arrive in the United States they will pick dollar bills from the trees."

Havana, once magnificent, now crumbling, has become Pompeii with people. Little of the city as it appeared in the early twentieth century remains intact, although the remnants of a city of taste and culture are stunning. So many of the stucco buildings, their pastel colors leached out, their exteriors crumbling, look like scratching posts for giant cats. Wrought-iron balconies are rusted husks. In Old Havana, eighteenth-century palaces constructed with twelve-foot ceilings have been reconfigured into twentieth-century slums with six-foot ceilings, providing twice as many floors for the impoverished to reside.

Whenever I met a Cuban citizen, I had a single goal: to try to comprehend what makes life in Havana not only bearable but, to many, defensible. A Socialist utopia Havana is not. The average citizen has insufficient food, little or no access to everyday necessities such as vitamins and toothpaste, minimum clothing, inadequate public transportation, no freedom of speech, genuine fear of tyrannical and arbitrary punishment, and a knowledge that life under Marxism has gotten progressively worse since the breakup of the Soviet Union (and the loss of its estimated annual subsidy of $5 billion to 7 billion). Yet of those I interviewed, only the medical-school professor sounded disillusioned. He told me that Cuba was close to a "social explosion" and only Castro's charisma was keeping the country together.

What Cuba does offer its citizens, in abundance, is education and health care (although the redirection of medical supplies to dollar-paying foreign patients may be eroding even that). Those benefits, along with a profusion of paramilitary police on street corners, have helped save Cuba from stumbling into a kind of *Mad Max*, postapocalyptic state, although there are signs that even the steadfast intellectuals who have been at the core of Castro's support are becoming weary. A seventy-year-old retired economist, a man who worked so tirelessly for the revolution in the sixties that it broke up his marriage, told me this joke: "A Cuban went to the U.S. and asked for political asylum. He was interviewed and proudly said that one of the achievements of the revolution was free health care and free education, the best in the world. He was asked, 'If it's such a great country, why are you leaving?' The Cuban replied, 'Because you are not always sick or studying.'"

There are few luxuries remaining in Havana, and none I came across that was equally accessible to tourists and citizens. In a mid-city park devoted entirely to the consumption of ice cream, tourists need not wait for their dollar-denominated sundaes, while Cubans stand in lines of more than two hundred for a chance to spend a few pesos on a treat. As I sat at a marble-topped table, Cubans in line only twenty feet away stood with their backs turned, ignoring me and my effortlessly obtained ice cream.

Havana does not offer many diversions, even for a tourist. Cuban cooking is a lost art, which is understandable, inasmuch as food is a lost staple. Although the city is almost surrounded by water, it has no beaches of note. I had no luck finding the kind of music I yearned for, the old Ricky-Ricardo-meets-Guy-Lombardo sounds, swarthy men playing songs of love. Havana certainly has the worst shopping in the world; its downtown stores are shells.

The real attraction of Havana is the opportunity to view an incredible, tottering, real-life Communist-led Socialist state: men and women walking around with ID cards, destitute children wearing almost no clothes, ration books corroborating near-starvation diets, nonworking appliances in almost every home, and a once-admirable cuisine reduced to sandwiches for one and all. In Havana a tourist can experience the sordid thrill of dispensing dollar bills to downcast citizens, much like John D. Rockefeller handing out Depression-era dimes. Ever since the Cuban government legalized the use of the dollar and sanctioned the establishment of so-called hard-currency stores that stock necessities unavailable for pesos, American banknotes have become the currency of survival.

The cost of my unconscionable breakfast buffet at the Melia Cohiba Hotel was twice Nilsa's monthly pension of $7.65, calculated at the rate of twenty pesos to the dollar. While the government might argue that what a Cuban citizen pays for food, housing, and utilities is minuscule, what makes such reasoning untenable is that everyone who lives in Havana requires dollars to live decently, and the only people with legal access to dollars are those with generous relatives in the United States and those with tourist-industry jobs that lead to tips. People in the street beg for dollars. They no longer want slivers of soap or spare toothbrushes; that state of innocence is long gone. The difference between what tourists have to spend on luxuries and what Cubans have to spend on necessities is so extreme that it seems impossible that the country can survive such seismic inequities.

The medical-school professor told me his salary in pesos was way above average, but he had difficulty living because he had no way to obtain dollars. He was wearing a ragged T-shirt, worn polyester slacks, and shoes crafted from unknown polymers. He said, "To me the end of the revolution started with the legalization of the dollar. I remember this day. On the night of 26 July 1993, Castro has spoken in Santiago de Cuba to explain the necessity of the revolution to survive. At this time, there were many people in jail because they had dollars and it is forbidden. From this time in Cuba, there are two different people: people who have dollars and people who cannot have dollars, and this is a very big difference. Today Cuba is a ghetto, enclosed not by bars but by dollars. If you have dollars, you go beyond that borderline."

I invited him to La Piazza, an informal Italian restaurant in the Melia Cohiba Hotel, where he ate pizza and drank Heineken beer ravenously and gratefully. His state of near destitution reminded me of another joke I heard—Socialist-state humor is almost always triggered by despair. The joke, told by my guide, went like this: "A guy is drunk in a public place, bragging to everybody that he is a porter at a hotel, that he has a lot of money. The police take him to jail, call his mother.

She comes to the station, explains to the police that her son has a drinking problem. They tell her how he was shouting, disturbing people, telling everybody he is the porter of the hotel. The mother says, 'He is suffering delusions of grandeur. He is just the director of the research center.'"

Everybody knows how revolutions start, with poverty, oppression, and tyranny. (Cuba had the bonus of a few too many American gangsters in residence.) But it is less clear how they collapse. My guess is that the end of Castro's Cuba will be the strains of tourism, the inevitable decadence that is already seeping into the most indomitable Socialist state remaining on earth.

To the hunger strikers, I was better than manna from heaven. I represented the American free press. I was exactly who they were hoping to see, even if my first question carelessly referred to their action as an "anti-Castro protest." To most Americans, Castro and Cuba have become synonymous. We think of him as the savior, the oppressor, the Wizard of Oz. A leader of the strike, Dr. Oscar Elias Biscet of the Lawton Foundation for Human Rights, gently pointed out that the five hunger strikers in the room were engaged in a "human-rights activity" condemning the imprisonment of persons who had protested government abuses.

I had telephoned the home of Biscet, a well-known dissident, and his wife suggested I visit him at the hunger strike. I took a taxi to the protest, an eight-dollar fare to go from a luxury hotel to the front lines of a nonviolent war against the Cuban political system. I arrived on the thirty-first day of the forty-day demonstration.

The small ground-floor apartment where the protest was taking place had walls covered with photos of international leaders who had refined the art of peaceful opposition: Raoul Wallenberg (who saved Jews from the Nazis), Martin Luther King, Jesus Christ, Mahatma Gandhi, Andrei Sakharov, and, stretching the definition of humanitarianism, Jorge Mas Canosa, the late leader of the Cuban American National Foundation, an anti-Castro organization that continues to operate stridently in Miami.

One of those in the small room was Juan Gregorich, a drawn, sallow man with deep lines in his face who had spent twenty-two years in jail as a political prisoner, although he admitted not all his actions had been nonviolent ones. He had burned a sugarcane field, written subversive graffiti, and aided anti-Castro guerrillas. For this he was sentenced to forty-nine years, but he was released in 1988. The four others were members of associations that track persons prosecuted and jailed for human-rights and political activities.

I pointed out how lovely everything in Cuba seemed to a happy tourist like me. Politely, careful not to offend, they informed me that they lived in a "terror regime" with paramilitary police and neighborhood informers, which is the reason I was able to enjoy the artificial calm that envelops Cuba.

Biscet called Cuba not a Socialist country but a totalitarian, Stalinist country, and said that he and his fellow protesters could go to jail for twenty years, or there could be "accidents" and they could be killed. They told me that in the old days they would already have been arrested, but the collapse of the Communist bloc and the loss of the subsidies from the former Soviet Union "have chained Castro's hands tight—that's why we haven't been shot."

I went directly from the hunger strike to El Floridita, the most famous and expensive restaurant in Havana. Sitting in the quiet circular room, surrounded by red-jacketed waiters, felt very prerevolution.

The food served at El Floridita might not bring about the downfall of Castro, but I'm surprised it hasn't liquidated tourism. It couldn't be worse. The forty-two-dollar lobster thermidor came in a generic white sauce and tasted as though it had been made from frozen lobster, even though the local lobster is so prized only government-certified restaurants are permitted to serve it.

The "tournedos of beef Papa," made with the limp, flavorless beef found in Cuba, were not edible. Ernest Hemingway has been elevated to the status of Havana's most marketable icon, with Che Guevara (found on the collectible three-peso note) a distant second. The bar of

El Floridita is filled with melancholy photographs of Hemingway with Spencer Tracy, Hemingway with Errol Flynn, Hemingway with Castro. In the photos, he looks blurry, out of focus. The Hemingway daiquiri, served ungarnished in a tall glass, was a yellowish, unsweetened, cold sludge.

Of all the government-run restaurants I tried, only El Aljibe was interesting, in part because it looks like a cross between a Seminole Indian lodge and a Connecticut Indian casino. The one huge room, with a ceiling at least thirty feet high, seats hundreds, and almost every-body eats chicken. When I suggested to my waitress that I would like something other than the highly regarded chicken, she panicked, deserted her post, and had to be replaced. I assured the substitute that I'd be happy with the chicken, which was lemony and good. I also admired an odd but appealing Chinese restaurant called Chung Shan Los Dos Dragones, located about a block from the center of Havana's tiny Chinatown section. It was always filled with customers, had a genuine liveliness no other restaurant could match, and offered the best dish for the money ($4.50) in Havana, lobster chop suey. I never was able to determine whether this place was sanctioned by the govern-ment or if the off-the-menu lobster chop suey was legal, but I went back several times.

The restaurants known as *paladares* are superior in almost every way to the government-run establishments, although almost none have air-conditioning, a debilitating deficiency. *Paladares* are twelve-seat (legal maximum) family-run (hiring outside help is forbidden) restau-rants of surprising competence located in the foyers and dining rooms or on the patios and terraces of private homes. At almost all I visited, the spaces were comfortable, the food at least satisfactory, and the service totally charming—invariably, the youngest and prettiest woman in the extended family is pressed into waitress duty.

When a *paladar* offered fish, that's almost always what I ordered, because fish cookery, for some reason, has survived in the home kitchen. A French-style *paladar* called La Chansonnier had the best food over-all, including rabbit in mustard sauce and admirable french fries. I also liked Puerto Isabela, for its open terrace, unusually large menu, and two particularly skillful fish dishes—red snapper *"primavera,"* with a layer of finely diced vegetables covering the fillet, and red snapper *"sobre-uso,"* with an oniony tomato sauce. Puerto Isabela served an incredibly sweet but appealing dessert, a strong, monastery-style cheese with a choice of guava or coconut puree.

Although Cuba professes to be a nation free of racial prejudice— one of Havana's wistful sights is dark-eyed black street urchins in rags splashing through puddles alongside blond, blue-eyed white street urchins in rags—I encountered almost no blacks working in restaurants. Supposedly, whites, blacks, and *mulatos* are all accepted as equals, but I don't recall being waited on by anybody who wasn't light-skinned. My search for a black-run restaurant took me to the wonderfully named Juana La Cubana, a *paladar* located in the rear of a building I never would have entered had my guide not patted my hand and assured me I'd emerge whole.

On the porch of this once-grand residence, shirtless men sat unsmiling in rickety chairs. They were not maître d's. I nodded ingratiatingly as we approached, and their expressions did not change. Inside, a long hallway was lined with makeshift miniature apartments built of plywood or other scrap materials, and the marble floor was littered with broken couches and wobbly tables. (In Havana, much should be thrown out but almost nothing is.) I felt as though I had wandered into a shantytown where the luckless emerge blinking into the sunlight to forage for food, yet this was the site of a well-regarded local dining establishment. So popular is Juana La Cubana, located in a relatively large apartment at the end of the hallway, that eighteen people were waiting for tables.

The dining area turned out to be a bedroom where the mattress and the box spring had been raised up and flattened against the wall, Murphy-bed style. A window air conditioner provided ventilation, of sorts. Prices were set in pesos, and forty pesos, the equivalent of two dollars, bought a meal of salad with avocado and impossibly tasty leg of pork. With me at dinner was a forty-nine-year-old scientific researcher with a superb terraced apartment, two children in university, and an unshakable belief in the ideals of the revolution. When I spoke of Cuba's shortcomings, including racism in the restaurant industry, she shook her head in denial and told me, "You should not look for the spots of the sun but the light that it gives."

By the last days of my trip, I was surviving on little more than pizza, a bad sign. I had not become one with the restaurants of the country. I sought out the Marina Hemingway's La Cova Pizza Nova, which proudly declares itself "the People Pleasing Pizza Since 1963." I hung out at my hotel's air-conditioned pizza shop, ordering pepperoni pies with Coke, a regression to childhood tastes.

I could no longer take the endless heat or the relentless red snapper. One day, shortly after noon, I was standing on a corner in Vedado, an upscale residential district of Havana, wondering where I could possibly go for lunch, when I received a sign. It was not a spiritual or a metaphysical sign. It was a real sign. I was standing in the shade of a banyan tree when an old man stepped in front of me and hammered a sign into the trunk of the tree. It read PIZZA, and it had an arrow pointing up the block.

Sure enough, two houses away I found another sign, this one reading PIZZA EXQUISITA. In the driveway was a tiny stand offering homemade pizza for six pesos, or thirty cents. The establishment seated one, on a broken-backed rusted iron chair, and the pizza looked like one of those individual-size pan pies sold in American airports.

They aren't so good. This one was worse. The red sauce was bitter, and I don't believe the cheese was really cheese. I nodded my thanks to the proprietor and explained that I would be on my way, eating my pizza as I strolled. As soon as I rounded the corner, I tossed it in a pile of uncollected garbage. I understood then what I should have much earlier, that there would be no hope for the cuisine of Cuba as long as a desperate need for money was the only reason why people cooked.

GQ, DECEMBER 1999

TORO! TORO! TORO!

I do not often go to the mountaintop, seeking the way. I'm not that spiritual, or that fond of exercise. But after spending several harrowing days in Los Angeles, the land of dancing sushi chefs and *"oy vey salmon sushi,"* I found myself soliciting the soothing company of masters, men who can find meaning in a single grain of rice.

Phillip Yi, vice president of the California Sushi Academy in Venice—where some rogue meat-eater had spraypainted FUCK SUSHI on the front door—spoke to me of a venerated chef in Japan who molds his sushi so exquisitely that the number of grains of rice in each piece never varies by more than three or four.

Nobu Kusuhara, chef-owner of Sushi Sasabune in West L.A., talked about his Edo style of sushi, the serving of cool fish on warm balls of loose rice. He said the Edo style was almost forgotten, but Japanese customers in their eighties remembered it from when they were children in Tokyo.

In southern California, a visitor can learn much that is right about sushi and experience almost everything that is wrong.

I am by no means a sushi ignoramus, even though I come from Euro-centric New York, not Pan-Asian Los Angeles. I know not to turn my little dish of soy (almost always *lite* soy in L.A.) into an off-brown sludge by stirring in gobs of wasabi (Japanese horseradish). I know to dip a little corner of the fish, but not the rice, into the soy if I wish to accent the flavor. I know it is permissible to use your fingers to eat sushi but never sashimi, which is unadorned raw fish. I know it is acceptable to order tuna and cucumber rolls, which are eaten in Japan, but no others. While I was in California, the words *California roll* never passed my lips.

Still, I was experiencing difficulties grasping all the complexities of sushi, even at Kusuhara's sensible Sushi Sasabune. Captivating as I found the establishment, his undisciplined little balls of rice were falling apart in my hand before I could get around to a second bite. Contrary to custom, I do not eat my sushi in one bite. I take two, or sometimes, in a demonstration of Occidental defiance, three. Kusuhara slowly shook his head and pronounced my sushi eating unacceptable.

"When you put the sushi in your mouth," he said, "you must close your eyes and feel the warm rice fall away, and then you bite into the fish." He said my style of eating was creating tension in my mind. "When you have two bites, your mind is not concentrating on tasting the fish. You are worrying about messing up the table." I nodded, bowed imperceptibly, and backed away.

To most of us, sushi is raw fish painted with wasabi and served on vinegared rice. In L.A., it can be anything. The proliferation of sushi restaurants in southern California began in the early 1980s, about the time the television miniseries *Shogun* glamorized feudal Japanese society. That was also the beginning of an era of Japanese hegemony over Hollywood, when the Matsushita Electric Industrial Company took over MCA and Sony grabbed Columbia.

Today, sushi is as intrinsic to the Los Angeles cultural scene as mud slides and SUVs. Sushi chefs and sushi sections are so much a part of supermarket shopping that a friend told me, "I was in a checkout line the other day, and a little boy sitting in the seat of a shopping cart in front of me—he was maybe three or four—started crying because his mother wouldn't open the sushi container for him."

Buffet tables at wedding receptions feature sushi. Children enrolled in the better private schools are offered sushi as a lunch selection—the designation on the menu cards that their parents fill out is "SU."

Sushi is eaten at business dinners because it is perceived to be a food of the elite, or at least of people with expense accounts, which in L.A. is the same thing. The California Sushi Academy has started training women to be sushi chefs, the equivalent of allowing women into the Catholic priesthood.

"The reason women never made sushi," explained Yi, "is that women wore perfumes and lotions that transferred onto the raw fish. Also, it was always said that women had slightly higher body temperatures and they would start cooking the fish with their hands. But mostly it was a male-dominated industry and they didn't want to let women in."

In L.A., and to a certain extent in New York, sushi made with *toro*, cut from the fatty belly of the bluefin tuna, has become the new beluga caviar. It is sold for as much as ten dollars a bite in L.A., sometimes three times that in Japan. At the tide-pool end of the edible-seafood aquarium are the implausible sushi rolls created to please customers who don't really like raw fish but understand that they must eat sushi to remain stylish. A friend of mine who writes for television, Roger Director, admitted to me that he still orders spicy tuna rolls, even though he's the only one in the business who still does. He said, "I started getting them three years ago, thinking they were the cosmic answer to my sushi conundrum, but they've worn out their welcome, and now I don't know what to do."

In the movie *The Fly*, Jeff Goldblum lures Geena Davis down an eerie alley to his laboratory, and to calm her apprehension he says, "It's cleaner on the inside." He could have been talking about the sushi restaurant R-23. I parked my car on a forlorn street in the old warehouse district of downtown Los Angeles and walked along some abandoned railroad tracks, searching for the spot that has become the most awesome sushi restaurant in all of L.A., at least for the week I was there. Across from the practically unmarked entrance—I suppose everybody that R-23 wants for a customer already knows the location—was a chain-linked fence topped with concertina wire. Nothing like flying three thousand miles to California just to find yourself in the South Bronx.

In addition to the bracing locale, R-23 is beloved for its cardboard chairs. Indeed, I soon found myself seated on an object that had much in common with a grocery-store carton, although it had a chair-*like* appearance and was not uncomfortable. My table, constructed of particleboard, was enhanced with a conventional white tablecloth. I thought nothing could be more depressing than the neighborhood I had just walked through until I noticed the artwork on the walls, mostly women in pain. I was seated directly under a painting of an elderly woman wearing a wedding ring, wrapped in a scarf, weeping in mourning. Kind of made me want to order fugu sashimi with the poisonous parts intact.

Our waitress had a thick Asian accent and insisted on speaking in a whisper, even though the noise level of the restaurant was incredible. I understood nothing she said until she raised her voice to push a special of pine-tree mushrooms. When I refused twice, she grew surly and service declined from unintelligible to intolerable.

The sushi was beautifully presented on a long, heavy faux-marble slab carried to the table by an extremely fit employee who must have been hired for his Olympian slab-lifting abilities. The fish was fresh and the rice so delicious that I decided to order a bowl of it. What came to the table, after a long wait, was a bowl of white rice overcooked to the consistency of gruel. Most of the other cooked food was similarly grim.

After the perils of R-23, the mundane strip-mall ambiance of Hamasaku, which is owned by legendary power-broker and sushi-eater Mike Ovitz, head of Artists Management Group, was welcome indeed. Almost all sushi restaurants are located in strip malls, which is not a remarkable observation, since almost all of L.A. is located in strip malls. The more minor the mall, the more grandiose the name, and Hamasaku is in the Santa Monica Plaza, a tiny oasis with byzantine parking rules—ten-minute, thirty-minute, and forty-five-minute spaces. Lucky me: I got one of the forty-five-minute spots.

I ordered marinated albacore tuna with "Hisao's special dressing." It turned out to be oversized chunks of tuna, some of them three inches long, awash in a sauce much like the creamy stuff served with pickled herring at Jewish delicatessens. Ragged slices of tasteless halibut came with a lip-puckeringly acidic *ponzu* sauce. Finally, I tried the sushi, made with fish that Arthur Treacher would disdain to fry. I had no difficulty leaving well within my allotted parking time.

Although sushi isn't always thrilling, the vast majority of it that isn't prepackaged is perfectly good. (Most plastic-encased takeout sushi is ruined by intolerable rice.) So far, much of the sushi I'd eaten in L.A. wasn't even up to New York standards. I moved on to the Hump, yet another fashionable spot. This one is owned by Brian Vidor, son of director Charles Vidor, and is located at the tiny, retro-feeling Santa Monica Airport. The Hump, with its fireplace, orchids, and bamboo plants, is perhaps the most attractive sushi restaurant in L.A. Nobody appears to care that *the Hump*—a World War II term for the Himalayas—refers to the struggle against the Japanese.

A few slices of red snapper sashimi were vibrant, and the *toro* was properly rich and fatty (if somewhat mushy), but the rest of the fish was uninteresting. The three of us didn't eat much, but the bill, including tax, tip, and a bottle of flabby Hawley viognier with perhaps the most bitter finish ever found in a California white wine, came to $289. I wasn't the least bit full, so I thought this was the perfect night to make a few unscheduled sushi stops.

I peeked into the Marina del Rey branch of Tokyo Delve's, acclaimed for a staff that supposedly breaks into spontaneous dance. As I walked in, "YMCA" by the Village People was playing, but the sushi chefs were doing nothing more interesting than making sushi. I left feeling cheated, like a tourist who visits Buckingham Palace and misses the changing of the guard.

Then I went to Crazy Fish, located on the outskirts of Beverly Hills and reputed to have lines out the door most of the day. Among the more than thirty kinds of sushi rolls offered, there is the Crazy Fish roll, which I could not resist. It was essentially several varieties of second-rate fish sticking out of some rice. Crazy Fish is the establishment offering the *oy vey* (Yiddish for "Oh, no! or "Oh, my!") salmon sushi, and it also features the Jewish roll of salmon and cream cheese. These appear to be transparent marketing ploys designed to lure unwary customers from the Harkham Hillel Hebrew Academy across the street.

The next day, I drove to Studio City to observe the wonders of Sushi on Tap, but I arrived to find it renamed Sushi Yasuke and the staff no longer willing to tap dance. It was practically empty, and when I suggested to the blond Japanese hostess that business must have been better before the music died, she giggled and replied, "Oh, yes, but we are really tired of tap dancing."

I had one more stylish restaurant to try: the environmentally correct Sushi Roku in Hollywood, which has a statement of guiding principles printed on the first page of its menu: "In our attempt to save the earth and its environment, Sushi Roku has been built with environment-friendly products and recycles in every way possible." The restaurant was done up in earth tones—no ozone-depleting pastels here. The menu was written in a style that recalls fifties restaurants specializing in Continental cuisine: Hot Appetizers From The Sea, Appetizers From The Garden (including one of my favorite farm-fresh garden appetizers, tofu), Cold Appetizers From The Sea, and so on.

I ordered the twenty-three-dollar Executive Bento Box, even though no Hollywood executive who wanted to preserve his reputation would ever order a box lunch. (Perhaps a better name, reflecting its bargain price, would be the Mailroom Bento Box.) Everything I tasted was bright, colorful, and decidedly on the sweet side. Virtually all the customers were Caucasian, the males wearing white T-shirts under unbuttoned dress shirts with the tails hanging out. If people are going to dress like that in restaurants, is Earth really worth saving? Next to me, a young couple appeared to be on a first date; he seemed calm from the waist up, but his feet twitched uncontrollably throughout the meal, vibrating with nervousness. At the end of lunch, he said to her, "You have an expense account or anything?"

At Matsuhisa in Beverly Hills, friends and I were seated at a plain wooden table adjoining a similar table occupied by gentlemen with tattoos, nose rings, and T-shirts. How fortunate I was to be dining alongside Korn.

Matsuhisa is the original American restaurant of Nobu Matsuhisa, the genius who invented Japanese-Peruvian-Californian crossbred cuisine. I seldom deviate from his signature items, even though they haven't changed much in a decade or so, because I'm always eating with friends who haven't been there, and I want them to taste everything I love. We had lobster ceviche, yellowtail dotted with a sliver of jalapeño, "newstyle" sashimi (slightly seared, in a light sauce of lime and soy, and not so new after all these years), halibut sashimi with a dab of red-chile paste, and Matsuhisa's ubiquitous and unforgettable black cod marinated in miso.

I returned by myself at 1:30 P.M. on a midweek afternoon, wanting to try the sushi bar, naïvely figuring I'd have no trouble getting a spot at such a late hour. After waiting thirty-five minutes crushed into a miniature waiting area, I finally was shown to a tiny seat. Where comfort is concerned, I could just as well have been dining in a subway during rush hour. The sushi, as I expected, was impeccable, but Matsuhisa has so many thrilling dishes, I don't recommend wasting your appetite on sushi. This is the one sushi restaurant where fish on rice seems an afterthought.

The establishment where sushi has risen to a place of glory and honor is Sushi Nozawa in the otherwise undiscovered Eureka Plaza in Studio City. Here you find Kazunori Nozawa, the so-called Sushi Nazi. He is known by no other name. He is the Sushi Nazi as surely as John Wayne is the Duke.

I have grown weary of "Nazi" as a culinary descriptor. It all started with the *Seinfeld* Soup Nazi, and these days any restaurant proprietor who fails to fawn over his customers becomes the Nazi designee of his cuisine. There are probably still a few genuine old Nazis out there, maybe hiding in Paraguay, and though I do not wish them well, I sympathize if they are offended by all of this.

Sushi Nozawa resembles a modern European sandwich shop. The only decorative touches are brightly painted red poles and a neon-rimmed fish picture behind the sushi counter, where Nozawa stands. I walked in just after 8 P.M. He glared at me and said, "Table or sushi counter?" I replied, "Sushi counter." He nodded in the direction of a sign that said TRUST ME. In sushi-counter vernacular, that meant I could eat only what he wanted me to eat, not what I might prefer.

Smiling ingratiatingly, I cleverly remarked, "You look trustworthy to me."

He stiffened at the unwelcome familiarity. I meekly took my assigned seat. The unique melding of sushi and sadomasochism had begun.

According to conventional wisdom, the sushi here is the best in L.A. Based on one visit, I'd put it in the ordinary-to-pretty-good range. The sushi rice was bland and served at varying temperatures, from cold to slightly warm. The albacore sushi came doused with a vinegary sauce. The crab in a hand roll was too salty. I liked the briny oysters and some wonderfully smooth sea urchin roe.

Throughout the meal, which was served very quickly, Nozawa stood unsmiling. To me he seemed a semitragic figure, a samurai sushi chef reduced to serving the peasantry. Because he does not take reservations, he has no way of keeping out people who are likely to annoy him. Most of his customers were badly dressed Caucasians, although two Asian women were the dates of badly dressed Caucasians.

The fellow sitting next to me at the sushi bar was wearing a black fuzzy sweatshirt, a black knit watch cap, and a bandage on his face. He ate the fish off the sushi, leaving the rice. He gulped water from a bottle. He soaked everything he ate with soy, leaving the counter a mess of rice, soy, and wasabi. Nozawa has a reputation for throwing out customers, but he didn't toss this guy. Throughout my meal, I was hoping he would.

Kusuhara, the chef-owner of Sushi Sasabune, worked with Nozawa at various times, and their styles are similar. If anything, his restaurant is less grand than Nozawa's. Outside, it has the appearance of two buildings cobbled together, one a stucco Mexican joint and the other an early California bungalow. Inside, the chairs are uncomfortable and the tables are the sort rolled out in function halls for special events. He has TRUST ME imprinted on the shirts of his waiters.

I trusted, and the food was nearly perfect. The sushi rice seemed a delicacy, even though no attention went into molding it into the perfect oblong shape found in punctilious sushi establishments. Most of the fish came in a variety of light, beautifully balanced sauces that tasted like *ponzu*, sweet vinegar, or honey. The salmon bore a sprinkling of sesame seeds.

When I returned the next day to introduce myself to Kusuhara, he told me that when he started out as a fish salesman in L.A., one of his early clients was Nozawa. "I was curious; maybe if I learned to make sushi, I would be able to sell fish to sushi restaurants better than anybody else."

Nozawa taught him, and in 1980 he opened his first sushi restaurant. Seven years ago, he and his wife, Ryoko, his high school sweetheart in Japan, opened Sushi Sasabune after finding the inelegant building they now occupy, located a few blocks from the San Diego Freeway. "When I saw it," he said, "I thought it looked terrible, but I knew that not many people would come in and I could start slowly, only my wife and I." He's forty-eight now, and for the past thirty years he's been going to the fish market every day it's been open, waking up at 4 A.M. and sometimes helping to unload the trucks. That's what happens when a man gets to the fish market before the fish.

No restaurant could differ more from Sushi Sasabune—in style, in locale, and especially in price—than Ginzo Sushi-Ko, located on a pedestrian walkway at the foot of Rodeo Drive in Beverly Hills. A friend and I took an elevator to the second floor of a tiny building, ducked under some annoying cloth flaps shrouding the doorway, and were politely shown to a semiprivate room containing two tables, each of them large but not particularly ornate. The base price of dinner here is $300 per person, and a nonrefundable deposit of $100 is required to guarantee a reservation. I couldn't imagine what they did to make raw fish that pricy, except sprinkle it with gold. And indeed they did.

I'll say this about my $850 meal for two, which included tax, tip, and a couple of tiny pots of cold sake: it was real good. In fact, considering that most $850 meals for two served in America today consist of two martinis, two jumbo-shrimp cocktails, two sirloin strips, creamed spinach, hash browns, and a $500 bottle of Cabernet Sauvignon, I'm certain it was better than most. The service was surprisingly casual but polite and almost perfect. The glasses, plates, and utensils were made of ceramic, porcelain, or lacquered wood, all lovely but probably not valuable. Our waitress told us the reason we didn't have one of the bright-red lacquered toothpick boxes on our table was that ours had been swiped by a previous customer.

There were nine courses, all chosen by the chef. (I count the sequence of sushi that concluded the dinner as one course.) Most fun was the foie gras–and-lobster *shabu-shabu*; least fun was being instructed to drink the seaweed-flavored *shabu-shabu* broth in which we'd cooked our foie gras and lobster. We ate Japanese "risotto" with white truffles—the oddly delicious rice reminded me a little of Italian risotto and a little of marshmallow fluff.

The sushi was magnificent, even though I had no real interest in eating some of it, such as the dangerous-looking red clam. (Although terribly chewy, it was otherwise harmless.) We had squid, Japanese mackerel, abalone, needlefish, and herring. The tuna and the *toro* here were the best I'd ever eaten. Chef Masa Takayama's raw *toro* was even better than Matsuhisa's, and his rich, fatty, melting, knee-weakening barbecued *toro* was superior to grilled Kobe beef.

Yes, we also ate fugu, the fish of death, which, if not prepared properly, can kill you. It came sprinkled with gold. The first fugu course consisted of raw fugu parts in *ponzu*. The second was a bite or two of fried fugu and reminded me of crab. That first course included baby chives wrapped in fugu intestines—very nice—as well as the liver of the fish, which I'd always thought was the deadly part. The chef came out to explain why we should eat it. I'm not sure I got this right, but I believe it had something to do with the fish being young and healthy and having eaten a balanced diet and the liver not having turned dark and evil and bloated and virulent.

Anyway, I ate the liver and survived. You think for $425 a person I wasn't going to clean my plate?

GQ, MARCH 2001

"AS LONG AS THERE'S A MOISHE'S, THERE'LL ALWAYS BE A MONTREAL"

"Françoise!" I exclaimed. "You have not changed a bit."

"William," she replied, averting her eyes and concentrating on Le Paris's *brandade de morue*. She coughed delicately, pretending to choke on a morsel of the sublimely creamy puree of salt cod and not on her obligatory lie: "Neither have you."

Twenty years had passed since we had last seen each other, twenty years since we were secret agents in the culinary world, restaurant critics writing under an alias for the *Montreal Star*. Together we had posed as a married couple named William and Françoise Neill, a well-bred, literate, and somewhat quarrelsome team of reviewers.

In reality she was (and still is) Bee MacGuire, a writer with impeccable epicurean credentials. I was (but in 1977 ceased being) the sports columnist for the *Star*, then the dominant English-language daily in Montreal. The reputation of the newspaper would hardly have suffered had Françoise Neill been unveiled as Bee MacGuire, but public disclosure that a sportswriter—a sportswriter!—had described the sole à *l'Armoricaine* at the beloved Castillion Restaurant of the Hotel Bonaventure as "a colorless dish . . . both for eye and palate" would have caused an outrage.

Admittedly, I was always looked upon as an odd sort of sportswriter, the kind of fellow who paid a little too much attention to the tea sandwiches served in the Forum press lounge between periods of Canadiens games and not enough attention to Guy Lafleur's shots-on-goal statistics. Still, nobody ever guessed that I was William Neill.

None of it lasted. Not our professional arrangement. Not Montreal's stellar dining reputation. Not even the *Star*, which went out of business in 1979. By then I had left to take a job in Boston, but I returned regularly to Montreal, faithful to a city that was so foreign and yet so comfortable and so close. And when the great restaurants started closing, as they did, I mourned.

Worst for me was the disappearance of Au Pierrot Gourmet, a tiny second-floor French restaurant on Notre Dame Street, whose chef and proprietor, Jean-Louis Larre-Larouille, had served as a bodyguard for Charles de Gaulle during World War II. Jean-Louis owned no shoes, only bedroom slippers, and he never left his restaurant.

By day he peeled tiny potatoes and watched televised soccer. By night he zealously patrolled his fiefdom, a mad monarch behind his ramparts, growling at customers who did not speak French or, even worse, did not order his daily specials. If a patron complained that the soup was too salty, which it often was, he'd reply, "This is not a hospital, monsieur." Then he'd throw him out. Even today I can recall the garlicky taste of his Gaspe lamb, cooked on a wood-burning stove. And I grieve that Jean-Louis returned to France and died penniless.

Had Au Pierrot Gourmet not closed, it is surely where Françoise (I'm more comfortable with the pseudonym) and I would have rendezvoused. A more than satisfactory alternative was Le Paris, a storefront bistro on Saint Catherine Street where we had eaten our first meal together as a reviewing team—and, for that matter, one of our last. The truth is that we rarely dined with each other while working, even though we pretended we had, because we agreed on nothing. We took others to dinner and wrote as though we had dined together, a faux spin on a faux marriage. I always thought of it as the culinary equivalent of separate bedrooms.

Le Paris was then and still is totally bourgeois, a place one might find across the street from the train station in an arrondissement of Paris where tourists do not go. It has dark red tablecloths, a linoleum floor, and a woefully inadequate coatrack by the front door. (Regulars know there is a supplemental rack by the toilets.)

My eye was immediately drawn to a single significant change: the curtains on the broad picture windows, once resolutely drawn to deter the eyes of passersby, were open. After our meal, I asked Guy Poucant, the proprietor and son of Maurice, who opened Le Paris in 1956, what event had brought about such a cosmic alteration. He explained that several years ago the curtains came down to be washed, and hundreds of potential customers suddenly took notice of the new restaurant in the neighborhood.

For me, Le Paris has always been irresistible, and it has become more so over the years. Its cuisine, which was already out of fashion in the seventies, returned briefly as "comfort food" a few years ago, but it may well be slipping from popularity again. Automatically, we ordered celery remoulade, mayonnaisey food that nobody asks for anymore. When I asked Françoise to remind me why we had, she replied, correctly, "You eat it to remember, not because you like it. It's a forgotten food."

In that spirit, we began with a wine called Pisse-Dru—it translates literally as "piss hard"—a thin and acidic Beaujolais that I have never seen anywhere but in Montreal. We recalled that it was equally thin and acidic twenty years ago. I suggested to Françoise that we quaff something more agreeable with our main courses.

"Anything you wish!" she exclaimed. Clearly, the years had softened her.

From the small wine list, I selected a Guigal Châteauneuf-du-Pape.

"No," she protested. "It's too much a slap in the face."

As always I let her choose the wine.

My pot-au-feu—boiled beef with turnips, potatoes, and cabbage—was savory and properly accompanied by sour little cornichons and mustard so good it should be in ballparks everywhere. Françoise selected calves' brains, though I begged her not to. I abhor looking at brains while I'm eating. Nonetheless, she had brains. Reluctantly, I tried them, and they tasted like capers and lemon juice floating on cotton candy.

This meal, as well as Le Paris itself, evoked the motto of Quebec, the one that is stamped on every provincial license plate (perhaps by English-speaking prison inmates jailed for running afoul of the province's ludicrous language laws): *Je me souviens* ("I remember"). The slogan can be thought of as sinister, fraught with political nuances and the promise of social unrest, but a gentler interpretation is also possible. That's what I prefer. To me the glory of Quebec and the wonder of Montreal is that they are both of a particular time.

By the 1970s, New York City already boasted the Four Seasons, Lutèce, La Côte Basque, La Grenouille, and La Caravelle. Today it is clearly the preeminent restaurant city in North America, but to my taste Montreal had the better dining twenty years ago. The restaurants were more egalitarian, more economical, and more French than those in New York, and back then French was the only serious way to dine.

Montreal's most esteemed establishment was Chez Bardet, which was absurdly located at the end of a subway line and served (as did all the finest Montreal restaurants) a menu of items punctuated by a surfeit of proper nouns. At Chez Bardet, there were *quenelles de brochet Nantua* and *gratin de volaille à la Bardet*—the latter, I believe, was ham, cheese, and roast chicken. There was Dover sole Waleska at Chez Delmo, rabbit Archiduc at Chez la Mere Michel, lobster tails Saint Denis (as well as a trio of strolling violinists) at Le Castillon, snails Château d'If at Le Mas des Oliviers, and, my absolute favorite verbiage, *coeur du charolais soufflé aux splendeurs du Perigord* at the Beaver Club, in the Queen Elizabeth Hotel.

To recall these places is to remember a Montreal that was filled with promise, a city that then-mayor Jean Drapeau, part visionary and part megalomaniac, boasted was "on its way to becoming the greatest city in the world. I can hear it as clearly as a composer hears a symphony." What he should have heard was a note of caution, as he nearly bankrupted the city with his arrogant and grandiose schemes, particularly the ruinous 1976 Olympic Games. In the seventies, however, fiscal reality was still a few years away, and the restaurant culture was so energetic it seemed invulnerable.

Even if the food served in many of my favorites is now out-of-date (it seemed that every dish was layered with cheese, finished with cream, and brought to the table in flames), it was perfect for the times. Nouvelle cuisine had not yet overturned classic French, and Montreal restaurants were fashionable as well as admirable.

The impending decline did not, for the most part, emanate from the kitchens. The chefs were not to blame. It came about as a consequence of Drapeau's mistakes and the policies of a new political order.

Quebec (which started out as New France) is about 80 percent French-speaking. That means 5 to 6 million Quebecers are living on a continent where hundreds of millions of neighbors don't understand a word they're saying. For decades, Quebec's English-speaking minority dominated the province, both culturally and economically. Then in 1960, in an attempt to reverse this situation, the so-called Quiet Revolution began. This reform movement turned into an independence movement, and the outcome was the Parti Québécois (PQ), which today rules the province and is committed to the separation of Quebec from Canada. While the idea of secession might seem abhorrent to Americans schooled in the lessons of the Civil War, it's not nearly so bothersome to Canadians, because the federal government recognizes the right of Quebec to separate. It just doesn't want it to happen.

In 1980, when the first separatist referendum lost by a few percentage points, the late and beloved PQ leader René Lévesque stood before his weeping acolytes, many of them draped in Quebec flags, and said, "If I understand you well, you said, 'Wait until next time.'" That time came last year, when separatism lost again, by a much closer vote, and the Parti Québécois suggested that they'd get it right the next time. Michael Boone, a former sportswriting colleague of mine on the *Star* who now writes a column for the *Gazette*, Montreal's last remaining English-language daily, explains it this way: "They're like frat guys. They won't take no for an answer."

Between the referendums came the Quebec language wars, with the ruling PQ passing unpleasant little laws mandating the use of French in the workplace and establishing an enforcement arm called L'Office de la Langue Française. This resulted in the creation of a funny little Quebec sublanguage invented by bureaucrats—the most infamous was the transformation of *hamburger* into *hambourgeois*. It could have been amusing, but it was not.

All of these burdens—financial, political, and social—caused Montreal and Quebec to decline economically. The culinary consequences were startling. I recall, early in the eighties, a fine dinner at a restaurant above La Brioche Lyonnaise, a candy store on Saint Denis Street selling uncommonly good chocolate-covered orange peel. On my next trip, the restaurant was out of business. Once I thought I had discovered a treasure in the working-class East End of Montreal—one with, of all things, a wonderful wine list. On my second visit, a transvestite stripper was performing. I quickly gulped my sweetbreads and my 1986 Château Sociando-Mallet, then departed, never to return.

Recently, I have sensed a comeback. Even though "The Situation," as the long-standing political unrest is known, is as discouraging as ever, and even though the city lacks money and leadership, the restaurants have a great deal to offer. The infatuation with nouvelle cuisine—that movement toward artistic, unsatisfying food that faltered quickly in France but hung on tenaciously in Quebec—seems about over. (Even today, should you see a *menu découverts*, or menu of discovery, in a Montreal restaurant, throw down your napkin and flee.)

Indeed, there are too many bistros, too many imitators of food made in New York, too many *menus découverts*, but now it is possible to visit Montreal and eat nothing but good food, food boasting of authenticity and prepared with passion. After two decades of waiting and watching, William Neill has returned.

When I asked Françoise to recommend the best restaurant in the city, she hesitated. I assumed this was because we never had agreed on much when we were critics for the *Star*, but I was wrong. Reluctantly, she told me about a storefront restaurant called Le Passe-Partout, located on Decarie Boulevard, a few miles from downtown. She warned me that the chef was a monster; the last time she went there they argued, and he threw her out. The chef is James MacGuire. If you recall, Françoise's real name is Bee MacGuire. They are brother and sister.

Le Passe-Partout (which has several meanings, including "pastry brush") is small, seating only about thirty, and open not nearly enough. MacGuire offers lunch four times a week and dinner only three. I found it difficult to get a reservation—I sure wasn't going to drop his sister's name—but I finally got a table on a Saturday night.

Entering the restaurant, I passed through a small retail shop offering wondrous baked goods, breads as flavorful as any in North America, plus all manner of extravagant luxury foods that nobody really needs, like wild-berry preserves from Saskatoon. In the dining area, the tables are dressed with damask cloths, the walls are a soothing peach-salmon, and a towering fresh-flower arrangement imparts luxuriousness. It's all perfectly charming, except for a perfectly awful chrome-and-glass front window that shatters any illusion that you might be in the countryside of France. The food, however, is the sustenance of such fantasies.

I started with a mussel soup so extraordinary in flavor and so modest in quantity that I had to restrain myself from ordering a second bowl. The broth was smoky, the potatoes firm. My main course was a venison preparation conceived at least a half-century ago, thick slices from the loin matched with a pale-yellow peppery *grand veneur* sauce that has been used with venison as long as the French have been hanging antlers in their hunting lodges. MacGuire, I was learning, is an absolute classic French chef.

With the venison came more observances of tradition: a puree of sweet potatoes, a few wide noodles, a sprinkling of cranberries nestled in a hollowed-out turnip. This man is the spiritual successor to Andre Bardet of Chez Bardet, but I suspect MacGuire goes to the market a lot more often than Bardet ever did.

MacGuire and his wife, Suzanne Baron-Lafreniere, who runs the dining room as well as a basement art gallery, have been partners in Le Passe-Partout since 1981 (but at their current location for only five years). I was surprised that I had not heard a word about them, and MacGuire explained, "We are such idealists, we said at the beginning it would be better if we had no articles about us. At the old location, we even had no sign. What happened was that the people who didn't like us wrote anyway, and the people who did like us respected our wishes and didn't write a thing."

MacGuire, who grew up in New York City, worked in a number of restaurants and patisseries in France, where his great inspiration was Charles Barrier, once a Michelin three-star chef. From Barrier he learned technique, precision, and discipline, culinary virtues that are ignored more than admired these days. He is able to emulate the food of much grander establishments by turning out a minimum of dishes each day. With one hot appetizer, one soup, one fish, and one meat dish, and with only thirty to forty customers at each luncheon or dinner, he and his two assistants are able to produce nearly flawless haute cuisine.

So much of what he does makes sense that I could not understand his sister's characterization of him as a monster—she likened him to the legendary Fritz Karl Vatel, a seventeenth-century majordomo entrusted with preparing a dinner for King Louis XIV of France and three thousand other guests who threw himself on his sword after learning that insufficient fish had arrived. MacGuire told me he had picked up some of his eccentricities from Barrier, who would sit in a glass-enclosed boothlike office in the center of his vast kitchen and bark orders at minions. "He'd use his microphone, and when his voice reverberated through the kitchen, it sounded like God," MacGuire recalled. Now forty-five, MacGuire avowed that he had changed, become less willful, less obsessed. "If there is a little too much salt in the salad, I don't say I have to make every salad, which I used to do."

As for his sister's overall evaluation? "Well," he said, "I can understand any chef who wants to scream."

Chef-owners like MacGuire were once the foundation of Montreal's restaurant tradition, though few like him remain. To be fair, fewer and fewer like him remain in France, too. The irony, of course, is that many French-speaking French-trained chefs who in past years would have emigrated to Quebec to cook and open restaurants have gone elsewhere, driven away by the political environment. They are not comfortable with the plan to make Quebec more Francophile.

Among those who came to Quebec before The Situation is André Besson of the restaurant Laloux, who arrived in 1975 and is, like MacGuire, one of the old-world monsters. His maître d' and sommelier, Marie-Isabelle DeVault, says, "Sometimes, for no reason at all, he screams—anything can get on his nerves." In his defense, Besson says that at least he screams and gets it over with, while MacGuire keeps it all inside.

Besson was born in Vienne, home of Fernand Point of La Pyramide, and so close was the Besson family to Point that the mythic chef cooked for André's baptism. Something took, for if Point could taste Besson's sauces, he would not be displeased. Yet to me, much of Besson's food tastes French-Canadian, particularly his game pie. This is both unexpected and welcome, because the old *habitant* cuisine of Quebec (the habitants were the old French-Canadian farmers) is badly represented in most of the city's other upscale restaurants.

Habitant cuisine centers around game, maple sugar, beans, and salt pork, and the only refined establishment serving such preparations that I ever admired was the long-forgotten Au Quinquet. In the seventies, Françoise reviewed it favorably in the company of a perfect dining companion, a woman born near the city of Rimouski, one of eighteen children whose mother died at age forty giving birth to twins. In French-Canadian Quebec, such a family scenario was not unique.

Today, when I want a taste of this classic heavyweight fare, I stop in at La Binerie, on Mont-Royal. I usually go for breakfast, taking a seat at the counter and ordering the number two, which comes with coffee, home fries, *feves au lard* (beans), a couple of eggs over, two slices of thick toast, and an assortment of odd meats (canned ham, a fatty pork pâté called *cretons*, crisp bacon, and a morsel of mushy but much-beloved Montreal-style hot dog), all served on a rectangular pale-green plate that looks like a treasure from a yard sale. The cost: less than three dollars.

Should you stop in later in the day, you can choose from among the dishes that helped very large families through very long winters: sliced veal hearts, yellow pea soup, meatball-and-pig's-feet stew, even *pouding chômeur* ("unemployed pudding"), a thick, coarse homemade cake soaked in syrup that's a leftover from the Depression.

For the daring, those interested in sampling the extremes of French-Canadian cooking, I suggest breakfast at La Binerie and dinner at Toque, which is located on Saint Denis Street. Toque, in this case, does not refer to the tall, traditional chef's hat. Here it means "crazy," which can refer to the decor, kind of post-Kandinsky modernistic, or to the food, mystical combinations arranged in perilous sculpted stacks. For that matter, it probably *can* refer to the chef's hat—Chef Normand Laprise sports a cap that looks like a cross between a yarmulke and a fez. If La Binerie offers essential French-Canadian staples, Toque's specialty is impressionistic French-Canadian fabrications.

Laprise, who comes from eastern Quebec, is the most accomplished of Montreal's new-style chefs, the ones who operate what Françoise likes to call "hard-surface bistros," small places without homeyness. The restaurants are multitudinous, but none are as successful as Toque. I went there with my friend Boone, the ex-sportswriter, who ate as though he hadn't had a good meal since the *Star* cafeteria closed. The most stunning dish was grilled salmon over chop suey over a grapefruit-orange salsa, and it convinced me that Laprise is the rarest of all chefs, an apparently out-of-control improviser with absolute command over his food and his impulses.

I selected two desserts—a warm crème brûlée filled with poached pears and a mille-feuille that turned out to be not a mille-feuille at all but a flourless chocolate cake enclosed in a thin puff-pastry crust, sort of an une-feuille. While Boone ate both, I asked Laprise how he could possibly find time to prepare such complicated food at lunch, and he answered, "This is not very complicated. We are more elaborate at night." Like most chefs in Montreal, he loves to boast that his food is *cuisine de marché*, or "market food," the freshest of the day. When I told him that every chef says this about his food, he replied, "Yes, they all say this about their food, but theirs is frozen."

. . .

"After you left," Françoise said to me, "about fifteen years ago, I got tipped off by a Greek teaching at the University of Athens about this man, Costas Spiliadis, who had a restaurant and is one of the crazy people. You know, there's a long tradition of divine madness in Greece. He's one of them."

Françoise was always the philosopher-critic, discerning high purpose in the eating process. (I sometimes felt that way, but only about Montreal's smoked meat.) When she learned about Spiliadis, she was the editor of *Montreal* magazine and wanted to write about him and his Parc Avenue restaurant, called Milos. He resisted. He was an outsider in the local Greek community, and he felt he would become even more of one if she wrote about his standards being higher than everyone else's. "He's into angst easily," Françoise said.

Spiliadis, whose Greek parents wanted the best for their son, came to the United States in 1966 to study criminology at New York University. He left for Canada, he says, without a smile, after everybody in New York City insisted on calling him "Gus" instead of Costas. When he finally settled in Montreal, he did what many Greeks do. He opened a restaurant.

Because he didn't care for the wholesale fish markets of Montreal, he'd drive twice a week to the Fulton Fish Market in New York City, a 750-mile round trip, with American cash in his pocket. He traveled in an old Chevrolet Impala that belonged to one of his waiters, and eventually he put so many miles on the engine and sloshed so much melted ice on the upholstery that he had to buy the worn-out, water-soaked, fishy-smelling car. He crossed the border so often that the customs officials started waving him through. "The joke was that I'd gone fishing," he says. "If not, they'd have made me fill out all these forms."

His obsessions never diminished. Ten years ago, a prominent customer, a judge, disparaged the bathrooms of Milos, so Spiliadis obtained marble from Greece—full slabs of Penteli marble, the softest and most feminine kind—and he built bathrooms from that. The rest of his restaurant is not nearly so formal. With its blue-and-white checked tablecloths, broad-beamed wooden floor, and displays of fresh fish on crushed ice, Milos resembles a Mediterranean restaurant reserved for the very elegant or the very wealthy. Actually, it does take considerable assets to dine here, because it is probably the most expensive restaurant in the city.

His fish is perfect. His vegetables are perfect. Everything is as perfect as mania can make it. When I asked him why he insists on such high quality, he replied, "Until people made me aware of that question, I never knew there was such a question." I went for dinner with Françoise, and when he recognized her, he brought her what I am certain was the best radish ever grown. What madness, for a man to be fixated on radishes.

The grilled shrimp were flawless, although he needlessly apologized that they were from the Carolinas and not the Gulf of Mexico. The octopus was slightly charred and so luscious in texture it reminded me of filet mignon. It was octopus from Tunisia. Only Tunisian octopus would do. Still to come was unrealistically fresh goat cheese from Ontario made by a family from Crete and topped with thyme honey, the richest honey I've ever tasted, from the island of Kythira, in Greece. You come to Milos, you not only get one of the best meals in Montreal, you also get a geography lesson.

Once, says Spiliadis, his mother flew from Greece to see the son she had sent to North America for schooling, the one who is only a thesis short of a master's degree. The visit worried him. "Greeks are notorious," Spiliadis said. "Send us to university, educate us, we end up opening a restaurant. She came in here, her head down, didn't look around, didn't say a thing." After she ate, I said to her, "'Did you like it?' She said to me, 'Eh.'"

He is forty-nine years old now, a bear of a man with a boyish face and an existence that Françoise describes as "an insane pilgrimage." His restaurant is among the most admirable in North America, what Le Bernardin in New York would be if it were a taverna. When Françoise said to him, "What is it that you are the first in all of Canada to accomplish?" he was ready with a reply. His expression was so sorrowful, I suspected the two of them had rehearsed their exchange, like an old vaudeville team. "Betray my mother," he said.

In recent years, the policies of the provincial government of Quebec have discouraged English-speaking immigrants and welcomed wholeheartedly those from other nations. I've always thought of this as part of the grand and misguided strategy of the Parti Québecois: in theory, downtrodden immigrants would be so grateful for admission they would plunge into French language classes and help turn Quebec into a neo-Gallic workers' paradise.

This master plan has failed to triumph, because what immigrants really want is to learn English. They're not dumb. They quickly figure out that English is a good language to know if you're going to live in North America. Those who cannot speak English tend to continue conversing in their native language, which isn't what the Parti Québécois wants, either. All these political and demographic changes have done nothing for the cause of French cuisine, simply because immigrants from places other than France are seldom fascinated by stuffed quails *à la gourmande*.

Not counting the English, the dominant ethnic minority in Montreal is the Italians, but I never think of them as a minority because Italian food is so mainstream. Most fascinating to me, perhaps because I'm irresistibly drawn to the cuisine, is the community of Eastern Europeans, many of them Jews. Back when immigration was measured by the boatload, Eastern European families made their homes on or near Saint Lawrence Street, which was once so relevant to the commerce and culture of the city it was referred to simply as "The Main." To this day, Saint Lawrence is an ethnic neutral zone, dividing eastern, French-speaking Montreal from western, English-speaking Montreal.

Saint Lawrence no longer feels like the first step in every immigrant's excursion into the New World, a place where *avant-garde* meant chicken liver light on the chicken fat. Today a restaurant customer is as likely to be offered a Bellini as borscht. In part the changes have come about because of a Jewish exodus from Quebec. The Parti Québécois has never done anything to Jews except encourage them to stay in Quebec, but whenever Jews find themselves in a culture that seems intolerant of linguistic and cultural diversity, they start packing. The Jewish population of Montreal, once well over one hundred thousand, is slowly but inexorably declining.

There have been reverberations. Montreal's legendary smoked meat, which tastes a little like corned beef and a lot like pastrami, hasn't been the same since the Parti Québécois came to power.

The one restaurant on The Main that has not changed is the Montreal Hebrew Delicatessen and Steak House, known everywhere as Schwartz's. The Schwartz brothers are long gone, but the fame of this delicatessen and steak house (it really isn't either) has never faltered.

Schwartz's has been in business since the 1920s, which is almost certainly the last time a decorator stopped by. The joint is long and narrow, with a single aisle that might have been the prototype for aisles in the coach-class sections of aircraft. On one side is counter service; on the other are tables with seats for six or eight. Communal dining works effortlessly here, because Schwartz's customers have been eating at Schwartz's for so long they understand the art of not annoying strangers.

The waiters are fine if you order what everybody orders at Schwartz's—smoked meat medium, Coke, french fries. They are too old and ireful to deal with variations. Each and every one has mastered the art of putting your food down in front of you and quickly turning away before you can ask for something extra.

The smoked meat is hot, thick, and peppery, and it looks just swell, but for decades I've been thinking it isn't as good as it used to be. Vic Vogel, an acquaintance of mine who grew up a few blocks from Schwartz's, always orders his with extra fat. You can specify lean, medium, or fat, but nobody I know asks for extra fat except Vogel, who is sixty and apparently in good health. He says as long as you eat a little pickle with it, the fat breaks down in your system. I wouldn't ordinarily believe such nonsense, but he says his mother eats just like he does and she's ninety-five.

The french fries are superb. I don't believe I've ever visited Montreal without stopping at Schwartz's for fries, even if it means double-parking outside and running inside for a bag. The Cokes are warm. They have always been warm, even back when they were Pepsis. It can be minus forty degrees Celsius outside (which is the same as minus forty degrees Fahrenheit, one of the things you learn when you live in Montreal) and the Cokes at Schwartz's will be warm. Should you attempt to get ice from your waiter, he will return ten minutes later with a glass holding the two smallest ice cubes you've ever imagined, ice cubes that will have no effect at all on the warmth of your Coke.

Up the street is Moishe's, a steak house that was once a lot like Schwartz's, but the owners put some money into fixing the place up. At best they had mixed results. Outside, Moishe's looks a little too much as if it's boarded up. Vogel calls the interior "Jewish provincial," a pretty good description. Moishe's was founded by the late Moishe Lighter. His sons, who now run the place, don't let you forget. Open the menu and the first thing you see is a full-page photo of Moishe. "Moishe was a very happy man," Vogel says. "As you were leaving, he'd hand you a candy and say, 'Don't go to Schwartz's.'"

If Schwartz's looks like it's from the twenties, Moishe's looks like it's out of the seventies, which isn't good, considering that it was remodeled in the eighties. Even the customers look like they're from the seventies. As I was walking in, the guy walking out was bundled in a massive fake-fur coat that he could have picked up at Joe Namath's garage sale. The customers, few of whom are youthful, tend to dress in business suits and sequined dresses. Vogel calls them "Jews of a certain generation." He's not Jewish, but he can get away with talking like that because everybody thinks he is.

Moishe's can be wonderful, especially if you get the right waiter, which we did. We got Franky, who has been there for forty-three years and still looks young, a testament to the curative powers of marinated herring in cream sauce. Proudly he told me, "In 1976 I served the pope. It was during the Olympics, and he wasn't the pope yet, just a cardinal, but he was a nice man. He had pickled salmon and a sirloin steak."

Good choices. I went right for the full Eastern European experience—hey, why do you think Cardinal Karol Wojtyla ate at Moishe's? My appetizer was irrationally salty schmaltz herring that tasted as though it had come right out of a barrel that had come right off a boat. Then I had the chopped liver, as dense and dark as chopped liver gets. Chopped liver is very serious food in English-speaking Montreal, and Vogel says the reason is that French-Canadian butchers had such a small appreciation of liver they'd practically give it away. "My mother would always give me a dime, send me to a French-Canadian butcher, and tell me to ask for the calves' liver for the dog," he says. "It was for us, of course."

I ordered a rib steak coated with garlic and pepper, the house specialty. It was not as good as Vogel's sirloin, which was as thick, tender, and beefy as any Manhattan sirloin strip. The food that had the most resonance for me was the tarts and pastries. These are filled with whipped cream so dense the kitchen must burn out blenders making it. When I told Franky I was amazed that the pastries were every bit as good as I remembered them, he said, "That's because the same man has been doing the pastries for forty years—Giovanni from Naples. He came a little after me."

Vogel, unabashedly emotional about Moishe's, says, "I'll tell you something. As long as there's a Moishe's, there'll always be a Montreal."

Restaurant critics are not supposed to be sentimental, but as William Neill, I always had a soft spot for Beautys, the best place in the city to start your day if your idea of breakfast isn't *feves au lard* and *cretons*. To appreciate Beautys, your idea of breakfast has to be an omelette containing hot dog, salami, green peppers, and fried onions. This is known as Beautys' famous mishmash.

I didn't know what to expect when I walked into the old place, a coffee shop on Mont-Royal, but I sure didn't expect to find Hymie

Skolnick at the cash register, precisely where he was when I left the city twenty years ago. "I'm still around," said Hymie, who is seventy-five.

He seemed as happy to see me as I was to see him, and he lavished upon me the mishmash omelette (*ahhh!*), the sandwich of smoked salmon and cream cheese on a toasted sesame-seed bagel from the great Montreal Bagel Factory on Saint-Viateur Street (oh, my!), and home-made rice pudding so rich and raisiny that Marvin Hamlisch himself praised it from the stage of the Place des Arts not too long ago.

Everything looked the same, only better, including Hymie. The overly spacious orange booths are now overly spacious royal-blue booths, but I couldn't see that anything else had changed. Hymie told me his customers are a little different because so many Jews have left Montreal—"the young people, not people my age." Business was still good. He got a plug on French television, and now French tourists stop in all the time.

He cleared up a few questions I never bothered to ask him all those years ago. I asked how the place, officially the Bancroft Snack Bar, came to be known as Beautys. He said that Beauty was the nickname he got because he was such a good bowler. "I got a couple of cups, as a matter of fact," he said. I asked him about the rumor that he walked onstage during one of Dean Martin's shows in Las Vegas to collect money that Martin owed him. He said it was true that Martin ran up a tab in the forties and ignored it—"Every day a mishmash, a hot dog," Hymie said—but he never went after the money, and Martin never paid up.

He said he had something to ask me.

"I forget your name," he said.

I told him my name, the one my parents gave me.

He said, "I always thought it was O'Neill."

I told him it was good to be remembered, and it was good to be back.

GQ, MAY 1996

SLICING UP NAPLES

I ask little of the great cities of Italy, no more than the presence of a few admirable trattorias scattered among the unheated museums, crumbling amphitheaters, and heroic statues with no noses. I'm content if the polenta is creamy, the Gorgonzola pungent, the artichokes tiny and fried just right. Is it wrong for me to want tasty Bolognese sauce in Bologna or savory Genoa salami in Genoa?

Simple though these needs may be, in-town dining in Italy rarely works out for me. Whenever I'm there savoring a magnificent meal, I can usually look out the window of the restaurant and see an old farmer in a pilled cardigan chugging by on his tractor. A mule stumbling along under sacks of *arborio* rice won't be far behind.

We all know Italian cuisine is the food of the home kitchen and, absent that, of the simple country restaurant with the wife at the stove and the husband out front, greeting guests and pretending he is the reason the place is doing so well. It is a cuisine of freshness and simplicity, which is seldom the strength of formal restaurants, yet that is not a satisfactory excuse for Italian food to suffer so acutely when exposed to the trappings of urbanity. After all, a restaurant owner has only to hire somebody with a fast car, of which there is no shortage in Italy, and instruct him to fill the trunk with ripe tomatoes, zucchini flowers, and artisanal sausages and drive in from the country once a day. He must also marry a stout woman who grew up in a household in which the mother cooked for the family, and there are plenty of those around, too.

Now and then, I have enjoyed meals in Italian cities. I love the wines at Don Lisander in Milan, the fish at da Fiore in Venice, and everything at Cibreo in Florence (except the gelatinous calf's foot, and I don't have to apologize for disliking that). I've spent a total of four to five months in Italy in my lifetime, and while I don't wish to appear ungrateful for those travel opportunities, few of my dining experiences away from the countryside have been memorable. There is much to recommend about Milan, Florence, Venice, Rome, and Bologna, but restaurants aren't among their virtues.

I've spent most of my time in the northern cities, but I'm gradually wending my way south. Most recently, I veered off toward Naples, an undertaking that had me buoyant with optimism. It is by reputation the birthplace of the red-sauce cuisine that defined Italian food for Americans throughout most of the twentieth century. Even better, the pizza of Naples is legendary, admired everywhere as the benchmark of the genre, even by citizens of northern Italy, who almost never speak of the people or the products of the south without a curled lip and a sneer of contempt. (It's mostly a work-ethic thing.) In Naples I would find pizza from wood-burning ovens, pizza sold in the shadows of perilous alleys, pizza that would expose as a cruel joke the pies we Americans have been eating all our lives.

Furthermore, I was thrilled to be visiting a city filled with the resplendence and detritus of history. Naples is a glorious relic, the most densely populated city of Europe, a survivor of conquests by the Greeks, the Romans, the Goths, the Byzantines, and the Normans. Naples was harried by the runaway slave Sparticus, placed under siege by the Germans, attacked from the sea by the Saracens, harassed by the Vandals, tormented by the Franks, forced into an alliance with the Sicilians, and, to hurdle a few centuries, bombed by the Allies. (It caught a much-needed break when Sophia Loren was born there, in 1934.) The Spanish, starting with Ferdinand and Isabella, ruled Naples for more than two hundred years. Under the influence of the Spanish and Bourbon kings, the cuisine of Naples began to evolve, helped along by an influx of New World products such as the tomato, the bean, and the pepper.

Naples is the base of the dread crime organization known by the old Spanish name *camorra*, far more insidious-sounding than *mafia*, which has come to reek of ineptness. In Naples I would learn if street crime and spaghetti go hand in hand, as American filmmakers would have us believe. I would gaze upon the killer volcano Vesuvius, destroyer of entire civilizations, walk dangerous alleys hung with ominous flapping laundry, inhale the sweet wood smoke of pizza ovens mingled with the sooty residue of everyday life. I eagerly awaited my visit, for I have wearied of traveling to cities so civil even the subways are safe at night.

The taxi driver bringing me from the airport excitedly pointed out the soccer stadium where Diego Maradona starred for Napoli in the 1980s—yet another reminder that whatever the century, Naples is forever living in the past. I told him I knew a man who knew Pelé, which must have impressed him, because he failed to overcharge me for the trip.

In the course of several excursions to the airport to collect my wife and some friends, all lured to Naples by my assurances that they'd experience the finest traditional Italian dining of their lives, I deciphered the system of extortion employed by drivers plying the airport-to-midtown circuit. It is ingenious and pervasive. They demand two to three times the fare registered on the meter, and should the victim protest, they offer a receipt that is four to five times what is on the meter. This way the driver cheats the passenger, the passenger cheats his company, and everybody prospers by participating in a satisfying life of petty crime.

I had booked a room at the Grand Hotel Parker's, which is up a winding hillside road from the Bay of Naples. My room overlooked the harbor, one of the world's great vistas, and waking up every morning to such a view made the trip to Naples worthwhile—even if the restaurants, as I was soon to learn, did not. A welcoming treat in my room was a waxed-paper bag of *sfogliatelle*, the world-class ricotta-and-dried-fruit pastry of Naples that manages to be crunchy, buttery, silken, and chewy, all at the same time.

For a good part of my life, I'd been looking forward to dining in Naples. I'd dreamed of it the way lovers fantasize about Paris, scholars about Heidelberg, and romantics about Venice. There is no more evocative scent to me than Pecorino Romano, the grated cheese that floated down upon every pasta dish served to me in the Philadelphia restaurants of my youth. Words such as *cacciatore* (cooked in mushrooms, onions, and tomatoes) and *saltimbocca* (sautéed with ham) are as emotionally appealing to me as any gastronomic terms, and I have always considered red-sauce cooking the food least likely to let me down. Back in the 1970s, when I was a sportswriter and traveled to major American cities without recognizable restaurants, I always knew I could count on places named Luigi's and Mama's to serve up satisfying plates of *chicken alla scarpariello* with *rigatoni alla marinara* on the side.

I hoped to visit a dozen restaurants during my ten days in Naples. I went to only five and gave up, dismayed. I tried five pizzerias, too, and I quit on them after discovering an awful secret: there are puddles in the pies, little lagoons of hot liquid that soak through the otherwise magnificent crusts. As troubling as I found this to be, it didn't shatter my confidence nearly as much as two restaurant meals I experienced soon after my arrival. The first was at a quietly fashionable spot called Ciro a Santa Brigida, near Via Toledo, the fashionable shopping street Neapolitans like to call Via Roma.

Ciro a Santa Brigida looks just right: nice tablecloths, simple wood furniture, the ambiance promising excellence without pretension. A friend and I stepped inside and were immediately shown to a tiny table in a cramped passageway next to a window overlooking a taxi stand. Then our waiter discouraged us from having anything we wanted, including the seafood stew that is supposedly the house special.

I ordered wine. He shook his head at my poor choice. "You like dry?" he asked. "Sure," I replied. He brought out a bottle called Asprinio di Aversa, which was dry all right. Perhaps it was the power of suggestion left by the unfortunate name, but the flavorless, flinty beverage seemed to leave a chalky film on my tongue, much like an unswallowed aspirin tablet. I insisted on the *gnocchi alla napoletana* because it sounded so right for my very first dish in Naples. To the waiter's credit, he warned against it. The gnocchi were gummy, probably store-bought. The sauce wasn't much more than canned tomatoes. We were offered no grated cheese, and when I asked why, the waiter replied, "I didn't know you wanted it." Never before had I come upon an Italian waiter mystified by the time-honored concept of cheese on tomato sauce. I insisted on the famous stew, which contained squid, octopus, mussels, and shrimp in an oily, garlicky sauce. I liked it well enough, although the shrimp had been overcooked to mush, which I subsequently found standard in *cucina napoletana*. My friend's grilled *orata*, a harmless local fish of minimal distinction, wasn't fresh. An arugula salad came soaking wet, and the leaves were too tough to chew.

It was a poor excuse for a meal, but worse awaited.

I had been advised by several heretofore trustworthy friends that Dante e Beatrice served traditional food untouched by time, and I looked forward to dining there more than at any other restaurant. After all, I had come to learn about the foundation of the Italian-American food that had sustained me for so long. My initial impression of Dante e Beatrice, like that of Ciro a Santa Brigida, was favorable. It's a tiny spot of two small rooms, with family photos on the pale-yellow walls and no frills except a guitar player whose discordant refrains turned out to be a perfect accompaniment to the invidious cuisine.

The moment the five of us were seated, a waiter brought out a slice of something he called *pizza rustica*, a sweet-and-savory ricotta cake laced with bits of ham. It was so appealing I was thrown off guard. When he suggested that we allow him to select our appetizers, I happily agreed. Out came eleven dishes, as fast as he could fling them on the table. The marinated yellow peppers were fine, and the carrots weren't too bad, although I can't say carrots take all that well to a long soak in vinegar. The other dishes were so outside the parameters of what I would call appetizing, I couldn't believe they were part of a cuisine that had established an unshakable foothold in the United States.

Most were so overly marinated my tongue shriveled on contact. The white beans were blessedly acid-free, but they were cold, bland,

and mushy, the only inedible white beans I've ever been served in Italy. The mozzarella was sour, clearly spoiled, but it was highly desirable compared to the marinated unidentifiable vegetable jerky, which in turn soared over the marinated small smelly fish.

I lunged for a menu, anxious to take this meal out of the waiter's hands. Listed was "tender roast veal." That sounded like a lifesaver, but my pleas were ignored. The waiter could not be stopped. He presented us with rubbery rigatoni in an insipid tomato sauce. We picked at it, and then I cried out *"Finito, finito!"* It was perfect Italian, the only time in my life I've pulled that off, but it had no effect. The cook came to our table carrying an oversize skillet. "Special! Fried spaghetti!" he said in English. I sagged at the announcement, but gamely replied, "Okay, but *finito* after that." The fried spaghetti was crunchy. There was nothing more to it. Then the waiter rolled out a serving table groaning under the weight of diverse animal products, most of them unidentifiable. We barely muffled our shrieks. The long, bony things were stringy. The fatty rolled things were tough. The meatballs had been cooked so long they had totally dried out, and yet, in a kind of perverse tour de force, they were absolutely cold.

There was more, as our futile *finitos* faded into hoarse whispers. Bitter, bitter greens. Some fruit nobody touched. Finally, a frosty pitcher of ice-cold *limoncello*, a local liqueur usually offered complimentary after a meal. Here it was reminiscent of lemon-flavored dishwashing liquid, and it was on the bill. In fact, everybody was charged for every course, whether the unwanted food was touched or not. In an effort to pad the check even more, a mandatory tip was added.

It is impossible to recover fully from that kind of gastronomic body blow. What made it worse was that the wretched Dante e Beatrice, surely the most terrible restaurant in Italy, had been touted to me as a place that would exquisitely guide me toward a greater understanding of the cuisine I had come to explore. I was stunned. I finally understood why everybody was always attacking Naples.

And I had yet to visit the pizzeria that would double my bill.

. . .

The pizzas of Naples emerge from ancient wood-burning ovens smoky, charred, and puffy around the edges. Although thin, the crusts are supple and chewy, not cracker-crisp like those on the thin-crust pizzas of America. The cheese is mozzarella, either *flor di latte*, which is made from cow's milk, or *mozzarella di bufala*, made from the milk of the water buffalo. The cow's-milk mozzarella is as good as the best mozzarella in America, but the mozzarella from the water buffalo is unsurpassed—creamy, tangy, and complex. (On the two occasions I ordered buffalo mozzarella in restaurants—not pizzerias—it was spoiled.) The tomato sauce used on Naples pizzas isn't much different from the tomato sauce in America, although occasionally chopped fresh tomatoes are added to good effect.

The pizzas cost almost nothing, maybe $3.50 for a whole pizza marinara (oregano-laced tomato sauce, chopped fresh garlic) that overflows an oversize dinner plate. I noticed that the women of Naples were able to handle these outlandishly large servings by leaving the wonderful outer crust untouched, an observation I passed on to Letizia Tancredi, the front-office manager at the Grand Hotel Parker's. She and I debated restaurants every morning. I would stumble down to the lobby, shaking my head in dismay, and the debriefings would commence.

When I mentioned to her that women were wasting the best parts of their pizzas, she huffed, "We do not!" When I presented her with my far more disturbing discovery about the wetness of the pizzas, she did not flinch. At Trianon, one of the oldest and best pizzerias in Naples, my wife had looked up in dismay from her tasty if fatally gooey *pizza margherita con bufala* (buffalo mozzarella, tomato sauce, basil, Parmegiano-Reggiano) and said, "It's soup." This was an exaggeration, although I wouldn't have been surprised to see small children with tiny boats floating them across their pizzas, reenacting Columbus sailing toward the edge of the world.

Tancredi shrugged off this disturbing flaw as irrelevant, although she did not deny its existence. "I like wet," she said. "That's because I dip the round (the outer crust) in the middle, where it is wet. We dip a lot in Naples. When we eat pasta, we dip the bread in the sauce. I have three babies, and they all dip. My husband dips. We dip a lot in our house."

After sampling nearly twenty pizzas, I figured out what made them so wet: everything. The cooks of Naples are generous with oil, and a lot of vegetable (not olive) oil is poured onto each pizza before it is baked. Mozzarella has a high water content, and so do crushed tomatoes. Add up all that liquid and what you get is a puddle in your pizza. Trianon, which had the most flavorful pizzas in Naples, also had the wettest. The even-more-famous Brandi, which has a photograph of Chelsea Clinton adorning its walls, made medium-wet pizzas. It also made the worst pizza margherita I tasted, which was unfortunate, since it claims to have invented the pizza margherita to honor a visit by the Italian queen Margherita in 1889. A lesser-known pizzeria, Luigi Lombardi a Santa Chiara, made admirable specialty pizzas topped with mushrooms or lightly smoked provolone cheese. We had a wonderful waiter there by the name of Ciro, but don't bother asking for him, because half the waiters in Naples are named Ciro.

The place that brazenly cheated on our check was Pizzeria da Mimi, on Via Speranzella in the heart of the Spanish Quarter, which slopes up from the Via Toledo and was built in the sixteenth century to garrison troops. A friend and I decided to explore the narrow, uneven streets, despite having been told the area was dangerous to outsiders. One of the streets of the Spanish Quarter, Via Concordia, is allegedly the principal habitat of the foot soldiers of the *camorra*. An elderly fruit peddler who spoke a few words of English—he told us he'd once been to New York with the Italian merchant marine—warned us to get out for our own good.

The Spanish Quarter reminded me of Boston's North End, particularly the shrewd efforts by residents to reserve parking spaces in front of their tenement buildings. One particularly resourceful woman had placed two clothes-drying racks filled with wet laundry on the street, end to end, taking up space just large enough for a car. About the time her husband returned, the clothes would be dry (if grimy from passing

traffic). This part of Naples respects the code of the *Curba Nostra*—
Our Parking Space.

Mimi's is on nobody's list of the best pizzerias in Naples, but my
friend and I sought it out after hearing that it attracted authentic citi-
zenry, not tourists like us. The place wasn't much to see: wobbly tables,
a hideous fake-stone vinyl floor, and freaky walls with tile on the bottom half and wood up top. We took one of the seven tables in the back
room and ordered two Cokes and one pizza to share. Almost all the
regulars were drinking Cokes from bottles. The waiter brought us two
holiday promotional cans decorated with pictures of Santa Claus, even
though Christmas was long past. Clearly, outdated inventory was being
unloaded on unwelcome guests.

Service was agonizingly slow, and not only for us. One elderly lady
called over a waiter (who was wearing a baseball cap with BRONX on it)
and said, "Today?" The pizza margherita, when we finally got it, was
about the same as the other pizza margheritas we'd been eating. Then
we were handed a bill that was twice what it should have been. When
I demanded an explanation, the waiter said, "Service charge." I paid up,
figuring we were being punished for trespassing in a section of the city
where tourists aren't wanted. Somebody had to teach us a lesson, and
Pizzeria da Mimi did it well.

Near the end of the trip, with my spirits plunging, I decided on an act
of desperation: I made a reservation at the only restaurant in Naples
awarded a star by Michelin, the French food-and-travel guide that likes
to put its inspectors in countries where they don't belong. Italian chefs
who cultivate the approval of the powerful Michelin guide invariably
cease refining their own culinary traditions and begin duplicating unnatural acts of French gastronomy, which is why their restaurants invariably disappoint. La Cantinella is located near a strip of deluxe hotel
properties, across from the harbor. It has the make-believe Polynesian-
paradise look of a chic Hollywood club from the 1950s: bamboo walls,
bamboo chairbacks, and tiki-style tin lamps hanging from the ceiling.
An orange-beaked tropical bird chirps away in the foyer.

The night I was there with my wife, the clientele was mostly well-dressed businessmen. They all seemed to be eating fried-fish platters and washing the food down with tannic red Tuscan wine, as inappropriate a food-and-wine pairing as exists. I ordered one dish that had genuine finesse, an appetizer of chilled seafood mixed with baby arugula leaves in a light lemon sauce. I didn't like anything else, including an appetizer of overly smoked swordfish slivers, a main course of baked fish and potatoes immersed in what I suspected was their cooking liquid, and a stunningly bad main course called Fantasia di Fritture. This turned out to be a collection of unappetizing miniature fish dumped from a deep-frying basket onto a plate. The meal contained no garnishes except for powdered sugar sprinkled on dessert plates containing cakes not worth mentioning.

Service until then had been mechanical, but after dessert we were ignored. Waiters wandered by. Waiters wandered away. None looked at us. After a half-hour, I suggested to my wife that we get up to leave, a generally infallible means of persuading a restaurant to bring the check. We slowly made our way to the cloakroom. We tipped the coat-check girl—the only female presence in most Naples restaurants. We strode by the bird—which also ignored us. We walked out the door. I expected to hear footsteps, but nobody came after us. The next morning, I returned to the restaurant to pay, and the son of the owner could not have been more charming or more apologetic. I learned something from this encounter: the people of Naples are at their best after altercations, win or lose. Most of the taxi drivers I refused to overpay were much friendlier after our arguments than before.

I did enjoy one restaurant meal in Naples. It was at a deceptively simple waterfront spot, Ciro a Mergellina, a large, airy, glass-enclosed structure across from a stretch of waterfront kiosks where almost all of Naples gathers to eat gelato on Sunday nights. The grilled fish was fresh and perfectly cooked, and the pizza emerged charred from a wood-burning oven. Most restaurants in Naples that serve pizza use electric ovens, which means their crusts have the texture of wallboard, which is the way we enjoy it in America. Ciro a Mergellina stays busy until well after midnight, and the scene is engrossing. Beefy young guys who should be named Sal or Rocco (and would be in South Philly) waddle in to eat with one another, and suave older guys who look like Vittorio Gassman strut in escorting girls who look as if they should be in parochial school.

What I realized after a week in Naples was how much I loved being there, except when I was going out to eat. Everywhere I wandered, I saw something that made me think of another place, a side effect of a city bursting with history. The high-rises on the hills reminded me of Hong Kong; the crumbling stucco villas, of Old Havana. I never felt threatened or uncomfortable, even when I was traversing the narrowest footstep-echoing alleys or challenging the surly staff at Pizzeria da Mimi.

I enjoyed walking around Naples, an activity that could only have been more pleasurable had the sidewalks been passable. The better neighborhoods have a dog-poop problem of Parisian proportions, and elsewhere the pavements are blocked with illegally parked cars. I invariably walked in the streets, which is a challenge, since the drivers are criminally indifferent to pedestrians. Now and then, I would duck into one of the magnificent Baroque churches to look around, and while there I would offer a small donation in thanks for not becoming a traffic fatality. The police, for all I know, are the darlings of Interpol, regular Eliot Nesses, but they appear to do nothing except stand around in clumps and reminisce about Maradona's debut against Verona in 1984.

I used to think Bologna had the worst restaurants in Italy, but Naples deserves the title. I suppose I should be disheartened, considering that I had arrived with such high expectations, but I am not giving up my quest to find an Italian metropolis with acceptable eating establishments. There remains one more major city on my itinerary— Palermo, the urban heart of Sicily.

I've heard wonderful stories about the food of Palermo. As I understand it, the port area is paved with trattorias that offer still-writhing fish from which one might select a fine lunch. I recently read that the sautéed breaded veal chops "in the style of Palermo" are unsurpassed, and I've long wished to try a few *cassata siciliana*, the famous pastries rolled in almond paste. Yes, I'm sure Palermo is the answer. It has to be. The next city to the south is Tripoli, and I'm not going there to eat.

GQ, MAY 2001

WAITER, THERE'S A FOOT IN MY SOUP

My friend Wing Nin Chan picked me up at the airport, and we drove directly to Xi's Garden, where he ordered pig's tail, chicken feet, duck tongue, preserved goose, dried marinated fish with scallions, sesame-flavored bean curd with pot herbs, dried duck intestines with pepper, wild-rice stems in oil, snails stuffed with chopped pork and snail meat, and a chicken soup filled with cubes of duck blood—a horror-film version of Jell-O.

Shanghai used to be called the Paris of the East. This kind of meal wasn't the reason why.

Fortunately, I was so tired from nearly twenty hours in the air I didn't know what I was eating. Anyway, only the bean curd repelled me, for I dislike tofu as I do no other Asian edible. The real shock came the next morning, when my tour of the city began. I rode a subway from my hotel to the "special economic zone" of Pudong, climbed the stairs, and stepped outside.

I was aware that Shanghai had been turned into the financial and commercial heart of an imminent New World Order. Now I was seeing firsthand what had come to pass. Never before had I gazed upon such vastness, ambition, and audacity of scale. It made the city I came from, New York, seem outdated, or at least old-fashioned.

To one side of me was the third-tallest building in the world, the Jin Mao Tower (1,380 feet), a kind of neo–Empire State Building, and on the other was the world-of-tomorrow Oriental Pearl TV Tower (even taller, but not a building and thus ineligible for world's-highest competitions). Encircling these monuments to aspirational central planning was a modernized district of apartment complexes and wide avenues. Soon to come, I learned, was the Shanghai World Financial Center, planned at 1,518 feet, which would make it the tallest building in the world. (In display models it resembles a fraternity pledge paddle, which will assure it not being named the most beautiful building in the world.)

Shanghai has always gleamed in my fantasies as a magnificent curiosity, one of the world's most alluring and mysterious destinations. I knew times had changed, but I was soon to find that the storied city I had traveled so far to explore had essentially vanished. It had been replaced by a metropolis I had no idea could exist, not in China or elsewhere. I had arrived at the anointed showplace of modern Asia.

A decade earlier, the economic district I was walking through was nothing more than primitive villages with black-tiled houses and rice paddies. Elsewhere, the transformation of Shanghai has been less startling but equally dramatic. The Socialist-modernist skyline of the new-sprung city has comic-book overtones—fanciful buildings topped with spires, fins, needles, and tiaras. Shanghai today is hubris unbound, and it has been constructed with such swiftness one might be tempted to believe the fragile and unholy alliance of capitalism and communism that spawned such a massive project could be the most efficient ideology of the twenty-first century, replacing the outdated fundamentals of tired old democracy.

The rebuilding of the city seems to have been for a clear purpose: to eclipse Tokyo, Singapore, and even China's very own (but secretly despised) Hong Kong as the preeminent city of Asia. Throughout the centuries, cities that have achieved world prominence have boasted historical importance, grand scale, an industrious (or easily manipulated) populace, and, not least, an impressive cuisine. (Every city but London, that is, where the principal culinary triumph of the empire was the importation of tea.) Inasmuch as millions of American tourists have returned from packaged trips to China complaining that the meals they ate couldn't compare to the delicious fried wontons drizzled with duck sauce they'd enjoyed back home, I decided to assume a great responsibility. I would find out whether Shanghai qualified as a culinary capital of the world.

The cuisine of Shanghai is unfamiliar to Americans, who are most comfortable with variations on the theme of Cantonese. That means a multitude of shrimp as well as sauces with plenty of cornstarch bounce. Shanghai was once known as the land of fish and rice, but its cooking has evolved far beyond such simplicity.

Restaurant meals invariably begin with cold, marinated appetizers that take some getting used to, because they're often made from animal parts unfamiliar to American palates. The courses that follow are more accessible, consisting of stir-fried dishes, hot pots, and dim sum. Steamed white rice is rarely consumed in restaurants, because it has come to symbolize both unseemly poverty and starchy corpulence. Glutinous rice, which is heavier and stickier than white rice, is often a component of casseroles, and black vinegar is a cherished condiment. Eels, turtles, and crabs are prized, and so is bony fish, considered sweeter than a simple fillet.

I tried snake, thanks to Wing. He owns nine Chinese restaurants in New York City, but one of the reasons he often visits his birthplace of Shanghai is to eat dishes he can't find back home. We were at Xiao Nan Guo, one of his favorite restaurants, which seats 1,100 and is a cross between a banquet hall and an amphitheater. The decor incorporates elements of latter-day Italy (Tuscan-like window treatments), merrie old England (rough-hewn stone walls), and contemporary Miami Beach (neon palm trees). The cuisine of Shanghai's Chinese restaurants is much more coherent than the decor of Shanghai's Chinese restaurants.

"How do you eat snake?" I asked Wing.

"Like eating spareribs," he replied.

Indeed, the chunks of snake did have a meat-on-the-bone quality, although snake meat is much chewier than rib meat, probably because snakes wiggle around a lot and pork ribs do not. Snake, despite what I've heard, does not resemble chicken. Snake eating encompasses elements of skate wing, beef jerky, and old cowboy movies.

A few days after this experience, I was touring an ancient garden when I attempted to impress an attractive young guide by boasting that I'd eaten some fine snake.

"I think if you want to eat snake," she said, "you should go to Guangzhou. It is very famous. They eat the cat, too. The cat is like the tiger, and the snake is like the dragon, so they eat it together in one bowl. But I don't like it. I am afraid."

I later asked Wing if he'd ever eaten cat in Guangzhou (formerly Canton). He had, of course. He'd been the guest at a dinner party with cat meatballs on the menu. His only complaint was that the stingy host had skimped on them. You know what they say about cat meatballs: Bet you can't eat just one.

I arrived in Shanghai, quite by chance, during the Asia-Pacific Economic Cooperation forum. In the United States, news of APEC generated the excitement of a tristate trade fair, but Shanghai was tingling. Two million pots of flowers and 7,500 trees had been planted along roads and in parks. American president George Bush showed up, and his scheduling people had already referred to one event as a "Chinese fire drill," but the Chinese were so pleased he'd come nobody became testy at the affront. He was reportedly eating room-service burgers after a tentative and unsuccessful foray into Chinese cuisine.

Westernized food can be found throughout Shanghai, mostly at Starbucks, KFC, and McDonald's, which have become almost as commonplace as stands selling pan-fried juicy buns, the justifiably beloved street food of Shanghai. A vigilantly patrolled, carefully regulated, painstakingly restored outdoor complex called Xintiandi is Shanghai's showplace of Occidental restaurants, bars, and shops. The first time I walked into Xintiandi—famous as the site of the birthplace of the Chinese Communist Party—a very efficient loudspeaker system was serenading visitors with Sister Sledge singing "We Are Family."

My first meal there was at Luna, which serves disastrously bad middlebrow Italian fare; its chorizo-and-chicken-liver linguine with a creamy meat sauce might be the worst Italian dish ever conceptualized. The jarringly chic T8 features an eclectic fusion menu; its sautéed mushrooms with shaved Parmesan and asparagus on "charred sourdough" came on bread so badly burned it was inedible. After those two meals, I couldn't help thinking how lucky I was that the "authentic Bavarian microbrewery and restaurant" about to open in Xintiandi was still weeks away.

My next Western-style meal was at M on the Bund, located a few floors up in one of the gorgeous early-twentieth-century buildings built by the British during their enslavement of Shanghai. The Bund is the embankment of the Huangpu, and the view from M on the Bund's open terrace across the river to the towers of Pudong is mesmerizing. Unfortunately, the food is not.

We arrived twenty minutes late for a six P.M. reservation and were informed that our table would be needed at eight P.M. I felt right at home, since this is how diners are treated in New York. Service was a disconcerting amalgam of fawning servitude and the bum's rush. The low-ceilinged main dining room, minimally decorated with a Chinese screen and a few Art Deco touches, was crammed with undersized tables so close together only the whisper-thin Chinese waiters could comfortably squeeze through. I shimmied sideways to get by. The "famous slowly baked salt-encased selected leg of lamb" was dry. Roast duck came with a sauce so sweet I regretted not having ordered this dish for dessert.

I tried two renowned Chinese restaurants that have received considerable attention because of how beautifully they are thought to cater to the needs of tourists. I found 1221 at the end of an alley. The background music was Mexican, and further noise was provided by a loud Brit on a cell phone. In keeping with the restaurant's reputation for coddling round-eyes like me, my waitress refused to let me order anything interesting. The sweet-and-sour pork was Manhattan takeout. Garlic shrimp was so tame an American friend eating with me happily compared it to the Red Lobster's popcorn shrimp. (He loves Red Lobster.)

Service was excruciatingly slow. Although the waitresses dressed like ninjas, in black outfits with red sashes, they didn't move like ninjas.

Club Jin Mao is the premier restaurant of the Grand Hyatt Hotel, which is in Pudong's Jin Mao Tower. It is located eighty-eight stories up, but the too-small windows are protected by steel grids, and looking out the windows is like peering from the cockpit of a DC-3. The tables are large and set with flowerless orchids. Napkins wrapped with tasseled cords are the only opulent touch. An optimist might find the Club Jin Mao understated. I found it cold.

My meal began with marinated peanuts, a standard Shanghai snack. These were superb, which was fortunate. My friend and I ate three bowls while waiting one hour for any of the food we had ordered to appear. At one point we stared longingly at the remains of a huge, sluglike sea cucumber ordered by businessmen at a nearby table. A man has to be ravenous to covet sea cucumber, a repellent creature that should be beaten with sticks and driven back into the ocean whenever it finds its way ashore.

We had, as the menu described it, stewed fillet of Yangtze River fish with sliced chicken and ham in a hot-and-sour sauce. It turned out to be little more than a bowl of hot-and-sour soup. I asked our waitress to point out the chicken. "It's in the soup," she said. I asked our waitress to point out the ham. "Sorry, we have no ham," she said.

The crispy duck wasn't crispy. The soup buns stuck to the bottom of the steamer, so when I tried to lift them out, they tore and the soup leaked out. The turnip cakes were perfect. I am a huge admirer of Shanghai turnip cakes, which have flaky shortbread crusts and are stuffed with a turnip filling so savory it could pass for meat. As fine as these were, they did not save the meal.

It was no surprise to me that the most satisfying dining in Shanghai turned out to be at traditional Chinese restaurants operated by Chinese. A reality of culinary development in international cities is that any restaurants that are not of local character need to arise naturally from the needs of a thriving immigrant community. Shanghai does not have that any longer. Back in the 1930s, when Shanghai was dominated by international settlements, it had about seventy thousand foreign residents amid a population of three million. Now it has less than half that number of foreigners in an official population of seventeen million. Even the fiercest central planning cannot make up for such an absence of cultural diversity.

I returned to Xi's Garden, the site of my post-airplane-ride entrail-eating experience. I went back because so much on the menu sounded delicious, particularly the food Wing had refused to order. My waitress was a young Chinese woman, Christine, who spoke good English and was infinitely patient when I started grumbling that the menu had changed and everything I wanted was no longer available.

She soon figured out that I hadn't been to this Xi's Garden but to a different branch. Instead of labeling me an idiot, which would have been understandable, she redoubled her efforts to see that I had a wonderful meal. Thanks to her I had pigeon that was sweetly lacquered, followed by the most entertaining food show in Shanghai: prawns marinating in rice wine dumped over hot stones, releasing a Vesuvian cloud of steam into the air. Next came fried, cumin-laced chicken with sesame-coated hot peppers and a whole fried fish prepared in such a labor-intensive manner it could have been the centerpiece of a banquet. The fish had been cut into chunks, deep-fried, then put back on the bone. In the Western Hemisphere, diners consider themselves blessed if chefs will go to the trouble to return mashed potatoes to the skin.

Christine hovered over me, fascinated by the presence of a Westerner, as few Chinese are these days. (When my wife telephoned and asked if I was being followed by Communist secret police, I told her that not only wasn't I being followed, I wasn't being noticed.) Christine seemed the perfect person to quiz about the nightlife of Shanghai, which is apparently limited to a phenomenon known as KTV bars. I saw dozens of them along Nanjing Road, the neon-lit promenade where concubines once window-shopped while sitting on the shoulders of coolies. I noticed them on street corners near my hotel. Everywhere I went I saw brightly lit KTV bars, and I had no idea what they were.

I hadn't come to Shanghai to wallow in decadence, but thus far I was disappointed with my social life. After all, Shanghai's lighthearted, East-meets-West lifestyle had long ago earned it the nickname Whore of the Orient. I asked Christine who went to these bars and she replied, "Bad girls. Bad men. If the man drink beer, maybe one bottle for very much money. Then the girl is dancing with the man and they sleep together. The man pay money for the girl."

To maintain my respectability, I scowled in displeasure.

KTV, which sounds like a network affiliate, stands for Karaoke TV. The notorious and legendary singsong girls of yesteryear who catered to certain manly needs have been replaced by young women practicing the art of karaoke, a notable downgrade in my opinion. I asked Wing to take me to one of these emporiums, and the next day he did.

We were greeted effusively at the door and led upstairs to a large carpeted private room furnished with couches, coffee tables, and a television monitor large enough to do justice to an American rec room. In came a string of girls, led by an overseer the girls called "Mommy," with trepidation in their voices. We were told to pick a girl, the way we would select a lobster from a tank. What occurred afterward was more ludicrous than libidinous.

My girl was an Asian Alicia Silverstone, which meant she was very pretty and going to fat. She went by the name of Yo-Yo, and I soon learned her father was dead and her mother had lost all their money playing mah-jongg. Our evening began auspiciously when she picked the seeds out of a watermelon slice and handed it to me. I thought, "Now there's a woman who knows what a man likes." Then she started singing karaoke duets with Wing. I suppose I should have been jealous, but I was concentrating on the watermelon, which was particularly sweet.

When she wasn't singing with Wing, she was singing solo. She must have sung the theme song from *Titanic*, "My Heart Will Go On," four times in two hours. When she wasn't singing it, a different girl was. I soon realized that one advantage of being on the *Titanic* was never having to hear that song. I later asked a Shanghai resident who seemed to know about such things to estimate the magnitude of the KTV phenomenon, and he guessed six thousand bars employing one million girls.

I learned a lesson that night. It's no fun spending an evening with a woman whose idea of pleasure is to listen to herself sing.

"I have a turtle foot in my soup," said one of my dinner guests, a Westerner who had recently moved to Shanghai but was still unaccustomed to the dining quirks. "A foot in your soup," he added, unnecessarily, "is not right."

We were at Merrylin, one of the megapalaces that dominate dining in Shanghai. At Merrylin, hostesses who look like Rockettes lead guests from the marbled entrance past Italianate statuary to private rooms decorated with oil paintings of Occidental women strumming ancient instruments.

This dinner had a dual purpose, to eat the famous hairy crabs (only the feet are hairy) of Shanghai and to meet Hui Ren Qiu, a lifelong resident of the city. She is an elegant woman, a former instructor of English who attended the finest schools of Shanghai, McTyeire High and St. John's University, and was forced to leave her home and reside in the countryside during the infamous Cultural Revolution of 1966. Hundreds of thousands of young Shanghainese endured similar humiliation. "I was ordered to seek reeducation from the peasants," she said, calmly and softly but still offended. "How can we receive education from the peasants? I picked up pig manure. While I am there, I am not allowed to read. It was not allowed. It was all a waste of our time."

She is a neat, trim woman in her seventies who came to dinner impeccably dressed in a brown blazer and camel-colored slacks. She wore a diamond pin from the thirties, or at least an excellent costume-jewelry replica of one, and appeared to have stepped out of a black-and-white movie, until I saw her hands. Under the fingernails of the thumb and first finger of her right hand was a fungus growth she picked up working in those fields.

Hairy crabs, which were in season, are taken apart with exquisite care in a formalized eating ritual that makes the banging and smashing of

Maryland's hard-shell varieties seem primitive. The result, in both locales, is a few bites of delicate lumps of meat, but the Chinese are more moved by the experience. They prize their crabs so highly they extol them in poetry ("Chrysanthemum glows in yellow blossoms and crabs are prime"). I chomped on my pair, one male and one female, liking the roe in the more exalted female but not overcome. Hui, a person of subtlety, ate one of hers with care and wrapped up the second to take home.

A few days later I walked into a small Taiwanese spot called the Bellagio Cafe, expecting little. The prosperous, sophisticated Taiwanese consider their cuisine rarefied and elegant. I consider it worrisome, because dried squid and similar subspecies are always appearing in their dishes. I ate a modest lunch, and it was a revelation. A dish called Garlic Explosion Shrimp, which consisted of heads-on shrimp buried in a mountain of bread crumbs seasoned with garlic, chili peppers, and bits of dried fruit was the most compelling food I ate in Shanghai. I rated the Bellagio Cafe's steamed pork dumplings unbeatable until I sampled the pan-fried ones, which were even better.

The restaurant seemed too trendy, too throbbing with music, too filled with young people in black T-shirts to be so concerned with food. The tables and chairs could have come from SoHo—they had fake-marble tops, aluminum arms, plastic seats. The waitresses were short women with short hair dressed in black-and-white schoolgirl uniforms.

The owner, Claire Lee, at first refused to speak to me. "I don't know how to answer questions. My English is not good enough. Maybe you come back in a half year." I explained how inconvenient that would be. She told me all the famous restaurants in Shanghai were the big restaurants and I should talk to those owners because they knew something about running a restaurant and she did not. I praised her cooking, and she replied that she didn't know how to cook; she hired somebody to do it for her. "When I told my officemates at China Airlines I was coming to Shanghai to open a restaurant, they said, 'You can only cook tomatoes and fried eggs and you are going to Shanghai to open a restaurant? You should be ashamed.'"

Lee is a small woman who walks stooped, which makes her seem unimposing, something she is not. The waitresses are munchkin versions of her, but she claims the intention was not to impersonate herself but to create a staff of women whom customers would enjoy but not lure away. Her brother Jimmy, who is one of her partners, explained. "This is an important concept in China. If you want waitresses, they must not be beautiful or ugly. You must have them in the middle. They cannot be ugly, because you must provide customers something for their eyes to enjoy. But if I am a rich man who comes in here and sees a beautiful waitress, I ask her how much she earns per month."

Added Claire, "I don't think a beautiful girl stays here long."

Bellagio Cafe has twenty-two tables, miniature for Shanghai, but it is open from eleven A.M. until four A.M. and the tables are turned, in restaurant parlance, nine times. I had five meals there, but often it was only a tuna sandwich. Americans occasionally require tuna with mayo on white bread, even amid the bounty of Shanghai.

I came upon remnants of old Shanghai by following the laundry. Near a few undistinguished streets, wash hung in alleyways or dangled from trees. I found these neighborhoods irresistible. I suppose those who mourn the passing of old Shanghai should be considered no more than sentimental wretches. I count myself among them.

Here I would find pan-fried soup buns offered for pennies apiece. The shops along these lanes are family run, or so they appear, and offer multiple services. My favorite combined bicycle repairs and unrefrigerated farm-fresh eggs. I regularly saw people walking about in pajamas because their only set of clothes was hanging out to dry.

Rickshaws no longer roam the streets, and at one time eighty thousand rickshaw pullers worked in Shanghai. Bicycles, including Shanghai's legendary Forever brand, are abundant, but Wing told me he expected bicycles to be gone from the streets within five years, supplanted by motorbikes. In restaurants women still place their purses on the seats of their chairs, leaning back against them, rather than on the floor. This is more out of habit than necessity, because the tradition of spitting in dining establishments is fading away.

My hotel was situated in the old French Concession, a remnant of the era when the Europeans bent Shanghai to their will. I came upon little that was remindful of those days, although a remarkable exception was the Old China Hand Reading Room, a dark, quaint, and curious retreat resembling the parlor of a grandmother who never airs out her house. I ordered a Coke float—standard Coke, terrible ice cream, magnificent ice-cream-parlor glass—for the high price of three dollars and browsed through stacks of old magazines. One of them, a 1991 copy of *China Tourism*, talked about the opening of the Yangtze River Delta and the displacement of the simple Pudong residents: "The way the villagers spoke was unaffected, which was in sharp contrast to the sagacity of the Shanghainese." The Old China Hand Reading Room is surely the original Barnes & Noble, the prototype of refreshment-ready bookstores to come.

So much is gone from Shanghai: the booming trade in silk, tea, and opium. British imperialism, French culture, Russian decadence. The pimps, hoodlums, drug runners, smugglers, and profiteers who came to ply their trades have turned to other Asian locales. Yet the future of the city seems assured. Only matters of the table remain in doubt. Hong Kong became celebrated for its food even though it offered little but Cantonese cooking, but Shanghai has officially embraced culinary diversity. Its leaders have made it clear that home cooking alone will not do. The Chinese food of the city is masterful, but the Western cuisine does not measure up, and there's too much of it to ignore. As an international dining capital, Shanghai falls short. To be fair, I cannot blame Communist authorities for all the dreadful Western food I sampled. No dish was more appalling than the goose-liver and chocolate terrine at the Peace Hotel, a dish that was probably on the menu back when Noël Coward took up residence and wrote *Private Lives*. For that foreign-devil food item, I blame the Brits.

GQ, JUNE 2002

The remark was breathtakingly frank. "We do not allow whites," said
the soft-spoken woman manning the phones at the Chicago headquarters of the Nation of Islam. Hearing me inhale, she diplomatically
amended her words: "Caucasians are not allowed in the mosque."

She could not have been more cordial. I had called the offices of
Louis Farrakhan's Muslim sect to find out how I might attend a
Sunday meeting at the national center, the Mosque Maryam. I
thought it would make an intriguing afternoon: lunch at the Nation's
new five-million-dollar South Side restaurant followed by services at
the mosque.

Once I learned I would be barred from the meeting, I wondered if
my plans to review the restaurant, Salaam, were also in vain. What if
no whites were allowed there? Restaurant critics seeking anonymity
have been known to employ disguises, but this would be a tough one
to pull off.

Actually, I didn't think even Farrakhan could get away with segre-
gating his restaurant—the Civil Rights Act of 1964 took care of that.
Still, I didn't want to be forced into some kind of reverse-discrimination
demonstration, sitting at the Salaam lunch counter, demanding service.

Back to the telephone I went, this time to call the restaurant. An
even more polite young woman answered the phone. Not quite knowing how to word this, I stammered, "Do you . . . ummm . . . accept . . .
ummm . . . white guests?"

This time, it was my words that caused distress. The woman took a moment to regain her composure before assuring me that indeed they did.

I learned something from all of this: racism isn't as simple as everybody thinks it is.

Not only am I white, I'm Jewish. Should you be under the impression that all white folks are equally distasteful to Farrakhan, you haven't been listening to his commentaries on the Jews.

When he's in a good mood, he likes to say that he has no problems with the Jews. Unfortunately, he's in a bad mood a lot. Want to really get him riled? Just remind him that the Jews are the Chosen People. The man can hardly get through a public appearance without Jews upsetting him. Now, Jews go out to eat all the time, and no restaurateur in his right mind would ever say such terrible things about such outstanding customers, but Farrakhan apparently can't help himself.

Farrakhan, who has predicted a holy race war in America, is surely the most unlikely restaurateur in America. For that matter, the Nation of Islam is certainly the most unlikely group to be sitting around with whites, breaking bread.

Founded in 1930 by W. Fard Muhammad, who proclaimed himself Allah reincarnate, the Nation of Islam is committed to the uplifting of the black man, as well as to the separation of blacks from whites. The sect is part religious, part paramilitary, part cult, and part Project Head Start. After Fard Muhammad, the Nation was led by Elijah Muhammad, who called himself the Messenger of Allah. He preached that whites were evil mutants of blacks and that Jews were a "race of evil people," wrote two books on food (*How to Eat to Live*, parts one and two), and fathered eight legitimate and thirteen illegitimate children. He died in 1975 and was succeeded by one of his sons, Wallace Deen Muhammad.

Wallace Deen Muhammad dismantled the Nation of Islam in order to take his followers on a more traditional path. Farrakhan, a formidable leader, rebuilt it. There are now an estimated 6 million Muslims in the United States; 2 million of them are black, and a modest percentage of those are followers of Farrakhan. So secretive is the Nation of Islam that estimates of its membership range from 2,000 to 200,000.

The grandiose restaurant Salaam, built in a weary, run-down section of Chicago dominated by storefront churches, unkempt shops, and vacant lots, is by some accounts Farrakhan's dream—he frequently visited the site during construction. It is a curiously ambitious project, since the only acclaimed food product previously produced by the Nation of Islam is its Salaam Bakery Supreme Bean Pie, prepared with navy beans, a favorite of Elijah Muhammad, whose food fiats carry a lot of weight in the Salaam kitchen. The pie is smooth, rich, slightly spicy, and altogether satisfying, but as good as it is, it is not a commodity to inspire a five-million-dollar investment.

Salaam is not one restaurant; it is a large, sparkling-white building housing a number of food-service enterprises—a bakery, a buffet, a cafeteria, three banquet rooms, and a "fine dining" section. Towering ninety feet high is a lighted Islamic star and crescent, giving a Vegas air to the undertaking. At the February 1995 opening ceremonies for the restaurant (or, as it is called on a tape available at Nation of Islam bookstores, "The Historic Opening Dedication of the Fabulous Salaam Restaurant—the Palace of the People"), Farrakhan explained how his "household name" would attract patrons, much as Michael Jordan's and Oprah Winfrey's have attracted customers to their Chicago dining establishments. Thinking of Salaam as a celebrity-owned restaurant with himself as the celebrity seems a profound reversal for a man who is usually intent on secluding himself and his followers from the rest of the world.

Dining there offers a chance to scrutinize Elijah Muhammad's diet and Louis Farrakhan's hospitality. It also provides a rare opportunity to look inside the very closed, very uncommunicative Nation of Islam, which in public presents itself as an angry speaker lashing out from in front of a phalanx of young, unsmiling, neatly groomed security men that Farrakhan calls the Fruit of Islam and I think of as the Bow Ties. Salaam is Farrakhan's calling card, perhaps even a genuine attempt to connect with a society that scorns him even more than he scorns it.

.   .   .

I'm seated at a comfortable banquette in the so-called fine dining section of Salaam. My guest and I have just received our appetizers, the
Salaam Fondue Supreme for her, the Sultan's Request for me. When I
look up, I see the posse arriving—coming off the elevator are more
than a dozen members of the Fruit of Islam dressed in dark suits, white
shirts, and bow ties. Four of them are seated by the maître d' at the table
right next to ours. I'm sure this is a coincidence. At least I think it is. I
decide not to let it bother me. I tell myself I am not like Farrakhan. I
am not the suspicious type.

Not letting them affect me turns out to be easy because they are so
quiet I am able to clock the pauses in their dialogue. Approximately every
five to seven minutes, one of them makes a comment and another one
answers. Then they lapse into silence. They might be fundamentalists,
but they aren't conversationalists. They're a little spooky, but at least
they're well behaved.

So far, we're enjoying Salaam, although our appetizers aren't as
advertised. The fondue, which is supposed to be served over an open
flame with three breads, has no flame, one bread, and no fondue fork.
Sultan's Request turns out to be zucchini boats stuffed with peppery
ground lamb and floating in a thick "Burgundy sauce." The sauce tastes
like canned brown gravy with some chopped vegetables added in an
unsuccessful effort to contribute flavor.

Although the kitchen staff is not impressing me, everybody else has
been cordial. At the front door, we were greeted by a Fruit of Islam
security man carrying a walkie-talkie. He politely handed us off to a
doorman, a middle-aged man festooned with Farrakhan buttons who
escorted us to the elevator while chatting amiably about the likelihood
of slaveholders being among our ancestors.

On the second floor, we stepped into a flamboyant function-room
atmosphere: carpeting with madly decorative burgundy, green, beige,
and white whorls; burgundy drapes; and innumerable chandeliers set
bright enough to blind. Over to welcome us came a young, sweet host-

ess who briefed us on Salaam and passed us on to the maître d', the sort of quiet, courtly, tuxedoed gentleman who is likely to find employment in hotel dining rooms of a certain age. He seated us, and we were promptly greeted by our waiter, who I am happy to report defied current fashion and did not introduce himself to us. My guest, however, found him so alluring, so Omar Sharif–ish in his dress whites—a tunic with a military collar, gold buttons, ensign stripes, and "Salaam" embroidered over the pocket in gold thread—that she insisted on asking. Noel had her enthralled.

So here we are, trying not to attract the attention of the nearly mute young men dining beside us, quickly gobbling the unflamed fondue before it cools, hoping for better luck with our main courses, when we suddenly realize something odd: hardly anybody seems to be having a good time.

Despite sprightly lounge music tinkling from a polished Yamaha baby-grand player piano and a perfectly gracious staff, Salaam has an aura of cheerlessness. Maybe it's because no alcohol is served and nobody loosens up. Maybe it's because the message of the Nation of Islam is one of responsibility and discipline, and followers confuse this dictum with having no fun. Maybe it's the overhead security camera, the kind that rotates to cover all corners of a room. That could dampen any mood.

I order a glass of nonalcoholic Chardonnay. It is so badly oxidized I send it back, which allows me to find out just how friendly the Nation of Islam wishes to be. "No problem," Noel says. The second glass, from a freshly opened bottle, is no better than the first, which tells me that wine storage at Salaam is about what you would expect at an establishment that doesn't approve of wine.

For her main course, my guest orders the Double Lamb Chops Morocco. I take Noel's recommendation and select North African Tilapia, which the menu promises will provide "an irresistibly delicious Motherland experience." Because the menu is so diverse, ordering from it is a challenge. It's impossible to figure out the specialties of Executive Chef Early Primus, who once cooked for Muhammad Ali. At the opening ceremonies for the restaurant, Farrakhan promised "an international menu where people of every part of this earth and culture can see themselves reflected in the menu." In other words, this is Continental cuisine taken to more continents than one menu has ever gone before.

There's Indian tandoori chicken, Jamaican jerk chicken, Italian lemon fettucine, Tex-Mex quesadillas, Chinese spring rolls, Caribbean grouper, and vegetarian barbecued ribs. (No nation would want credit for that.) I don't believe Farrakhan's chef can pull off a menu like this. I don't believe Alain Ducasse could pull off a menu like this.

Although tilapia is not a particularly interesting fish, and I suspect freezing has further blunted the flavor of my entree, I enjoy the dish. It isn't spicy, as it is supposed to be, but the bland white sauce is fine. The lamb chops, ordered medium-rare, arrive overcooked and rather cold. What's worse, they're accompanied by the same accursed Burgundy sauce that ruined the zucchini boats. It is even more awful this time because it has congealed.

"Having dessert?" asks Noel.

We're tempted not to, since the first two courses have dragged on for two-and-a-half hours. That's a long time to sit at a dinner table and not drink wine. Still, the Salaam bakery has a good reputation.

"Of course," I say.

He offers us a choice of either bean pie or crème caramel. Well, nobody ever said the Salaam bakery produced a cornucopia of fine products. We select the crème caramel. Wrong choice. It takes fifteen minutes to show up and has a tough, thick crust.

Afterward, on the way to the Salaam parking lot across the street from the restaurant, I notice the Fruit of Islam with the walkie-talkie watching us. He is making sure we get to our car safely. I don't know many other restaurants that care about the well-being of patrons once they've paid the check.

At the Respect for Life Bookstore #1, just across the street from Salaam, I pick up a nice selection of items: the two Elijah Muhammad books on eating, a tape of the opening ceremonies for the restaurant, and a video of Farrakhan's 1994 speech at the University of Massachusetts, Amherst, titled, to be precise, "(The Furor of Farrakhan) 'The Controversy with the Jews: The True History of Slavery in the Americas.'" A young man in a bow tie working the cash register studies my selections and singles out the tape featuring Farrakhan berating the Jews. "That's a good one," he says.

Although I inform him that I am from out of town, he says he will accept a check. My guess is that not a lot of customers stiff the Nation of Islam.

Despite the menacing appearance of some of Farrakhan's militant followers, I've been treated well whenever I've dealt with his group. Back in 1985 I attended Farrakhan's infamous rally at Madison Square Garden. Many other white people who were there expressed horror, while the mainstream press was apoplectic—*The New Republic* compared the event to the Nuremberg rallies of Nazi Germany. For me, it was hard to take seriously.

Farrakhan had, Casey Kasem–like, gathered together all sorts of golden oldies. In this case, they were grizzled Jew-bashers from around the nation, everyone from Russell Means to Stokely Carmichael, bit players in a variety show featuring gospel, prayer, militarism, lies, hatred, love, neatness, faith, fascism, paranoia, wit, and megalomania. Farrakhan was his usual self, pointing out that "the germ of murder is sown in the hearts of Jews across the world." To me, everything sounded staged.

Widely reported was this exchange:

Farrakhan: "Who were the enemies of Jesus?"

The crowd, excited as kids at a birthday party, gleefully screamed the expected reply: "Jews! Jews! Jews!"

What I don't remember seeing in print was Farrakhan's own answer to his question: "The scribes."

I'm white. I'm Jewish. I write. I don't think there's much about me that Farrakhan would like.

I'm sitting in a booth, reading my morning paper, enjoying fresh but weak coffee and a fresh but bland Danish. It's just like every other morning, except my breakfast comes from the Salaam bakery and my paper is *The Final Call*, Farrakhan's house organ.

I've read newspapers that are more offensive—a number of New York tabloids come to mind. Still, *The Final Call* has its malevolent moments. The National News Briefs section is reporting the arrest of a Hasidic rabbi for allegedly fondling a teenage girl on an airplane. Although the paper comes out only every two weeks and has space for only three national news briefs, the rabbi makes the news. I suspect there are many cries of "Stop the presses!" whenever the editor of *The Final Call* comes across an item about a wayward Jew.

It's quiet here, peaceful. My booth is in a sunny room decorated with cartoon fish on tile walls. I could be in the family restaurant of a mid-priced hotel chain.

Immediately after such a light breakfast, I decide to have lunch. I've had my eye on the cafeteria's rotisserie chicken, which comes with macaroni and cheese, greens, and a roll for $5.95 (white meat) or $5.49 (dark). There are no greens today, so the white-jacketed server offers a substitute. I ask for a little cabbage and a few candied carrots, and I have to stop her from filling my tray to overflowing. Portions are more than generous at Salaam.

I take a table in Elijah's Garden, a glass-walled interior dining area with a marble fountain, patio furniture, and two overhead television sets. The carrots are soft and sweet. The cabbage is limp from sitting too long in water. The macaroni and cheese is nicely flavored but a little dry. My flimsy plastic knife bends double when I try to cut the chicken. For that matter, it bends double when I try to cut the carrots.

The chicken is juicy, meaty, and sweet. I wonder if it was raised in accordance with the principles of Elijah Muhammad, who decreed the superiority of penned-in chickens that eat what you give them to barn-yard chickens that eat bugs and worms. Say what you will about Elijah Muhammad, he was Frank Perdue before Frank Perdue.

Elijah Muhammad's writings on food, published in the late sixties and early seventies, are inspired by eminently sensible Muslim customs and beliefs and then veer off into the oddball. He recommends fresh fruit, cooked vegetables, and the food of Orthodox Jews. He also advises against sweets, fats, tobacco, pork, alcohol, and processed, canned, or fried foods. He also recommends butter over margarine, putting him decades before his time.

His less coherent moments come when he finds fault with freshly baked bread and explicitly endorses small fish over those weighing fifty pounds or more. He warns his followers against eating too much or too quickly, because then the food will not be digested and they will become "small and skinny."

I am reminded of one of his more eccentric culinary tenets—"There is no such thing as stale bread"—at the start of my second fine-dining experience: the waiter presents us with a dried-out half-loaf. My guest is reminded of something else—lip gloss—when she tastes the Salaam special butter, which is whipped up with honey, orange, and lemon.

I decide to make this dinner a true international feast, leaving virtually no cuisine unexplored. After two satisfactory nonalcoholic fruit drinks, greasy vegetarian spring rolls, an order of vegetarian somosas that contain meat, heavy-duty quesadillas good enough to entice Texans to join the Nation of Islam, tandoori chicken topped with that vile Burgundy sauce, a chopped Cobb salad that arrives unchopped, first-rate broccoli with hollandaise, and a couple of fabulous nonalcoholic blender drinks made with Häagen-Dazs ice cream, we decide it is time for dessert.

"You're kidding," exclaims William, our waiter. I like him as much as I liked Noel, maybe more. That's because he isn't as good-looking as Noel and doesn't distract my date.

William walks away looking over his shoulder, waiting in vain for us to confess that our dessert order is a gag. The bean pie is excellent, as always.

"I know you're finished now," says William.

We concede that we are.

"I'm tired," he says. "I've been on my feet since ten o'clock this morning."

He tells us he has a long train ride home to Evanston ahead of him, but he is thinking of stopping on the way for a beer. That answers one of my questions. You don't have to be Muslim to work at Salaam.

It's Sunday afternoon, a beautiful day. I return to the cafeteria, eager to try the $5.99 seafood combo plate. Again I carry my tray into Elijah's Garden, which I'm beginning to think of as my private place. Nobody seems to eat here except me. The BellSouth Senior Classic is on both overhead TV sets. I wonder if anybody is going to believe me when I tell them that I sat at Louis Farrakhan's restaurant watching old white guys in green pants hit golf balls.

The broiled perch is frightening. It smells old and spoiled and is the single worst item of the entire Salaam dining complex except perhaps the Burgundy sauce. After lunch I head for the two P.M. meeting at Mosque Maryam, located about four miles from the restaurant. I've got on my best blue suit. My shoes are shined. I've eaten so many meals at Salaam in the past week I feel like a member of the Nation of Islam, or at least like somebody who deserves to get into services on a guest pass. I'm wondering what will happen when I try to walk in.

The mosque is not an inviting building. Located across a wide avenue from a strip mall, it's all stone slabs and sharp angles, an intimidating fundamentalist façade. Electronically operated sliding gates block the entrance to the parking lot, so I leave my car on a side street and approach on foot. It's 1:55 P.M.

I walk up the steps behind three women wearing traditional loose Muslim garb. At the front entrance, a young Fruit of Islam stands guard. He opens a door for the women. I ask if I can go in.

"No, sir," he says courteously.

I ask why not.

He says I should go around to the side door. He explains that the front doors are for women only.

I turn back down the stairs. A black man in a lemon-yellow suit passes me. I look over my shoulder. He's walking in the front doors.

I don't know what's in store for me at the side doors. I'm not expecting ecumenism.

When I get there, I'm stopped. The person doing the stopping is a small girl, maybe five years old. She's adorable, and she's selling *The Final Call*. I tell her I've already got it.

The second person guarding the door is her mother. She says to the girl, "Tell him thank you, honey." The girl says, "Thank you."

The Nation of Islam isn't so tough after all.

I walk through the door, into an anteroom where about a half-dozen security men stand watch. The guy in the lemon-yellow suit is being frisked. Much to my surprise, I'm not escorted out. I'm told to empty my pockets, lean against the wall, spread 'em. What is this—a house of worship or an episode of *Cops*?

I hold out my keys, my wallet, a couple of pens, and a spiral-bound reporter's notebook.

Whoops.

I await cries of "Get the scribe!" Nobody says a thing. I'm patted down, asked to register. A kindly gentleman at the sign-in desk asks me how I heard about the services. I tell him word gets around.

I nod to the guards, walk through another door. I'm in. I don't know why I've been admitted after being explicitly informed of a ban against whites. Maybe it's because Farrakhan isn't speaking this Sunday and they figure I'm not there just for a show. Maybe they've seen me at Salaam and figure I'm genuinely interested in the Nation of Islam. Maybe I don't look Jewish.

Inside, Mosque Maryam is spacious and bright, with theater-style seats. The women sit apart from the men and outnumber them two to one. Everyone is very still. No chatting. No looking around.

The mosque is about one-fifth full. I surreptitiously glance around. I seem to be the only white person. I'm seated between two young men, neither of whom looks at me. Almost everybody is neatly and carefully dressed, although I notice some young men in hooded sweatshirts.

Several of the Fruit of Islam stand facing the audience. A few minutes after two P.M., they slam themselves into their seats like plebes at a military academy dining hall. The service begins with a short prayer, and then an introductory speaker sets the stage for Ishmael Muhammad, one of the sons of Elijah Muhammad and the assistant minister of the mosque.

He bids all of us "*As-salaam alaikum*," and the response from many of the men in the audience is a militaristic "*Wa-alaikum salaam, sir!*" Ishmael Muhammad speaks for about an hour and a half, emphasizing family values.

He is in favor of more home cooking and fewer soap operas and talk shows. "Oprah and Montel won't make you a success," he exclaims. The only whites he impugns by name are Betty Crocker and Sara Lee—he wants women to cook, not just open packages. His anger at what white people do to black people is restrained. His admiration of what white people do for one another is intended to be a lesson: he wants black people to treat one another equally well.

He is particularly concerned about the disciplining of small children. He says his mother "popped" him as a child, and the children of today would grow up better if they were popped more often. He recommends decisive action against children who squirm while having their diapers changed.

From the meeting, I take away this message: Those who have the most to fear from the Nation of Islam are two-year-olds who are not potty-trained.

On the way out, I receive a smile and a friendly nod. It is from the same Fruit of Islam who did not allow me to enter through the front doors.

On the basis of my five meals at Salaam, I know this: The bakery is adequate. The casual-dining areas are clean and comfortable and, perch aside, offer tasty food. To me, the mystery lies in the effort to offer "fine dining." I do not believe many of the followers of the Nation of Islam can afford the prices—lamb chops without vegetables cost more than twenty dollars, once the mandatory 15 percent tip is added. I cannot find any attraction for people who are not members of the Nation of Islam.

Farrakhan has publicly stated his intention of restoring the food-service strategies of Elijah Muhammad, who opened a series of modest Salaam restaurants in the sixties and seventies. (The last of them closed in the late seventies.) He has announced plans for five more Salaam complexes, costing at least $2 million each. He intends to buy up a million acres of farmland.

None of this explains why he requires a restaurant with gold-trimmed salt-and-pepper shakers and golden fixtures in the bathrooms.

He is a proud man and quite likely a vain one, fond of silk suits, Italian alligator shoes, and gold jewelry. Perhaps he feels only a palace can adequately reflect the national figure he has become. He is a doting father, and his daughter, Maria Farrakhan Muhammad, designed and supervised the building of Salaam. "She's quite an artist, and she does make things quite expensive," he said, fondly and forgivingly, at the opening ceremonies. Perhaps it is too much to ask an indulgent dad to rein in his beloved daughter.

In my five visits to the restaurant, I saw only one other white person, a white man dining with a black woman. I can only guess at Farrakhan's motives for building Salaam. If he did it with the admirable goal of reducing the isolation into which he has guided the Nation of Islam, his plan is likely to fail.

GQ, SEPTEMBER 1995

OLDEST LIVING JEWISH WAITERS TELL ALL

What I said to the elderly Jewish waiter working the lunch shift at Ratner's in New York was this and nothing more: "Your partner here is very nice, but I wish our waiter were you."

I meant no disrespect, but I had forgotten the first commandment of conversing with an elderly Jewish waiter: Watch your words, because what the customer says is rarely what the waiter hears. I was speaking in English, the language of the happy-go-lucky Pilgrims, and he was listening in Yiddish, the language of the long-oppressed Jews of Eastern Europe.* As Leo Rosten points out in his classic work *The Joys of Yiddish*, the language "lends itself to an extraordinary range of observational nuances and psychological subtleties."

Mostly, it lends itself to sarcasm, which is why the waiter instinctively took offense. By him, I was a *momser*.† I felt his eyes bore into mine for an endless three seconds as he reacted reflexively to a lifetime of aggravating customers, perceived affronts, and insufficient esteem. My friend Merrill Shindler, a Los Angeles food writer who grew up in the Bronx, had warned me about the wrath of the Ratner's waiter, of provoking a look that would "chill every cell," but I was unprepared for such Old Testament scorn. The stare was accompanied by absolute

---

*If you think the Puritans had problems, you don't know from problems.
† Wide-ranging pejorative, from smarty-pants to bastard.

silence, which was just as daunting, because everybody knows that a silent Jew is not a happy Jew. Finally, he spoke, his words cold and flat: "Enjoy your meal." His voice, devoid of inflection, knotted my *kishkas*.*

At the time of my visit, Ratner's was about to close after ninety-five years as the Lower East Side's high temple of the soothing kosher dairy lunch. Throughout most of the twentieth century, a meal at Ratner's was an immutable Sunday tradition. Jewish shoppers would pick through the *chozzerai*† piled in the stalls along Orchard Street and then pour into Ratner's, filling the 344 seats, even lining up along Delancey Street to wait their turn.

Neighborhoods change. The Jews have moved away, and the newcomers do not have a taste for baked vegetable cutlets, nor do they bring their children in for a nice glass of chocolate milk with whipped cream. The passing of Ratner's is heartbreaking, but to me it signals an event of even greater consequence—the end of the era of the professional Jewish waiter.

Once, they were innumerable, a multitude of Yiddish-speaking men who came off the boats from Europe and helped feed tens of thousands of Jewish immigrants with big appetites and little English. Only Jewish waiters understood such delicacies as broiled kippered herring.‡ Only they could properly pronounce *knish*.§ They became fixtures at waiter-service delicatessens and Eastern European–style restaurants that flourished in New York from the early twentieth century into the 1970s.

Ratner's waiters, many of them on the job for most of their lives, became legendary, more famous than Ratner's cuisine. They were emo-

---

*The human intestine, but also a culinary oddity, a Jewish beef sausage made with so much filler it tastes like beef-flavored breakfast cereal.
†Technically, junk, although everybody but me always found wonderful bargains on the Lower East Side.
‡Dried, cured, smoked, darkened fish that has much in common, aesthetically, with the dead, bloated seafood found in evaporated tide pools.
§A small, heavy, overly romanticized pastry at its worst when filled with buckwheat groats.

tionally complex and disturbingly moody, tormented by a belief that they had more promise, more dignity, and more intelligence than their profession deserved. When I took the F train down there, it was to pay my respects to them, not to eat, although I figured that while I was in the neighborhood, it couldn't hurt to have a little something.

I helped myself to a few of the incredibly fresh and fluffy onion rolls, then ordered a plate of the famous cheese blintzes, which tasted awfully un-Jewish to me—the thin crêpe wrappers were reminiscent of Amish funnel cakes.* The person serving me was a young, dark-skinned, exceedingly gracious Ethiopian Jew who told me she was the first woman hired to wait tables at Ratner's. When I mentioned that the elderly waiter working in her section seemed more in the classic Jewish mold, she called him over to meet me. I was trying to act like a *mensch*,† pay my respects, but I thoughtlessly offended him. I forgot that a Jewish waiter without thin skin is like a *latke* without apple sauce.

Back in the early to middle twentieth century, quite a few decades before anybody was discussing food trends, or even, for that matter, food, everybody who was Jewish talked about Jewish waiters. Dining out came down to this: you couldn't live with them, and you couldn't get a tongue sandwich without them. My father, who is eighty-six and started eating blintzes at Ratner's in the 1930s, remembers the waiters as "a sour bunch of people who walked around with towels under their armpits, and then they'd use those towels to clean the tables." When I argued with him that they couldn't all have been that way, his answer was, "I remember it so clearly because we'd talk about it all the time. They'd been working there ninety years, and none of those ninety years was any good."

Jewish waiters didn't just pick on Jews. They were nonsectarian, sparing nobody. In January 1961, as reported in *The New Yorker*, the

---

*I could have expressed my displeasure by crying out, "This is a *blintz*?"—the question-that-is-not-a-question being among the most devastating forms of Yiddish-style criticism.

†A fine fellow, although a step down in the Jewish pecking order from "a real *mensch*."

great British actress Dame Edith Evans, then in her early seventies, was taken to lunch at Ratner's. She asked for pancakes.

"Blintzes," the waiter replied. "What kind?"

"What kind do you have?" Dame Edith asked?

"If I told you, would you remember?" the waiter snapped back.

Ronnie Dragoon, who owns a chain of nine Ben's delicatessens in the New York area, recalls that the era of the Jewish waiter was already coming to an end when he entered the business in 1972. While he never appreciated their overt crankiness, he admits "they created a certain ambiance that's missing today." Bob Stein, an owner of Eppes Essen in Livingston, New Jersey, says, "They may not have been the greatest waiters who ever lived, but they had a feel for what the customers wanted, and they had an answer for everything."

I always cherished them, no matter how disdainfully I was treated, because they were a comforting connection to my Jewish heritage. I knew that if I could somehow get off to a good start with them, which was no cinch, I was in for an unrivaled dining experience, one that incorporated traditional food and bad jokes.* If you ate what they told you to eat—and you risked hard feelings if you did not—they might even stop to talk to you, and the best of them combined the folk wisdom of Sholem Aleichem† with the resigned weariness of the shtetl.‡

The uncritical affection I felt for them is almost certainly a result of my unconditional failure as a Hebrew school student. My inability to learn the ancestral language, combined with a desultory performance at my bar mitzvah, caused me to be scorned as a dimwit in the Jewish community. I ended up uneasy with religious formality, but I loved the

---

*A waiter walks out of the kitchen, carrying a steak. A second waiter says to him, "Moishe, what's your thumb doing in the meat?" Moishe replies, "What, you want I should drop it again?"

†Pen name of nineteenth-century Yiddish humorist Sholem Rabinowitz—which, by the way, is my mother's maiden name, not that I've seen a penny in royalties.

‡The isolated, backward Jewish communities of Eastern Europe, inspiration for many a sardonic joke that begins, "The rabbi of the shtetl was walking along when . . ."

waiters, who were living Judaic artifacts. That they came forth bearing food helped, because my family, like most Jewish families of Eastern European background, confused food with affection. The primary Jewish token of love isn't a bouquet. It's a brisket.

"Henny Youngman was a lovely guy," says Jack Sirota, recalling the famous funnyman and Carnegie Deli regular, "but as a tipper he was a bum. He said to me, 'Aren't I a good tipper?' I said to him, 'If this was 1935, you'd be great.' He said, 'Jack, I tip a dollar here and a dollar at the Friar's Club.' I said, 'You're a bum here and a bum there.'"

After forty-one years waiting tables at the Carnegie, Sirota has become almost as much a symbol of the Manhattan restaurant as the eccentrically grandiose sandwiches—number thirteen, a turkey, corned beef, swiss cheese, and coleslaw combo, has been known to weigh in at three pounds. He's six feet tall, and back in the days when he weighed 310 pounds, he was photographed holding an oversize sandwich for a promotional poster. The caption read NOT ALL THE SKYSCRAPERS IN NYC ARE MADE OF GLASS AND MARBLE. Woody Allen, who used to be a Carnegie regular, cast him as a waiter (no stretch there) in Broadway Danny Rose, but Sirota says, "Since he married Soon-Yi, I don't see him."

A lot has changed at the Carnegie over the years. The sandwiches are bigger. Sirota is smaller, having taken off forty pounds. Most of all, the regulars don't come around as much, now that tourists line up outside and the wait can be forty minutes on weekends. "Now it's ninety-nine and three-quarters percent transient trade, and maybe one percent Jewish," he says. "We put out matzohs on Passover. They take a bite and say, 'What's this?'"

Sirota was born in Brooklyn and started his career as a waiter in the Catskills, the modest mountain range north of New York City where Jews went to breathe fresh air but ended up spending most of their time in the dining rooms. The Jewish waiters who worked up there remember those days with affection. They were all young, slim, handsome, and made a very good living. Sirota recalls, with a rueful smile, that he weighed 150 when he worked at the Avon Lodge.

"During summertime the hotel was quite busy, with five hundred guests," he says, "but after the Jewish holidays* I'd go to Canada, fishing and hunting. In 1955 I bought a brand-new Oldsmobile; it cost me twenty-eight hundred dollars and included a tank of gas. I had two guns, two fishing rods, and no shortage of girls. When I say I was a ladies' man, I didn't take them for pizza. For steak. I made a lot of money and lived well. In those days, three drinks cost a dollar.

"It was the best time of my life. One of my special guests in the hotel was Sid Caesar. He was a great guy, very nice. I even played pinochle with him. Sid Caesar was quite a marksman. I would go into town, buy cans of shaving cream, and he would shoot them to see how high they would go. He had a .357 Magnum and a high-powered rifle. He wouldn't kill a fly, but he loved to shoot. His best friend owned the Joyva halvah† company. They'd fill the halvah tins with seltzer, shoot at them. If you have money, you can do anything."

Finally, Sirota met the woman he wanted to marry, the cousin of his brother's wife. She didn't want to live in the mountains, so they returned to New York City, and he went to work at Mirko's Guitar Room, where he once waited on Carl Sandburg. "You can't get any bigger than that," he says.

His life is quiet now. He works only three days a week, this sweet, shambling man who seems at peace with the world. While I'm talking to him, a Chinese-American waitress who has been

---

*Jews divide the year according to the standard Gregorian calendar when speaking to Gentiles, but "before the holidays" and "after the holidays" when addressing other Jews.

†A delicious sesame-seed candy that rightfully belongs to the Arabs, unlike Jerusalem.

*at the Carnegie for fourteen years interrupts several times, angrily
and forcefully, to point out how difficult Sirota was when she
first arrived. Speaking of all the old Jewish waiters at the Carnegie,
not just Sirota, she says, "They were so mean, they killed me."*

*He lets her speak, and then he says, softly, that times were
different then. He had supervisory responsibilities, and it was
his job to make sure the customers were treated right. He tells
me the things he used to say to her he wouldn't say anymore,
but just to be certain I know he hasn't become a pushover, he
adds, "Maybe I was that way because circumstances warranted."*

The professional Jewish waiter was as much an American original as
the workingman who drove herds of cattle, laid railroad tracks, built
skyscrapers. He just moved a lot slower. Bobby Trager, the chef of Nate
'n' Al's delicatessen in Beverly Hills, recalls frequent visits to Ratner's
with his grandmother, who would always buy him the vegetarian
chopped liver he loved. "No waiters ever walked like them," he says.
"They walked like they were old, even when they were twenty-five. It
was almost like they had a walker, but they didn't have a walker."

To my friend Shindler, Jewish waiters were the American equivalent of the imperious Paris waiters who looked down at all who came
to their tables, although he points out that "the French waiters smelled
of truffles and the Jewish waiters of *schmaltz*."* Their motives, of
course, were different. The French waiter utilized his sneer to empha-
size the superiority of his national cuisine, while the Jewish waiter was
only letting you know that his soul was suffering, to say nothing of
his feet. "You know," says Marvin Saul, seventy-one, owner of Junior's
in Los Angeles, "Jewish feet are not great feet for being waiters and
waitresses. They got bunions. They got flat feet." Adds Seymour Altman, seventy-four, owner of Altman's Delicatessen in Baltimore, "I can

---

*Rendered chicken fat, an essential dietary component for any male wishing to
achieve the Jewish masculine ideal of 250 pounds weight and 250 milligrams
cholesterol.

picture today how they *schluffed** their feet, like they had weights on them."

The professional Jewish waiter was not a pretty sight. He was often short, balding, and bent over. He did not introduce himself, but if you were seated at one of his tables often enough, you would get to know him by name, and he would get to know the food you preferred. He was neither impersonal nor polite, as servers are today. He wasn't quite a Renaissance man, but he was, in his own way, well-rounded. He often fancied himself a playwright, a songwriter, and a gambler; that he was unsuccessful at all three endeavors did not diminish his self-esteem. He suffered, and not silently, for the horses that ran slow, and for the artistic works he created that remained unpublished or unsung.

Jack Lebewohl, an owner of the Second Avenue Deli in Manhattan, remembers the illegal second-floor poker parlors that flourished along Allen Street on the Lower East Side, set up to attract Jewish waiters. "They were called goulash joints, because they got goulash for free while they were playing cards," he says. "In Las Vegas and Atlantic City you get free drinks, but in the Jewish gambling houses it was free food." Larry Leiter, one of the owners of Moishe's in Montreal, recalls one Jewish waiter who had other vices between shifts. "He'd work lunch, walk downtown, find a broad, take her out for a drink, be back at five-thirty for the dinner shift, work the night shift, go out and party. And he was no young man, either. He was doing it up to the end, and when he left here he was seventy years old. A Romeo, and his wife never knew."

Today, there are still Jewish waiters, but most work part-time. They don't go to the track. They go to graduate school. Moishe Teitelbaum, thirty-three, owns a tiny kosher dairy restaurant, Matamim, in Brooklyn, that has no old Jewish waiters. He says, regretfully, "Waiters like that don't have any value to the new generation. The new Jewish waiters are all strictly business. They get what you want; they bring it with a smile; they get their money and their tip. Nobody wants the old waiters,

---

*A deliberate form of locomotion commonly seen on Mississippi work farms where prisoners are restrained by ball and chain.

the ones who would talk with the customers about their grandmother's recipe for matzo-ball soup. Nobody has time. The young Jewish customers have cell phones, beepers, and two or three jobs."

"The young Jewish guy of today, he's above this kind of work," says Norman Moss, seventy-five, who was born on the Lower East Side and is the oldest professional Jewish waiter I could find. *"He's more educated, travels more, and he's into the twenty-first century, which does not include waitering anymore."*

Moss has been at the Stage Deli in Manhattan for about a quarter-century, pretty good for a man who has always thought of himself as an entrepreneur, not a waiter. Before coming to the Stage, he owned a Chock Full o' Nuts restaurant, an ill-fated franchise operation created by a pre-Starbucks coffee company. The specialty of the house was cream cheese on date-nut bread.

From this he made a living? He did not. After that unsuccessful endeavor, he came to the Stage, where he credits his success to attentive service. He doesn't say he was the best Jewish waiter he ever saw. That would be Max Silver, now retired to Florida, who took such good care of regulars that whenever one of them asked for raisin-pumpernickel bread, which the Stage never offered, Silver would go into the kitchen with a handful of raisins and press them into the pumpernickel.

"I've seen a couple waiters here, they believe if you put down a pastrami sandwich and a Dr. Brown's cream soda and send out the check, that's the job. But there's more to it than that. Keep an eye out, extend yourself, and hope for a decent tip."

He's not sure how long he will remain a waiter, because he and an associate have plans. They've invested in a website with the name zygesunt.com,* *a sure moneymaker. "I'm into the twenty-first century,"* he says.

        •   •   •

---

*Zy gesunt: A sweet old Yiddish farewell, meaning "Stay healthy." Bill Gates should live to be a hundred, he would never think up this website.

To understand what made Jewish waiters so unhappy, it's necessary to grasp this fact: in his heart, no Jew is a servant of another. The Bible is filled with stories of the rich and powerful who thought they could subjugate the Jews, only to find out otherwise.* The Jewish waiter may have *schlepped*[†] between kitchen and dining room, but inwardly he knew he was destined for greater accomplishments. He was undereducated, which he regretted, because Jews revere the scholarly. He was relatively poor, which was a tragedy, because all around him Jews were becoming big shots.

For an answer to the pain this must have caused, I turned to Jackie Mason, comedian and verbal historian of Jewish folkways. He told me, "Jews always feel they have to get somewhere, and the waiters came here without an education and resented that they had to adjust. Gentiles felt it was okay to be working class, but Jews to this day come to this country, have to stand out, become somebody important, not just a working stiff.

"They were independent characters who had to be waiters, and they adjusted, but they resented their jobs, and they were left with hostility and frustrations and humor laced with a little venom. They convinced themselves that the whole world stunk, and so that it didn't stink all by itself, they took it out on the customers. They were sure the restaurants weren't what they once were and customers weren't what they once were and nothing was like it once was. They adjusted, tried to make a comedy out of their jobs, translate their lives into vaudeville acts. It was their only outlet, but if that didn't work, they took it out on their customers."

If the professional Jewish waiter became the master of contrarian service, then much of his behavior could be traced to the customers he was required to satisfy. "The people made them that way," says Morris

---

*God to Pharaoh, biblical oppressor of the Jews: "Have some boils. Wear them in good health."

[†]To move at minimum speed over a modest distance while uttering maximum complaints.

Breitbart, seventy-eight, a manager at Ratner's for fifty-one years. Seymour Paley, seventy, owner of Corky's, a Jewish-style restaurant in Fort Lauderdale, agrees. "Who can take the Jewish customers?" he asks. Harry Rasp, owner of the restaurant Essex on Coney in Brooklyn, agrees. "The trouble with the Jewish customer is that the restaurant is only as good as the last meal he had. He has no memory of the previous five hundred good ones. If the last one was not so good, I hear, 'Harry, you're not running it the way you used to.'"

"It was the customers," says Joseph Weingarten, sixty, when I ask him why he left the Concord, one of the greatest of the Jewish resorts in the Catskills. "The chutzpah, the attitude. Always, it was the fardreyen kop."*

Currently a waiter at New York's Smith & Wollensky steak house, Weingarten was born in Romania and came to America in 1959. His first job was waiting at Grossinger's, the snootiest of the Catskills resorts, and then he moved to the Concord, where he stayed for twelve years. A top waiter like him would be responsible for thirty to fifty customers at each seating, all of them demanding immediate attention. After all, they were paying thirty dollars a day for room, entertainment, activities, and three meals.

"The food was tremendous," he says. "Fourteen different juices, twenty different eggs, pancakes, waffles with vanilla ice cream, cheeses, fishes. How much could you eat? And they complained—oh, my God, they complained. It was amazing, and it broke my heart, because I came from World War II. I ate mamaliga† during the Russian occupation, 1945 to 1949, until I went to Israel, in 1950.

"The customers would come in to breakfast. I remember this

---

*Making trouble for no reason whatsoever; in Weingarten's interpretation, "busting chops."

†An entropy-defying Eastern European cornmeal mush that always burns the tongue, no matter how long it sits on the table to cool.

one lady, she said to me, 'Do you have oatmeal?' I said yes, I had oatmeal. She said, 'I'll have Wheatena.' Then she started on the eggs, what kind you got? I told her, 'I got all kinds, soft-boiled, scrambled, hard-boiled, omelettes.' She said, 'Give me shirred.' It went on and on. There was another guy at one of my tables, one morning I had to give him a message. He read it, said, 'Joe, my brother died, can I have a cup of coffee?' I bring him a cup of coffee, there's always a piece of coffee cake that comes with the coffee, it's on the dish. He looks at it and says, 'Is this the only kind of cake you got?' How can he eat after that? Your brother died, you take your car, go home, why are you worried about the cake?

"One customer, a lawyer, he had an appetizer, a salad, a bowl of matzo-ball soup, then he asked me what he should have next. I suggested roast capon with vegetables. He finished that, and the stuffed veal, and the pot roast with Yankee beans. After the pot roast, he wants pepper steak. I'm thinking, Is he an animal? I've got fifty other people I have to wait on. I say to him, 'Can I have a break now?' He went to the maître d', said he was insulted."

Still, Weingarten loved life in the Catskills—the women, the horses, the air. Jews spend so little time outdoors they tend to be exhilarated by oxygen, much like Gentiles inhaling the heady scent of a pickle barrel for the first time. "It was hard work, sometimes three weeks without a day off, and I was the number-one waiter, people asked for me," he recalls. " They liked me because I got a good line with people; they like my jokes. One of my customers, a Jewish undertaker, he had a nice place on Ninety-first Street. He leaves on a Sunday, hands me an envelope, shakes my hand, says, 'I'll be seeing you.' I said, 'I hope when you are seeing me, I should be able to look at you.'"

Eager to find as many elderly Jewish waiters as possible, I started calling. I telephoned likely restaurants in Dallas, Berkeley, Las Vegas, Philadelphia, Los Angeles, Beverly Hills, Baltimore, Chicago, Denver, Boston, and Washington, D.C. I tried Connecticut, thinking some old

Jewish waiters might have inexplicably migrated north to the Nutmeg State. I called all over New Jersey. I was certain I'd find a few in south Florida, but I did not. Not one in Miami or Miami Beach. If there is not a single elderly Jewish waiter at Wolfie's in Miami Beach or at the Rascal House in North Miami Beach, is this not the apocalypse?

I called places with names like Saul's, Hymie's, Murray's, Zaidy's, Rubin's, and Larry's. Except for New York City, I got *bubkes*.* I started telephoning Quebec and didn't find a single one at the famous Montreal Jewish restaurants Moishe's and Schwartz's.

After calling more than thirty restaurants and speaking to dozens of owners and managers, I was certain only a few elderly Jewish waiters remained, all of them in Manhattan. Yet one authority disagreed with me. Jackie Mason, whose convictions about the state of Jewish waiters cannot be ignored,† insisted I would come across "eighty to a hundred twenty" of them if I looked in Brooklyn. He pointed to the resurgence of kosher restaurants and Jewish community life there.

I didn't think he was right, but I went anyway. I drove through Flatbush, Borough Park, and Williamsburg, the Jewish heartlands, and a few lesser-known Jewish areas in between. I poked my head into more than a dozen kosher and kosher-style restaurants, and almost everywhere the owners shook their heads, smiled and said they had no waiters like that anymore. Finally, I found Essex on Coney.

Technically speaking, none of the waiters there qualified, since they didn't meet my minimum requirement of sixty years of age. Still, they were too perfect to pass up. Luis Margulies, fifty-one, the youngest of the old-style professional Jewish waiters I came upon, immediately placed a dish of *cholent*‡ in front of me, just so I'd have a taste. Another waiter,

---

*Once defined as "insultingly trivial," now accepted as "absolutely nothing."

†When I asked Mason, who is revered by Jewish waiters, if he tipped them more than he tipped non-Jewish waiters, he replied, "I'm not going to tip a Jew more than a non-Jew. That sick I'm not."

‡A phenomenally dense, infrequently encountered, slow-cooked Sabbath stew traditionally prepared before sundown on Fridays and left in the oven overnight, where it thickens even more.

Norman Wasserberg, one month shy of his sixtieth birthday, told me he knew of no more than six or seven waiters like him still working in Brooklyn.

Margulies and Wasserberg were wearing semidressy outfits—open-collar white shirts, black vests, black pants, black shoes—splattered with food stains. They apologized for their appearance, explaining that neatness was impossible with the clientele they had. Nobody who ate there wanted to sit for more than twenty minutes, and waiters had to dodge customers and one another as they scurried between kitchen and dining room.

This was all new to me. I understood that Jewish families of Eastern European descent weren't obsessed with table manners—Jews were always too busy learning ethics to bother with manners. Nevertheless, I'd always believed that Jews ate slowly, since holiday meals, such as the Passover seder, are long and contemplative. At Essex on Coney, I watched Jews eat as though the Cossacks* had just come through the gates.

"See those two?" says Wasserberg, nodding covertly toward two well-dressed, middle-aged Jewish women sitting at a table behind us. "They're waiting for another woman, but they won't wait. They'll order."

Three minutes later, they have their food and are eating. Their friend shows up, gets a menu, orders, appears not at all upset that her friends have started without her. She just eats faster, and the three finish together, as though the meal were choreographed.

"Throw it at the people, they eat it," Wasserberg says. "Soup, main dish, they want it all at once. The other day, I had a special event, twenty-seven people. I served twenty-seven stuffed cabbages, twenty-seven soups, they chose from three appetizers, they had a choice of five main dishes, they had dessert, and

---

*They should rot in hell, and their horses, too.

they were out in an hour and a half. And that was with two speeches."

He and Margulies start telling stories, trying to top each other.

"I have people walk in," says Margulies, "and while they're walking to the table, they give you the order. Soup, appetizer, main dish, they want it all at once."

"I give them the check sometimes before I serve the food," Wasserman says.

Margulies tells me about the time he was taking an order at one table and a customer at the next table started pulling on his pants leg, too impatient to wait his turn.

Wasserman says that with some families, if the man finishes first, he gets up and leaves the restaurant.

They both recall a wedding where the guests started grabbing food from trays being brought from the kitchen.

They tell me the only people who ever eat slowly are young men and women meeting for the first time. Marriages are arranged in this Orthodox community, and the first meeting must take place decorously in a public place, not in a movie theater or in a car. If there is no magic, the young man and woman eat and are out in ten minutes. If they like each other, they might sit talking until the restaurant closes.

"They go home, tell the person who arranged it that they want to see each other," Margulies says. "They're engaged in a week, married in three months, and have the first baby nine months and a week later."

Still, no waiters were quite like those at Ratner's. They had more to offer. Like footwear. Charlie, one of the most famous, kept boxes of shoes in his basement locker and sold them tableside while taking orders. Nobody could try them on, and nobody could get a refund. Whenever a customer came back to complain that the shoes he bought were too tight, Charlie would say, "Put them in water to stretch."

Susan Friedland, a cookbook editor, says that in 1970 she took a soft-spoken, non-Jewish friend to Ratner's, and he asked the waiter to substitute mashed potatoes for the boiled potatoes that came with the dish. The waiter said it came with boiled potatoes, her friend kept insisting on mashed potatoes, they kept going back and forth and finally the waiter said, "I'll get you mashed." The dish came out, and it had four boiled potatoes on it. My friend said, "Don't you remember? I asked for mashed." The waiter picked up a fork, smashed down on the potatoes, and said, "There, you have mashed."

Seymour Paley, the owner of Corky's, says the reason he always preferred to hire Jewish waitresses for his place was his experience with Jewish waiters. "I couldn't stand them," he says. "I once walked into Ratner's with my twelve-year-old nephew, ordered lox and eggs, no onions. The kid couldn't eat onions. The waiter brought it out, it had onions. I said to him, 'Didn't I say, sir, no onions for the kid?' The waiter said to me, 'C'mon, be a sport.'"

The oldest Jewish waiter at Ratner's turns out to be Alex Hersko, seventy, the very fellow I offended on my earlier visit. His partner, the Ethiopian woman who tried to introduce us, explains his rejection of my friendly overture: "That's the way he is. When you're that way for thirty years, you never change."

He either fails to recognize me or is polite enough to pretend that he does not. He tells me he was born in Romania, came to New York in 1970 by way of Israel, and shortly after his arrival here was fortunate enough to be offered a job at Ratner's. When he started, only one of the waiters wasn't Jewish. "I can tell you, a Jewish waiter in a Jewish place, a Jewish customer comes in, he feels very comfortable, he feels it is like home. A Jew goes into a restaurant and the waiter is Gentile, he doesn't feel the same. Start talking Yiddish and you're friends immediately."

Hersko's hairline is receding, which is not news where elderly Jewish waiters are concerned, but his six-inch graying ponytail makes him one of a kind. He explains, "My wife started cutting my hair after I went to an Italian barber twenty years ago and he cut it like a German soldier's. She cut it for fifteen years, then one day, a few years ago, she says she doesn't want to cut my hair anymore, I should find a barber. I said, 'Okay, I'll let it grow.' Now my steady customers, they ask for Alex with the ponytail."

And so the epoch of the Jewish waiter ends. Hersko was everything I had hoped to find—a little too cranky and a little too caring, all at the same time. He even writes songs, not that they've done so well. For me, he represented thousands of waiters, tens of thousands of orders of fried cheese *kreplach*,* millions of trips to the kitchen and back. I asked what it meant to him to be the standard-bearer of a century of tradition, to be the oldest and quite possibly the last elderly Jewish waiter working on the Lower East Side.

"It doesn't impress me," he replied.

GQ, OCTOBER 2000

---

*Ravioli-like dumplings that at Ratner's, I have to say, tasted even more Amish than the blintzes.

PETE JONES IS A MAN AMONG PIGS

Oddly enough, restaurants in most sections of the country feel obligated to offer a variety of sandwiches. That's because not everybody has learned how to make any one kind of sandwich so perfectly that no others are required.

Here in New York City, for example, we have more kinds of sandwiches than we have people carrying lunch pails. I was lamenting this situation not long ago while nibbling a caviar-and-smoked-salmon *croque-monsieur* at Le Bernardin. As I absentmindedly munched on the egg-battered sandwich, I found myself thinking not of the citified seafood combination in my hand but of an incomparable sandwich experience in my past. I vividly recalled the rhythmic crack of cleaver on cutting board, the glorious vision of wood smoke belching darkly into the sky, the heady scent of vinegar infused with Texas Pete Hot Sauce.

I realized that my memories of the sandwiches made with hand-chopped pork that I'd eaten in eastern North Carolina had become clearer to me than reality. Almost fifteen years had passed since I'd last walked into a barbecue spot down there and said, "A sandwich, please." No further expression of my needs was necessary, since no other sandwiches were available. On a few awkward occasions a waitress—never a man, not in those parts—would ask if I wanted coleslaw on it, and I would tell her that of course I did. It should never be served any other way.

I thought sadly of the lengths to which we New Yorkers have gone to transform sandwiches into culinary adventures. Even our bread has become complicated, whereas the eastern North Carolina sandwich requires only a packaged sandwich bun. Knowing that other good things come on hamburger buns, like hamburgers, for example, I had tried suppressing my desire for chopped pork by eating chopped beef as often as possible, but that didn't work. So thoroughly had I mythologized the eastern North Carolina sandwich in my mind that even the hamburgers I once loved had become a cruel joke.

I'd started proselytizing, informing those few friends who would listen that the eastern North Carolina sandwich was America's greatest regional dish, surpassing even the jumbo-lump crab cake of Maryland's Eastern Shore. I welcomed debates on the importance of the sandwich in the panorama of indigenous American food. Others championed fried chicken, lemon-meringue pie, even bacon-lettuce-and-tomato sandwiches. I conceded any of them second place. A friend suggested a freshly picked ear of corn, and I mocked her for advocating a foodstuff that could be stored in a silo.

My fixation became so overwhelming that I realized only a visit to North Carolina would end it. I prepared to go, even though it was the dead of summer and I recalled that the establishments making the sandwiches I so loved had little in the way of ventilation other than the hot breezes stirred by a few haphazardly placed electric fans. It would be me, a sweating pitcher of sweetened ice tea, a fat sandwich wrapped in wax paper, and a few flies torpid from the heat. I so looked forward to the trip. I could consume unfathomable numbers of sandwiches in the course of determining who made the best, not that I expected any to be less than magnificent.

Barbecue, of course, is America's greatest gift to the culinary world. The French, the Spanish, and various others seek praise for inventing it, but we perfected it. I speak now of meat slow-cooked over wood or charcoal, not supermarket cuts of beef incinerated in backyards by suburbanites cooking over briquettes soaked in lighter fluid. By selecting the eastern North Carolina sandwich as the beau ideal of barbecue, I was placing it above pork ribs and beef brisket, the industry favorites.

I had no qualms about my commitment, for this sandwich is barbecue at its most sublime. I believe the reason it has never received proper acclaim is that it is little known outside the coastal regions of North Carolina, which are seldom visited, except by devastating hurricanes.

Before setting off, I tried to make certain I wouldn't make the calamitous mistake of eating barbecue prepared with gas or electricity. Barbecue without wood is like French food without butter, inappropriate and insulting. I wanted to detour around all such cookery. In addition, I decided I would only seek out places east of U.S. 1, the north-south highway that passes through Raleigh, the state capital.

I have at times enjoyed a meal in central and western North Carolina, where the hush puppies (undersized deep-fried cornmeal cakes) are superior to those in the east, but the barbecue there is fatally tainted by ketchup. Long ago, settlers in eastern North Carolina feared the tomato, believing it to be poisonous, and they were right, at least where barbecue is concerned. When a piquant vinegar-based sauce is mixed into chopped pork, the sweet, wood-cooked flavor of the meat is intensified. When the heavy, tomato-based sauce obligatory in central and western North Carolina is added, the flavor is masked. It goes without saying that either is preferable to the mustard-based sauce of South Carolina, which makes a chopped-pork sandwich taste like a ballpark hot dog.

I telephoned every barbecue spot east of U.S. 1 that I could find and asked this question: Do you cook with wood, gas, or electricity? I reached fifty-nine of them, and fifty-six were kind enough to give me a straight answer. By that, I mean they didn't insist that I telephone their public relations firm, which is what every New York City restaurant would have done. At Bunn's, the fellow who answered the phone pugnaciously replied, "We don't give out our secrets, but we'll put our barbecue up against anybody's." Now, I understand the South has a lot of secrets it doesn't want us Yankees to know, but there is no secret to how barbecue is cooked. If there isn't a pile of wood behind the place, the owner isn't cooking with wood, and if the pile of wood is so neat it looks as though it hasn't been touched, it's probably there to fool people like me into thinking the cooking is done with wood.

The woman who answered the phone at Betty's Smoke House Restaurant ambiguously said, "We use smoke," which could mean anything, including a cook with a three-pack-a-day habit. The woman at Big Nell's Pit Stop allowed that hers was "open-pit," a coy barbecue come-on. Open-pit is a non-fuel-specific term used to crowd-pleasing effect in the South, in much the same way that chefs up north label their own cooking as "gourmet."

Thirteen people assured me that they used wood, although in this region wood cooking is usually indirect. Oak or hickory is burned down to charcoal, and the charcoal is then moved to the open pits where the whole hogs are cooked. Smoldering charcoal adds less smoke flavor than a flaming log, but the fires are easier to control, and charcoal cooking seems to give a creamy, soft texture to pork. Regardless, wood in any form is better than gas. With wood I imagine delicate tendrils of smoke and heat encircling the pig, massaging it, caressing it, permeating it. With gas I imagine Audie Murphy with a flame-thrower, charging a Kraut bunker.

A number of owners who were cooking with wood warned me that their way of life was dying out, which they blamed on nefarious state regulators. The man who answered the phone at Murray's blamed "the bureaucrats" for driving out people like him. Exaggerating quite a bit, he added, "I'm the last that's left, and I'm going to be gone." Laziness could be another cause of the proliferation of gas cooking, because turning a valve is easier than chopping down a tree. Whatever the reason, less and less barbecue is being prepared with wood, and I was somewhat dismayed to learn that I could count on finding only thirteen sandwiches I was certain to like. It didn't seem nearly enough.

To ensure I wouldn't go hungry, I made up my mind to look into the impertinent "we'll-put-our-barbecue-up-against-anybody's" boast issued by the little-known Bunn's, in Windsor. I also decided to include Big

Nell's and Betty's, the only establishments in the southeastern part of the state that hinted at the possibility that they might be using wood. I also wanted to eat at B's, in Greenville, which I'd heard about. B's is so famous it apparently has no use for a telephone.

I understood from past adventures with barbecue that it was unlikely I'd actually eat at B's, even if I found it. Going out of your way to visit a barbecue spot you aren't absolutely sure is open for business is never a good idea. The proprietors of barbecue places wouldn't be the proprietors of barbecue places if they liked to work regular hours. Odds are they aren't going to be at work if there is any excuse for them not to be.

I took a plane into Raleigh-Durham International Airport, which straddles the vinegar-ketchup line of demarcation, picked up my rental car, and set off. What I didn't know at the time but was soon to discover is that all the best vinegar-based chopped-pork-and-coleslaw sandwiches—I'll just refer to them as sandwiches from here on—are around Route 70. It should be renamed the Barbecue Beltway of North Carolina. My explorations took me as far north as Albemarle Sound and as far south as the South Carolina border, and it turned out that all the sandwiches I preferred were either right on Route 70 or no more than thirty minutes away.

I'd set aside six days for the trip and ended up driving an effortless 936 miles in four days. The eastern North Carolina I recalled from my last trip to the region, back in the eighties, had quite a few back roads, but the transportation grid has been upgraded from asphalt to Autobahn. North Carolina has always loved wide highways (one of its nicknames is the Good Roads State) and just about every road I traveled was a four-lane divided highway, even when it didn't seem to make economic sense—Interstate 40 has one exit leading to Jones Sausage Road. The bridges of eastern North Carolina are even more astounding. They are soaring, arching, futuristic structures much like the kind I used to see in the Flash Gordon comic strips of my youth. Call me an envious Yankee, but we New Yorkers pay $3.50 to go from the Bronx to Queens, and not once in all my North Carolina travels was there a bridge or highway toll.

The lavish distribution of federal highway funds to this modest region astounded me, but there were other sights to behold. While waiting in a long line to board a ferry, I decided to remain in my car after spotting a DANGER: QUICKSAND sign. I can't think of a more effective deterrent to nature walks. While driving along Route 172, I suddenly found myself entering Camp Lejeune, a Marine installation. The sentry looked in my car and seemed taken aback to see the backseat covered with Moon Pies, a packaged cake made in Chattanooga, Tennessee. (I became addicted to them years back in the course of researching why people would eat something so awful.) Every so often, while driving through the camp, I'd pass a diamond-shaped yellow traffic sign that read TANK XING, which gave me a thrill of anticipation, until I realized I had no more chance of encountering a tank than I did of coming across a moose at one of those MOOSE XING signs all over Maine.

After heading out of the airport on day one, the Buick set on cruise control, I quickly came upon the first assurance that I was in barbecue country: a pork-packing-plant billboard beautified with a cartoon of a pig wearing a crown. Most of what I saw after that was cornfields, churches, double-wide trailers, and way stations for refilling propane tanks. The prefabricated building thrives in this part of the state, in part because of the ever-depressed economy and in part because of last year's Hurricane Floyd, which brought waters twenty to thirty feet high. I occasionally passed long-abandoned farm buildings, grayish brown and mummified. The miracle is that they still stand despite the eighty-mile-per-hour winds that have shaken them so many times over so many years.

My first stop was Goldsboro, an hour's drive east of Raleigh, where I showed up at Guy Parker's yellow-brick eating spot a half-hour before the opening time of ten A.M. It was closed. Instead of giving up and leaving, I walked around back and started poking my head into windows and doors until Parker heard me trespassing and invited me inside. "C'mon in, we're open," he said, explaining that he'd been on the premises since three A.M., cooking pork.

Parker's place had once been a service station, pretty common in the barbecue business. He'd remodeled it himself, adding overhead fans, wood-grain booths, brown vinyl benches, pig paraphernalia, and baskets of artificial flowers. His sandwich was filled with plenty of chopped pork, and it was correctly served at room temperature, which I believe is a holdover from the days when refrigeration was a luxury. On top of the pork was a dollop of decent coleslaw.

Up to that point, the sandwich was pretty standard, but there were two modifications I'd never seen. The bun looked as though it had been placed on the grill with an anvil set on top of it, because it was a little warm and a lot squished. Then there was Parker's tour de force, a slice of crisp skin atop the chopped pork. I've eaten plenty of chopped pork laced with bits of skin, and I've always admired the resulting crackle and crunch, but this was the first time I'd seen a whole slice added to the sandwich the way a slice of American cheese is added to a burger.

"How do you like that?" asked Parker, when he saw me take the skin from the sandwich for a closer examination. I just nodded, not wanting to tell him that the skin seemed a distraction. I ended up eating it separately, munching it like a wafer. The real problem I had with his sandwich was vinegar-related. Parker bottles and sells his own brand of vinegar sauce, and he is too generous with it, sprinkling in so much that his sandwich tastes more like vinegar than pork.

Still, I was so thankful to be sitting there, I smiled happily throughout my meal. When I paid the bill, I noticed that the sandwich came to $2.12, and his explanation of how he settled on that sum was too complicated for me. Mostly, the eastern North Carolina sandwich sells for $2.00–$2.50, and there is no reason to stop anywhere that charges more.

About twenty minutes away, right on Route 70, was Wilber's, a near-legend in barbecue country. Just past Wilber's, off on the other side, was McCall's Bar-B-Que & Seafood. McCall's worried me, not because of the way it spells *barbecue*—it's the same food, whether it's written *barbecue, BBQ, or bar-b-que*—but because it doubles as a fish restaurant. Barbecue owners who sell fish tend to forget they're in the pork business. I'm particularly wary of the ones who fry croakers, whatever they are, because there's nothing worse than sitting down to a meal in a barbecue place that smells like a fried-croaker place.

Wilber's wasn't a whole lot more promising. There was a sign outside offering two specials of the day, one of them spaghetti with tossed salad and the other a fish plate that came with two vegetables. I don't like to see greens on barbecue menus, although I understand that cabbage is required for coleslaw.

To my surprise, each made a first-class sandwich. I'd rate Wilber's slightly better, because the pork was chunkier and more peppery. At Wilber's, I had my second and last sweetened ice tea of the trip. I'd promised myself that I would drink only sweetened iced tea, because that's what the locals like, but after a big glass at Parker's and another at Wilber's, I was trembling from sugar shock. Sweetened iced tea in North Carolina isn't a beverage; it's an intravenous glucose drip. From then on I drank unsweetened tea—identified as "untea" on my check at McCall's.

I was way ahead of schedule at this point, because eating in New York had made me forget how quick and efficient service can be everywhere else. Waitresses who work the barbecue circuit have a routine. Once you're seated, they take your order within thirty seconds. A minute later they're back with tea, utensils wrapped in a paper napkin, and an apology for keeping you waiting for your meal. Two more minutes pass and your sandwich arrives. I had eaten three lunches in Goldsboro, and it wasn't yet one P.M.

I had one more stop, a catering firm known as Alton's, open to the public only three days a week. I figured any place that exclusive had to be worth finding, even if it was on the road leading to the Goldsboro-Wayne Municipal Airport, and nobody I asked had ever heard of the Goldsboro-Wayne Municipal Airport. It took me almost an hour of high-speed driving before I found what I believe is the world's only unmarked municipal airport, and the more lost I got the more certain I was that I was in for the barbecue experience of my life. That's the sort of optimism required when searching for a remote restaurant you're sure you'll never find. When I finally arrived, I saw that the barbecue was being prepared in some sort of pig cooker on wheels. I liked the idea that locals never go anywhere without dragging their barbecue behind them.

As I walked inside, I heard the sweetest of sounds, the *thunk* of a cleaver chopping away at pork. Alton's resembled a Grange hall hired for a family reunion. There were long tables set with plastic tablecloths, and the chairs looked to be the kind that fold up for storing in a shed, although I tested mine and it refused to bend. Every table had four unmarked bottles of sauce on it, but I ignored them. I never add sauce to barbecue sandwiches, figuring it will be interpreted as an insult, the way shaking salt on a *plat du jour* angers fancy French chefs.

The sandwich at Alton's was tasty enough, although it came on one of those horribly squished rolls and contained so little meat it was about as filling as an hors d'oeuvre. The iced tea was weak, like most iced tea in this part of the country, but I suppose I can understand the reluctance of proprietors to spend a lot of money on tea when what their customers want is plenty of sugar. On the way out, I picked up some oversize, homemade, brown-sugary chocolate-chip cookies, three for a dollar. I was planning to keep them in the car and eat them throughout the trip, but the chocolate started dissolving in the heat. That can't be said of Moon Pies, which are covered with an unimaginably terrible chocolate product that refuses to melt.

The luncheon portion of my first day concluded, I headed northeast to Farmville, looking for Jack Cobb's, which is open only three days a week. This was supposed to be one of them, but the lights were out. I was sorry to see that, because I liked the ambiance: a rusty old JACK COBB & SON sign, a pig painted on the front window, and railroad tracks running alongside. I drove on in search of the well-regarded B's, in Greenfield, and found it on the edge of town, on B's Barbecue Road. That's about as fine a tribute as a barbecue spot can get, having the road it's on named after it. B's was closed, even though it wasn't supposed to be, according to the hours posted outside. Somebody had scribbled a note on a white paper bag and left it between the front door and the screen. It read: "Sold out of food." I pushed on, headed for Bunn's, the place that bragged it would put its barbecue up against anybody's.

Bunn's is located in Windsor, which looks like the kind of town that had parades and ice cream socials until the four-lane bypass got built and sucked the life right out of it. Bunn's is a pleasant place, in a hoary, country-store sort of way, although a refurbished seating area in a side room, apparently modeled after hospital cafeterias, couldn't have been more depressing. The sandwiches cost $1.50, which is fifty cents less than anybody else's, and came on a hamburger bun that was a whole lot worse than anybody else's. The pork was respectable enough, although I didn't detect any hints of wood smoke, and I couldn't figure out where or how it had been prepared. The tiny charcoal grill out back was way too small to hold a hog.

I reached the town of Ayden about noon the next day and went looking for the Skylight Inn, which, I remembered from a previous visit, was on Route 11. I drove up and down the road for a couple miles each way and was frantic with worry when I couldn't find it, because I remembered the sandwich there as one of the most memorable eating experiences of my life. It turned out that Route 11 had changed, and I was driving on the all-new, four-lane version. The Skylight Inn was where it always had been, but the road was no longer Route 11.

Almost nothing had changed. In back was an alpine pile of split wood, so huge it reminded me of those mountains of used tires scattered throughout the Northeast. A sign read UPHOLDING A FAMILY TRADITION OF WOOD COOKED BAR-B-QUE SINCE 1830.

The funny little dome atop the one-story brick building was still in place, denoting the Skylight Inn's claim to being the barbecue capital of the world, which it might well be. Inside I noticed a self-service soda dispenser that wasn't there in the eighties and more gumball machines than ever—four in all. Barbecue places have a lot of gumball machines because local booster clubs are always asking if they can put one in to raise money to send kids to summer camp, and barbecue owners don't have the heart to refuse. Behind the counter, a man with a cleaver was chopping pork, although he wasn't the same fellow from fifteen years back.

I gradually made my way to the front of the line, where Pete Jones, the owner, was assembling sandwiches and trays. The $2.50 tray gets you coleslaw, cornbread, and more pork than can fit in a sandwich. I was tempted but ordered the usual. Working quickly, Jones scooped up a mound of chopped pork from a huge pile on the counter behind him, added a smaller serving of coleslaw, and put both on a Sunbeam hamburger bun. He wrapped the sandwich in waxed paper and handed it over. My first impression was of heft. As I started into one of the side rooms to find an empty table, I noticed a fellow with a NRA belt buckle and a Pepsi-Cola cap tidying up. I asked him how much meat went into each sandwich, and he replied, "All we can cram in."

The dining area I selected didn't have a lot going for it, as far as customer satisfaction was concerned. Every place I'd been before here had invested seriously in air-conditioning, upgraded the comfort level from sweatbox to meat locker. The air-conditioning in the Skylight Inn's side room was barely perceptible. Wisps of a pork-scented breeze drifted about. The tables had brown Formica tops, the chairs had brown vinyl seats, and the floor had brown-speckled tile. A couple of Rubbermaid Brute garbage cans stood in one corner. All these ambiance issues became immaterial the moment I bit into the sandwich. I couldn't stop myself. I ate it so fast I had to go back and get another one right away.

The pork was creamy and soft. The crunchy bits of skin were done just right, which meant they encompassed the yin and yang of barbecue, the crackle of carmelization and the ooze of fat. The vinegar was barely noticeable, and the presence of hot sauce was undetectable until it touched the back of my throat, leaving a tiny burn like the finish of a Napoleon Cognac. The coleslaw was fresh, elegant, and fine, containing a hint of mustard, so little that it seemed to influence the color more than the taste. I tried to eat my second sandwich slowly, but I gulped it, too, and I was too full to have a third.

I walked over to the counter to pay my respects to Jones and was told he had gone home for lunch, a shocking admission. If a man can eat this food every day, why would he choose to eat anywhere else? The fellow taking over for him said I should go to the house across the street and knock on the kitchen door. I walked across South Lee, which had hardly any traffic as a result of its no longer being Route 11, and through a yard, passing some pens containing turkeys and others with dogs. I knocked hard so Jones could hear me over all the gobbling and barking that started up when I went by.

He was in the kitchen, having fish for lunch. His doctor had told him he had to stop eating barbecue six days a week, which he'd been doing for fifty years. Jones said he'd been diagnosed with a cholesterol count of about 800, which is a pretty effective warning sign for a seventy-two-year-old man. "Actually, I'm just guessing the number," he said, "but I went to the doctor, and he took all these tests, and when he got the results he called me and said, 'Come into my office as quick as you can. You're supposed to be dead.' He wouldn't tell me what it was, but a little while later he said I'd gotten it down to 375, which was about half." His daughter had fried the fish in olive oil, and he was washing it down with cranberry juice, a meal he didn't seem to be enjoying all that much. He just ate steadily and slowly, and then he smoked a cigarette.

He said nothing had changed at the Skylight Inn since last I'd come around, other than himself, and that was due to age. He was still cooking barbecue the same way, on charcoal made from 85 percent oak and 15 percent hickory, more oak than hickory because he likes a less smoky taste. I asked him a lot of questions about the coleslaw, which was even better than I recalled. He said he'd been offered ten thousand dollars for the recipe but that there was no recipe because every batch had to be made differently. "No two bags of cabbage are the same, and I go by smell," he said. He agreed to reveal one secret. The mayonnaise he uses is Kraft.

I asked him if there was any barbecue he liked as much as his own, because I hadn't found any, and he said that a second cousin of his by the name of Bum Dennis had a restaurant in the center of town I should try. "His granddaddy and my granddaddy were brothers," he said. I drove over to Bum's Restaurant, which is across from the police station and one store over from a shop called Guns Unlimited.

Bum had admirable air-conditioning, a relief after the Skylight Inn's. I can't praise much more than that. The sandwich was so poorly put together almost all the meat fell out when I picked it up. That made me all the more appreciative of the assemblage at the Skylight Inn. Jones is like one of those artisans who can build a stone wall without mortar that lasts for centuries.

The next morning, I headed for the southeast corner of the state, passing Lane's Barbecue House. It was closed, but with good reason. It had burned down, which is one of the potential drawbacks to cooking with wood. Just south of Camp Lejeune, I came to Betty's Smoke House Restaurant. I walked around the building and didn't see anything resembling smoke. Nor did I see wood. I felt it was a little too early for lunch, so I decided to poke around the gift shop, which made the hostess anxious. She yelled across the room, "Can I help you, sir?" I got the message: Get out of there and get to your assigned seat. I did so, immediately.

I ordered quickly, then asked permission to keep the menu at my table, just to look it over. In less than two minutes, the hostess returned and snatched it away. Dillydallying isn't encouraged at Betty's, which moves at such high speed the dining-room chairs are on rollers, like office furniture. The sandwich cost $3.50, which was too much, and it came with french fries, which it shouldn't have. The pork tasted fine, but the fries were the mundane kind served at coffee shops.

Just before the South Carolina border I came to Big Nell's Pit Stop, which backs up to a trailer park. I opened the door and walked into a fawning tribute to NASCAR. The walls were covered with stock car–racing posters, and all available shelf space was filled with racing-related bric-a-brac, like a Kellogg's Corn Flakes box with a picture of Richard Petty. Augmenting the decor was a handwritten sign taped to the men's room door that read, IF YOU MAKE A MESS, CLEAN IT UP! I guess that was Big Nell's way of saying *bon appetit*. The sandwich was remarkable in one respect: it was inedible. The pork was so watery and tasteless it could well have been made from reconstituted meat, the stuff of Camp Lejeune training missions. It was the only sandwich I didn't finish, the only eastern North Carolina chopped pork sandwich I've ever disliked.

The proprietor might have mistaken me for Jeff Gordon, so quickly did I accelerate out of Big Nell's parking lot. I started back north on Route 17, then performed another feat of daredevil driving when I noticed a Cheerwine soda dispenser on the far side of the four-lane, gleaming like a Cape Hatteras lighthouse, just outside a tire store. Cheerwine is pretty much the sweetest soft drink ever made, and in my opinion the greatest accompaniment to barbecue ever produced, although nowhere I ate on this trip offered it. I ripped the car into a U-turn, tore into the parking area, and had an ice-cold, twelve-ounce can that tasted just right, a little like Dr Pepper with cherry syrup stirred in. Except for a Moon Pie, I can't think of another food that provides so much pleasure for forty cents.

I had three stops scheduled for my final day. The first place let me down, considering how perfect it looked. Smoke was pouring from an open pit when I arrived at Murray's, a white-pained cinder-block building in a rapidly gentrifying suburb of Raleigh. Yet the pork was oddly bland, tasting of little except vinegar.

Stephenson's, which lists its address as Willow Springs but isn't even in the same county as Willow Springs, wasn't promising at all. It was way too fancified. The tables were varnished pine, and mine was situated next to a glass wall overlooking a little garden of flowering trees and bushes. I couldn't figure out why I felt so uneasy, until I realized I had never been in a barbecue place with landscaping before. The shrubbery was excellent, and much to my surprise, so was the sandwich. The coleslaw was magnificently ingenious, a challenge to the slaw made by Pete Jones. Some wild-eyed innovator in the kitchen had added a few bits of finely chopped pickle, just enough to give the slaw extra piquancy and a pleasing crunch.

Grady's was even harder to find than Stephenson's. Allegedly in Dudley, it was five miles from the town center at the intersection of two roads not found on any map I had in my car, and I had three of them. There was nothing near it but open fields and a tractor. Grady's had seating for about twenty-five, a cooler filled with soft drinks, some frilly curtains, and a gum machine. The pork was so delicious I found myself contemplating the possibility that it was even better than the Skylight Inn's, although the coleslaw wasn't in the same league. I wanted to ask the woman stirring a pot how she made such a wonderful sandwich, but she let me know she was too busy to talk and I should find her husband, who had all the time I needed.

Stephen Grady told me he had opened in 1986, back when he was employed at a sawmill and could get all the wood he needed for free. At the time, his wife, Gerri, had been laid off and needed work. "I bought it to make her a job," he said, smiling, "and does she ever have a job." He's sixty-five now, and he and Gerri expect to work for five more years. That will be the end, he said, because nobody will want to undertake the costly upgrades the state demands of a new proprietor. A long-term owner is allowed to ignore many newfangled regulations, and so can a relative who takes over a family business, but none of Grady's eight children from a first marriage had shown interest in barbecue, and his wife's children weren't lining up, either. "You got to work hard at this," he said. "This is not one of those easy livings."

Worried that the end was near for wood-cooked North Carolina barbecue, I reached a supervisor in the state's environmental-health services. Bart Campbell, one of those much-feared regulators I'd heard about, insisted the state wasn't trying to put anybody out of business. It just didn't want walls covered with soot, cinder blocks soaked with grease, and flies coming through unscreened windows. He didn't sound unreasonable. "We don't want people cooking on bedsprings they put across the top of their pit," he said. "We're trying to keep people away from things they can't clean."

He assured me that the state of North Carolina still stood behind wood-cooked barbecue, which was the right thing to say. Without barbecue there would be no reason for citizens to attend church suppers or gather at political rallies, both fundamental to the well-being of any southern state. "Life without good barbecue would be bad," Campbell said.

I returned home to the land of toll roads, satisfied. I had eaten too much of the best barbecue I'd ever tasted, and I felt reasonably confident that wood cooking would endure, provided future generations of barbecue owners didn't resent having to run hot-water pipes out to their pits.

I had eaten a dozen or so sandwiches during my four days on the road. While some people might think that was too many, all I know is that the morning after my return, I woke up realizing I had a long day ahead of me and not a single sandwich to help me get through it.

GQ, NOVEMBER 2000

ALICE DOESN'T COOK
HERE ANYMORE

This is a story about the celebrity chefs you adore: Wolfgang, Emeril, Rocco, Alice, Todd, and Mario.

It has a flaw, however, and I wish to acknowledge the fact immediately, lest you think I'm trying to get away with something. This is not the equivalent of one of those sneaky magazine profiles where the movie star refuses to give an interview and the writer hides the truth as long as he can.

Here is my confession: Although I am writing about celebrity chefs, the ones beloved by TV audiences and foodies nationwide, no actual celebrity chefs will make an appearance. I suppose it is the journalistic equivalent of mock turtle soup.

I tried to find them. I looked everywhere. I did what every glued-to-the-tube food fanatic wishes he could do. I traveled around the country visiting their signature restaurants. I made my way to Beverly Hills (Wolfgang Puck's Spago), Berkeley (Alice Waters' Chez Panisse), Boston (Todd English's Olives, in Charlestown), and New Orleans (Emeril Lagasse's Emeril's). I also ate near home, in New York City (Rocco DiSpirito's Rocco's on 22nd and Mario Batali's Babbo). I went 0-for-America.

Not one of them was in his or her restaurant when I showed up. There was a time when cooking was a calling, and chefs believed they should be nowhere but in their restaurants. André Soltner, chef-owner of Lutèce, lived above his and missed five nights of work in thirty-four years. These days, chefs are more likely to be out taping a show, getting photographed, or preening at a food festival. Yet truancy has done nothing to diminish their popularity. It wasn't easy making a reservation at any of the restaurants, and when I finally did (under a false name), it was rarely at the time I would have wanted to eat. Finding one of these chefs behind a stove is hard, but dining in one of their restaurants at eight P.M. is even more difficult.

In this country, celebrity dining has three interpretations. (The French and Italians may think they're superior to us in culinary matters, but they're way behind in celebrity cuisine.) We have celebrity-owned restaurants, which boast some sort of financial or promotional involvement by a well-publicized figure and are generally short-lived. Arnold Schwarzenegger's Schatzi on Main in Santa Monica is one that has endured, although once he became governor it changed from celebrity-owned to politician-owned. We have celebrity-patronized restaurants, which are dining spots where famous people go to reaffirm their right to occupy the best tables, even if ordinary people have begged for them weeks in advance. Le Cirque 2000 in New York is one such restaurant, as is The Ivy in L.A.

Unlike the other celebrity-dining phenomena, the celebrity-chef restaurant is mainstream, a melding of food and fame directed at the common man. Because of franchising, it is enormously influential—at last count, English was a partner in seventeen restaurants. And thanks to your local supermarket, you need never deny yourself the pleasure of dining on celebrity-chef food, even if you're merely opening a jar of Lagasse's pasta sauce or heating up one of Puck's famous pizzas. Due to television, celebrity chefs are more recognizable than news anchors.

The six chefs whose restaurants I visited are certifiable stars, although not all in the same way. At age sixty, Waters is above it all, a celebrity with a cause, that being "sustainable agriculture." More than any other chef-owner, she has forged bonds between restaurant and farmer. Her good work started with the opening of Chez Panisse more than thirty years ago and continues with the Chez Panisse Foundation. DiSpirito, thirty-seven, had embarked on a conventional career path, concentrating on running the kitchen at Union Pacific in New York, when he signed up for the NBC reality show *The Restaurant* and opened Rocco's on 22nd. In doing so, he provided a rapt American viewing public with an unlikely adventure, a red-sauce Italian restaurant careening out of control. No man before him has ever looked so bad in a television series in which he starred.

English, forty-four, almost single-handedly altered the moribund Boston restaurant scene with his inexplicably tasty, pile-it-on presentations, more heap o' cuisine than haute cuisine. With a cooking style perfectly suited to the ever-expanding tastes (and waistlines) of American diners, he has emerged as the most entrepreneurial of the celebrity chefs, with restaurants in hotels and airports and on the *Queen Mary* 2. Batali, forty-four, is the most successful interpreter of Italian food ever to work in this country and the host of three (at last count) Food Network shows, the most beloved being *Molto Mario*. He is sure-handed in all things except his short-pants-in-winter wardrobe. Puck, fifty-five, is the man behind Spago, the most renowned American restaurant west of New York. He introduced designer pizza, recast American food as casually chic, and established California cuisine as a benchmark of fine dining. Finally there's Lagasse, forty-five, host of *The Essence of Emeril* and *Emeril Live* and the most triumphant television cook since Julia Child. Lagasse is as warmhearted as his television image, and, despite a penchant for pork fat, far more gifted at the stove than is generally believed.

The problem with celebrity chefs is not their skill; every one of them has created praiseworthy, crowd-pleasing food. What is worrisome about the trend toward idolization of chefs is that the more beloved they become, the less likely they are to be found in the establishments that benefit from using their names. To me, dining in a restaurant where the chef never shows up can be more discouraging than dining in a restaurant where the green beans are canned. For some of these chefs, a bad day is one when they aren't on the road opening another bistro.

.   .   .

The original Spago, in West Hollywood, transformed fine dining into A-list entertainment. That Spago is gone. The new Spago, in Beverly Hills, is a California-European-Asian fusion restaurant with a few Austro-Hungarian items, such as goulash, from Wolfgang Puck's past. When I arrived, I was immediately shown to the sort of table I always get—the worst in the house. There is something about me, perhaps a look of passivity, that tells maître d's I have come to be abused.

Spago has a number of convivial dining areas, but I was seated in the gloom of a passageway leading to the men's room. When I expressed dismay, I was told my table was the favorite of Academy Award–winning actor Red Buttons, the fourth-funniest man named Red (behind Skelton, Foxx, and Auerbach). I can only surmise that Red enjoys reliving the misery of the dining room scene from *The Poseidon Adventure*, one of his more memorable movies. I asked to be moved and was immediately seated among my betters, at a table near the open kitchen, where I could watch cooks in white doo-rags bustling about. I didn't see Puck, but I noticed executive chef Lee Hefter and executive pastry chef Sherry Yard, well-known culinary figures in their own right.

Hefter was supervising the kitchen staff, while Yard was doing the rounds of the dining room, greeting regulars, at the moment seated in a booth with friends. When a plate of steamed mussels arrived, she clapped her hands gleefully and waved the aroma their way. For my friends and me, no applauding chefs. Still, the standard complimentary *amuse-gueules*, spicy tuna tartare in a miso-infused cone followed by foie gras over chopped figs, were remarkable.

Then Yard recognized me, or at least suspected she did. She utilized a very clever find-the-food-critic maneuver. She stood in front of me, stuck out her hand, and introduced herself. What else could I do except confess? That's when I got the kind of treatment Red Buttons could only dream about: out came enough food to satisfy the midnight buffet line on a cruise ship. Our waiter asked if we had enough room, and offered to expand our table if we felt cramped. I could have had it all.

I was tempted to demand the removal of the lowlifes at the table adjoining ours—their clinking silverware was annoying me—but I took pity on them. I could have insisted on Sinatra instead of the grating techno-rock, but then I came to my senses. I had become a celebrity food writer for a moment, giving me a glimpse of the corruption inherent in fame.

Between courses, I asked Yard why Puck wasn't in the restaurant. She said he was usually around. Actually, it hardly mattered. Hefter, a Jersey guy, is such a masterful chef that to me Spago doesn't suffer when Puck takes a night off. I can't think of another celebrity-chef restaurant with a deputy as talented as Hefter.

I asked Yard what influence Puck has on her desserts, and she went into mimicry mode. She puffed up her cheeks, and said in a very inept Austrian accent, "Make it bigger. Bigger!" Her reply to him? "Wolf, this isn't a diner." For dessert, I had Persian mulberries that Yard found at a farmer's market. I didn't know there were mulberries in Persia. I didn't even know there was a Persia. I always thought mulberries were underachieving blackberries, but these were explosively sweet. With perfect mulberries, who needs a celebrity chef? Who even needs a chef?

Up north, just outside San Francisco, is the long-running restaurant of Alice Waters, a celebrity chef against her will. She has done little to exploit her reputation as one of the pioneers of new American cuisine except put out cookbooks. She has one restaurant, one vision. What Puck did for pizza, she did for produce. She is a consecrated figure, a hearty helping of Julia Child with a pinch of Mahatma Gandhi.

Obtaining a reservation downstairs at Chez Panisse is nearly impossible. I did it by accepting a table upstairs (where more casual food is offered) and asking to be placed on the downstairs waiting list. The menu there is straightforward: one set meal at one set price is served each evening. What I'd heard is that people with downstairs reservations check the Chez Panisse website to learn if they like what's being served the night they've booked. If it's Tunisian night, or something like that, they cancel. The night I went, it wasn't something like that. It was Tunisian night.

That has to be how I got my table. Everybody read that they had to pay fifty dollars for Tunisian short ribs plus salad and pie and decided pizza at home sounded great. I got a 9:15 P.M. slot, late for California but probably very chic for Tunisia.

I was thrilled. Finally I was to eat at a restaurant I'd admired from afar for decades. I admit that I wasn't entirely open to the idea of eating food from a country that doesn't have any good restaurants. And I'm pretty sure the last time Tunisian short ribs appeared on a menu was during the Second Punic War. Short ribs are profoundly heavy fare, a cut of beef favored by folks who enter pie-eating contests at state fairs.

Chez Panisse—the word *chez*, with its snazzy French connotations, is misleading—looked nothing like what I expected. The exterior is cluttered with vines on overhead trestles, making the restaurant resemble some cheesy Italian red-sauce spot. There was also a peace sign fabricated from garlic bulbs left over from a Bastille Day celebration. My first impression after walking inside was that the place needed some serious livening up, the sort that could be provided by the presence of a spirited celebrity chef. I asked the sommelier when Waters would be arriving, and he said, matter-of-factly, "She has a lot of projects going on." I glanced into the open kitchen. The cook doing most of the work had a funny beard and could well have been Amish. I told the waitress I was hoping for Waters, not some dour-looking guy specializing in funnel cake. She told me that Waters "never cooks here. She's hired chefs who she trusts. She might come in and taste, but the restaurant runs itself."

Chez Panisse is not a conventional restaurant. It's an ideology, a way of life. It's not about idle pleasure. It is about proper nourishment. It teaches you what is good for you. Do Americans need such lessons? Sure. Do we appreciate such lessons? Not often, but once in a while we listen, especially when Waters is preaching to us.

The three little salads that made up my first course were better than the three little salads I invariably sample when I make my first pass through a Sunday buffet line, but that's as much praise as I can muster. The short rib was a mere morsel, an Eve-sized portion consisting of one rib. It was tender, meaty, and fatty, so I suppose a single rib was Waters' way of saying that fatty meat is fine if you don't eat too much of it. It came with a mild green sauce that reminded me of South American *chimichurri*. For all I know about Tunisia, it might be in South America. The pie—okay, it was a tart—had a nice, buttery crust.

I didn't leave happy. Or full. I had eaten a perfectly satisfactory but oddly perfunctory meal, one brimming with rationality but devoid of entertainment. I understand that Waters has become a mother figure to all of us, a voice of responsibility, but even meals at home with Mom had more laughs than this one.

"Where's Todd?" I asked the waiter as he led me to my table.

By saying only his first name, I hoped to present myself as an inti-mate friend, a confidant of the chef. I'll do anything to get waiters to talk.

"He was in earlier," the waiter replied.

I was surprised. English has so many restaurants, I figured there wasn't much chance of him being at this particular one.

"Why did he leave?" I asked.

I already knew the answer. Celebrity chefs don't mind being in their restaurants, providing they don't have to stay long. For them it's like stopping in at a book-signing or a charity event.

"I don't know," was the reply. "He came in, yelled at all of us, and left."

Olives, in the Charlestown section of Boston, a few blocks from Bunker Hill, is English's flagship restaurant. The original opened in 1989, a block from its current site, with a no-reservation policy. It was such an immediate sensation that lines formed, filled with outsiders who would not ordinarily have been welcomed on the mean streets of what was then America's most racist community. I always believed Olives was a significant influence in altering Charlestown from the redneck ghetto it was into the yuppie enclave it has become. Say what you will about yuppies, at least they're friendly. These days Olives accepts reser-vations, charges $15 for valet parking, has doubled in size, and presents an elegant countrified ambiance. The clientele, being from Boston, tends to dress in shorts and flip-flops.

My meal was a mess. The famous black-truffle-and-foie-gras flan was ice cold in the middle. The accompanying sauce was warm. This caused my innocent dinner guest to ask if English was trying to make a point by contrasting hot and cold. The only point this dish made was that the hot-appetizer station wasn't very skilled at reheating food. Obviously, English hadn't yelled quite enough.

Black olive dumplings stuffed with creamy goat cheese were wickedly rich, as the food here so often is. Two of us couldn't finish a half order, which led me to ask the waiter if any person had ever downed a full order by himself. He said, "It's insane to try." Absolutely disastrous were the "handcut pappardelle noodles," a puddle of flour and goo. Roast pork, cleverly accompanied by fig jam, was unbelievably overcooked, a few degrees from dust.

As bad as Olives turned out to be, it left me rapturous compared with dinner at Rocco's on 22nd, of *The Restaurant* fame. This was the series that turned waiters into household names and made a cult figure out of Rocco DiSpirito's mother, Nicolina. She threw her heart, her love, and her frail little body into the labor of making meatballs for her son's restaurant, which would have been wonderful except they weren't very good. They're more like underspiced miniature meat loaves.

Four of us went on a Saturday night in August, just after the final episode of the first season was aired. Because DiSpirito knows me, I sent my three friends in first to see if he was there.

Number one said, "I didn't see Rocco."

Number two said, "I didn't see anybody working there I recognized from the TV show."

Number three said, "I didn't see anybody I've ever seen in New York before. Everybody is from out of town."

I asked our waitress, a small black woman wearing an oversize belt buckle that read GOOMBA, why Rocco wasn't in the kitchen. "He's busy doing press because of the show," she replied.

She told us he stops in a few times a week to "check things out." Clearly, food preparation is not on his checklist. In a city where the standards of Bronx-Italian cooking aren't particularly high to begin with,

Rocco's on 22nd served some of the worst red-sauce dishes I've ever encountered. After tasting the strip steak *alla pizzaiola*, absolutely unrecognizable as beef, I swore I'd never eat meat in an Italian restaurant again.

That vow lasted less than a week. Soon I was lurking outside Mario Batali's Babbo, awaiting the arrival of friends. I planned to repeat the scouting mission so successful at Rocco's on 22nd, send them in as forward observers. My scheme failed when the restaurant's wine director, David Lynch, spotted me and came outside to ask what I was doing aimlessly walking up and down. I made some feeble excuse about loving fresh air, which I don't, and asked him if Batali was in the kitchen.

"He won't be here tonight. Too bad. It's his day off," Lynch said.

Critics are almost always given complimentary dishes once they're spotted, and mine was pig's-foot *milanese*. Snicker if you will, but Italian oddities that almost never find their way onto American menus are what Batali does incredibly well. The pig's foot was a thin, crisp cutlet, all crunchiness and fat. I liked it a lot.

During dinner, I got into a conversation with a Los Angeles couple at the next table, and I asked them if they were disappointed that Batali wasn't cooking. The answer, I thought, was a compliment to the food. "Is he the chef?" the woman asked. They came to the restaurant whenever they were in the city not to see a chubby man with a red face running around in implausible clothing but because they admired the cuisine. They didn't care who was preparing it. "It's wonderful," she said.

She was almost 100 percent right. I enjoyed every dish except the breast of veal, a special of the day. I remember how wonderfully well my mother made her breast of veal, and this dish wasn't nearly as tender, moist, or luscious. For the second time, a celebrity-chef meal had reminded me of dinner with Mom. This was not how I expected this adventure to work out.

Getting a table at Emeril's isn't as difficult as it used to be, but satisfying the reservation clerk is demanding. She wanted the number of my hotel (I hadn't booked one) or my cell phone (I don't own one). She told me when to reconfirm and how to dress. Although it isn't expressed explicitly, the idea behind the dress code at Emeril's is that restaurant patrons not resemble the studio audience at *Emeril Live*.

Somehow I got through the qualifying tests. Although I had made a reservation for two, I came alone. (A beautiful young blond prostitute solicited me on the streets of New Orleans while I was walking to Emeril's, but unfortunately it was a guy.) The hostess said, "I've got a great spot for you at the chef's food bar, overlooking the entire kitchen." I'd purposely asked for a table, not the so-called food bar—I don't like perching on a stool while I eat. I decided not to argue. The open kitchen at Emeril's is supposedly a laugh riot, every night remindful of Mardi Gras.

The night I arrived, Lagasse was not among the kitchen cut-ups. Seated to the left of me were Sally and Bill from Newburyport, which is just north of Boston. Seated to the right of me was a local couple from nearby Metairie, just engaged. I asked Sally if she was disappointed that Emeril wasn't around, and she replied, "Oh, I knew he wouldn't be here. He owns three restaurants around here. He's never at any of them."

She then proceeded to relate a celebrity cautionary tale involving two of her children: one went to a celebrity lacrosse camp—who knew that lacrosse even had celebrities?—and the famous player was barely there. "He said two words and that was it. He wasn't on the field. He wasn't cheering the kids," she said. The other attended a celebrity hockey camp featuring Mario Lemieux, and he was around for "maybe five minutes."

Sally, relentlessly upbeat, had decided that Emeril's kitchen staff needed a lot of cheering up. "They're pretty down guys," she said. She pointed to the salad guy, whom she described as really glum. Hearing that, the young blond on my right, who identified herself as Emmily (yes, that's how they spell "Emily" in Louisiana) chipped in. "I thought there would be more interaction, like at a hibachi," she said.

I ordered the "*dégustation*," or tasting, menu, and everybody else's food was a lot more fun than mine. Such a menu has many small portions, and tiny food is not what Lagasse does best. I got to try a lot of Sally's dinner, and it was wonderful, particularly the grilled rib-eye steak with foie gras butter.

I learned a lot from Sally. She ordered better than I did, and she knew more about celebrity pitfalls. Although it was her first visit to the restaurant, she understood what to expect, a lesson those who patronize celebrity restaurants should bear in mind. "If you're sitting here thinking Emeril is going to show up," she said to me, "it isn't going to happen."

Did it matter that none of the chefs were at their restaurants? As far as food preparation was concerned, it did only at Olives, the restaurant of Todd English. His recipes are knockouts, and a competent chef watching over the underachieving kitchen would have made an enormous difference. The food was up to par at Spago, Chez Panisse, Babbo, and Emeril's. Even if Rocco had been on Twenty-second Street, he couldn't have rescued Rocco's on 22nd.

Where gratification and pleasure were concerned, their absence did make a difference. Perhaps if we went to restaurants to sustain ourselves nutritionally, it wouldn't matter if they showed up—and if that were the case, Chez Panisse might then be thought of as the finest restaurant in America. But that isn't why we dine out.

We go for a breathtaking experience, much as we go to the theater, to be part of something spectacular. Without the star cooking the food, or at least striding through the dining room, there's only a fraction of the expected thrill. Or we go to be coddled, to take pleasure in being someplace where we'll be welcomed. For most of us, a visit to a celebrity restaurant is a once-in-a-lifetime experience. We're never going to get to know the maître d' or the waiters or the girl who brings the bread, so only the presence of the celebrity chef can make us feel special.

I thought I'd be immune to all this. I set out believing that I didn't care about celebrity chefs. I'd had enough of celebrities back when I was a reporter for *People* magazine. Yet I felt something was lacking everywhere I ate, even at Spago, where the food could not have been better. What was missing was the chefs.

It seems absurd to me that I should have been affected this way. I know celebrities are generally the most remote and unapproachable individuals on the planet, rarely bursting with love. I realize everyone who patronizes celebrity restaurants is supposed to be grateful for the opportunity to taste celebrity cuisine, even if the sous-chef is preparing it. Still, I felt cheated. Seeing those famous faces is important. We can go anywhere if all we want is a hot meal.

MARCH 2004

Ten Commandments for Restaurants

1. Don't Underestimate Our Intelligence—or Our Math Skills

I once ordered the three-dollar cheese plate at a New York restaurant and got an ungarnished chunk of "cave-aged" Gruyère so tiny that I shook my head in despair. The waitress huffed, "It's a *full* half-ounce." Maybe the cheese was raised in a cave, but I wasn't. Using my junior high math skills, I calculated that the Gruyère was going for a mere $96 a pound, the sort of markup that would make even truffle salesmen blush.

2. Don't Put Me On Hold More Than Once

Maître d's (sorry—*reservationists*) have mastered this art. "May I put you on hold?" asks Chad, who punches the button before you can reply. I'll put up with this once, but when Chad does it again, I hang up and never call back. Restaurants that continually have customers listening to Kenny G's greatest hits should have a truthful recorded message: *"We're so popular we don't give a damn if you come to our restaurant, so we're putting you on hold again and again, and if you even think of complaining, your name will go on our blacklist and you'll forever be deprived of our ninety-dollar 'market menu' consisting of small portions of stuff the chef got cheap."*

3. Don't Banish Us to the Bar as Punishment

The all-too-common phrase "Your table isn't quite ready" invariably means the customer is sent off grumbling to a packed bar. Restaurants that can't honor reservations on time should offer some sort of consolation to inconvenienced guests, even if it's nothing more than a complimentary glass of the not-very-good house wine. The first kind word to a customer shouldn't come after he's seated, when the bread boy asks, in various fractured languages, "You want the chapati, the focaccia, or the ficelle?"

4. Don't Push the Austrian Zweigelt Unless You Know Something About It

Wine lists are becoming packed with obscure bottles from all over the world. Having a Portuguese Castelão on a list is fine as long as there's a sommelier on hand to describe it, but too many restaurants are leaving the job to waiters who have no clue—no restaurant would put barramundi on its menu without explaining that it's an Australian game fish. By the way, both the Zweigelt and the Castelão are red.

5. Specials Should Never Be Expensive

Nothing is more annoying than an off-the-menu *côte de boeuf* special for two that turns out to cost $38.95 per person, way out of line with other prices. Granted, the waiter who lovingly described the steak to you shouldn't have to announce the price—that makes everybody feel cheap and creepy. But if a maître d' with a phony Italian accent is going to shave white truffles over your tagliatelle, the dish shouldn't cost $72, unless everything else does. Nobody should have to take out a home equity loan just to afford the venison of the day.

6. Knock Off the "Day-Boat" Routine

Sure, like I really believe there's an armada of fishing boats sailing off every morning at daybreak and returning at dusk, just so every restaurant in America can put day-boat halibut or day-boat cod on its menu.

7. Waiters Must Never Ask *"Who Gets the Soup?"* While I'm Regaling My Guests

I know, I know, our waiter is very busy. A lot to do. There isn't a waiter alive who doesn't believe the restaurant would close without him. That's why he can't wait for me to finish my sentence before he interrupts my lively conversation to ask the eternal question, "Would you like fresh pepper on that?"

8. Don't Ask "Is Everything All Right?" Unless You Want an Honest Answer

In a world filled with perfunctory gestures, this is the worst. When the restaurant owner comes by the table to ask this question, he wants us to tell him that his joint is unrivaled. Sure it is. The chef is putting canned pâté on the tournedos, the sommelier is into the cooking wine, and the carpet in the dining room hasn't been replaced since 1973. And we're supposed to tell him everything is all right?

9. Ban the Banquette

What is this, the Last Supper? I hate sitting side by side with my friends (and their coats), all of us up against the sticky red Naugahyde cushion. Why is it that everybody hates the middle seat on an airplane but doesn't mind banquettes? (At least on airplanes, the sparkling water comes free.) By the way, I don't like booths, either, but I know everybody else does.

10. Bring Back the Dress Code

I'm tired of putting on a jacket to go out to dinner and finding myself surrounded by velour tracksuits. At the very least, announce your lack of standards with a sign: WE WELCOME SLOBS.

SIDES

MY BEEF WITH VEGANS

My first contact with hard-core veganism occurred in the offices of
GQ, heretofore never thought of as a breeding ground for countercul-
tural doctrine. An editor who is a fierce vegan sent me a note urging that
I repent and "see that meat eating has grim consequences that extend
beyond the health of the individual omnivore." I can see why I might not
be a vegan icon, considering my predisposition to lurk hungrily in the
foyers of butcher shops.

Included with his overture was a guide to veganism ("Think of all
the exciting new foods you'll be trying") and a pamphlet entitled "101
Reasons Why I'm a Vegetarian." It was indeed informative. I learned that
the combined weight of all the cattle on earth is greater than the combined weight of the entire human population. The solution, as I see it, is
to eat more cows.

Vegans do not eat meat, of course. Nor do they admire anyone who
does. They are the radical arm of the vegetarian movement, ill tempered
all the time. One of their fundamental tenets, that it is immoral to
eat eggs, milk, butter, or any of the fruits of animal labor, makes them
seem a few beans short of a burrito. Another of their goals, to put an end
to cruelty in commercial slaughterhouses, is compelling enough to make
me uncomfortable.

As they lurch between acts of insanity and acts of humanity, vegans seem no better or worse than any of our domestic extremists, the
ones I do my best to ignore. What appalls me about them is that they

are not content to exorcise pleasure from their own dinner tables. They insist that everybody who enjoys eating join them in their odd brand of masochism.

Not all people who decline to eat meat are like them. Macrobiotics, who share the vegan affinity for food colored unattractive shades of brown, are kindly souls who believe in the Zen principle of not irritating everybody with whom they come in contact. The way I see it, macrobiotics is the art of prolonging life, whereas veganism is the art of making life not worth prolonging. The ovo-lacto-vegetarians we see around all the time are much more tolerable. They are actually happier than most people, since all they eat are giant chocolate-chip cookies.

I've always felt vegans are best avoided, and they have certain attributes that make them easy to identify and evade. First is their grimness. At the vegan restaurant Angelica Kitchen, in New York's East Village, I asked my waitress, an attractive young woman with green fingernails, for some of the best vegan pickup lines tried on her. She replied bluntly, "Vegans aren't funny." Another is their pallor, a minor side effect of existing on a diet that cannot sustain human life. A third is the miso stains on their hemp wear, while the fourth is the terrifying attitude they assume.

I have heard stories, all reputedly true, of the outrages perpetuated by the worst of them. A vegan invited into a home throws open the refrigerator door and announces that children are being poisoned. A vegan served honey by a kindly host denounces it as "bee puke." A Memphis rib joint is spray-painted, the owner warned that his family could be the next to suffer. An Austin, Texas, newspaper columnist receives a death threat after poking fun at them. It would be nice to believe these are the deeds of isolated rogue vegans, but I'm skeptical. I suspect I have just made a list of what vegans consider a good time.

I myself have sat beside vegans, eaten with them, listened to the horror-movie mantra they utter lifelessly to one another upon meeting: "Where did you get your protein?" I have tales to tell, stories that would curdle the very milk vegans forbid their children to drink. The most terrible one is of a beautiful young woman I know who turned vegan and immediately fell for her yoga instructor.

Since vegan women eat nothing and are therefore as skinny as super-models, they are unusually attractive to men, but there is no sense in ordinary men pursuing them. Vegan women all fall hopelessly in love with their yoga instructors. These are spindly yet extraordinarily flexi-ble guys who project an irresistible air of serenity and piety. Yoga instructors don't have students; they have harems. Here is the story of my friend and what became of her.

A Vegan Cautionary Tale

She used to be just like you and me. She was normal and ate foie gras. Then she became one of them and started eating tempeh. She took a yoga class. She moved in with the instructor. This is one of the saddest stories I've ever heard.

These days she claims her previous life was never any fun. She says she suffered from anxiety disorders and was a "supershallow breather." Listening to her made me wonder if all vegan recruits are shipped to reeducation camps.

She met her new boyfriend at a big-deal Manhattan yoga center called Jivamukti. She says she went there looking for peace. At the con-clusion of a class, all the students maneuvered themselves into a yoga position known as the "corpse pose," which entails lying on a mat with hands and feet comfortably apart. This, she told me, is what happened next:

"The teacher goes around and, as a gesture of generosity, rubs aro-matic oils together, makes heat in his hand, massages a temple or maybe gives a shoulder rub. At this point, he took oil, made it warm, picked up one of my feet, gave me a foot massage for three minutes, then the other for three minutes, massaged the lines out of my forehead. Then he was gone, disappeared."

I was sure she had called the police. That's what any intelligent, suc-cessful, no-nonsense New York woman like her would do. I was about to congratulate her on helping stamp out sexual harassment in yoga classes when she said, "I was turned on. I couldn't believe this man had done this to a complete stranger."

She did not pepper-spray him. She went over and thanked him for his foot massage. She fell for the whole thing. Not long afterward, he told her she was the woman he was destined to marry. On their first date, they went to Zen Palate, where, she recalls dreamily, "We had some really good tofu with black-bean sauce." They now live together.

It must be good to be a vegan yoga instructor, roughly comparable to being a drummer in a rock band.

While sitting in Angelica Kitchen, an immensely popular restaurant that must gross more money than Lutèce, I said the three little words I never expected to say in a vegan restaurant. I turned to my friends and announced, "This is delicious." I was eating marinated tofu on mixed-grain bread. The bread was an unhealthy-looking speckled brown, and while I dislike indiscriminate speckles in my food, the bread was fresh, which is not all that common in vegan restaurants. The tofu was doing no harm, which is all I ever ask of that product, the roasted carrots added a sweet crunch, and the parsley-almond pesto was vibrant. *Vibrant* is another word I never expected to utter in a vegan restaurant. I was almost as pleased with the soup of the day, split-pea that could not have tasted better had a beef bone been used for the stock. In my newly devised four-tier classification of vegan food, I rated both the sandwich and the soup Worth Ordering Again.

I was never quite as satisfied with anything else at Angelica Kitchen. Let me put it more precisely: I hated everything else.

I want to be fair about this. Nobody is more close-minded than me when it comes to vegetarian cuisine, regardless of whether it's vegan, macrobiotic, or vegetarian. I think vegetarian restaurants generally prepare vegetables worse than nonvegetarian restaurants. Vegetarian restaurants have little respect for the individual properties of their ingredients, only a realization that one takes longer to get soft than another. I've always suspected that vegetarian chefs toss their turnips, potatoes, and cabbage into the same pot and follow a one-line recipe that reads: "Turn up the heat."

I find vegetarian restaurants both smug and culinarily unsuccessful. Still, I have always been inclined to allow vegetarians to go about their business without interference from me. But I don't feel quite the same about vegans. What infuriates me about them is their self-righteousness, their insistence that we miscreants give up our enjoyment of food and eat what they eat. I set out to determine if their dogma made any sense at all, if I was mistaken about the inferiority of their cuisine. To do that, I decided to eat at three of the most esteemed vegan restaurants in New York—the aforementioned Angelica Kitchen; the branch of Zen Palate located on Ninth Avenue; and Hangawi, in Midtown.

Angelica Kitchen is something of a vegetarian cliché, with insufficient room between the plain, varnished-wood tables, place settings that include chopsticks for no good reason, a friendly but ineffectual staff that might well have trained on some alien plant world, and all the staples one would expect—carrot juice, sesame sauce, miso soup, mulled apple cider, and the like. Near the entrance is a community help board offering assistance with the essentials of life, such as channeling, massage, and meditation, and a lot of notices promising rewards for the return of lost animals. Vegans seem to lose more than their share of cats.

After Worth Ordering Again, my next vegan gastronomic rating is Just Plain Bad. In that classification I place Angelica Kitchen's three-bean chili, one of those profoundly unsuccessful attempts to make a dish that ordinarily relies on meat taste as though the meat isn't missed. Also Just Plain Bad was the overly spiced, overly smooth humus served with a lump of cauliflower plopped in it, a carrot-apple juice melding two incompatible flavors, and a translucent fruit-and-gelatin parfait that looked like baby food but would frighten any child who tasted it.

Making my third vegan category, Bad Beyond Belief, was a "daily seasonal special" called Scary, Posh, Baby & Sporty. It had lots of everything, including tofu sour cream, yellowed cauliflower, gnarled radishes, and what seemed to be weeds. On a second visit, my special of "baked ginger tofu triangles with udon noodles in a silky peanut sauce" arrived with sweet potatoes, broccoli, kimchi, mizuna, peanuts, and sesame seeds but without the tofu. In real cooking, unlike vegan cooking, main ingredients seldom if ever are forgotten by the kitchen.

If Angelica Kitchen satisfies the repressed hippie yearnings of the vegan community, then Zen Palate addresses a different psychological need, a longing to connect with the mystical East. The decor of the Ninth Avenue branch is surprisingly trendy, with oversize sconces, sponged walls, and dimmed lights, but any decorative effort is overwhelmed by a drab, indifferent staff. The kitchen is determined to cook food quickly rather than well, and the outerwear of customers is strewn about, making the place look like a suburban rec room on NFL game day.

I ate one dish Worth Ordering Again, a plate of delicate ravioli stuffed with a not unpleasant mixture of soy protein, bamboo shoots, and snow peas and topped with a subdued sesame-wasabi sauce. Very nearly Worth Ordering Again, but I wouldn't, were the "sizzling medallions," which I liked until the monotonous texture of the chewy little orange-flavored wheat-gluten blobs tired me out. Bad Beyond Belief were cardboard-like scallion pancakes with no scallion taste, pan-fried vegetable dumplings filled with a repugnant brown mash, and a dish called Dreamland. I thought Dreamland had promise. It contained deep-fried linguine, black mushrooms, and marinated ginger. This dish severely tested my karma, because after a single bite, I wanted to throw it across the room.

Hangawi, a Korean vegan restaurant, turned out to be so much more admirable than the other two places that I would put it on a totally different spiritual and culinary plane. I didn't love what I ate there, simply because the food suffered mightily from the limitations of the vegan diet, but I did find the cooking impressive.

I approached Hangawi warily, because like most Americans, I find Korean cuisine a little too unconventional, with its emphasis on steaming, marinating, and casseroles that aren't anything like the ones our mothers made. I yanked open the imposing outer door to the restaurant and entered a tiny anteroom. Then I had a choice to make: go forward or flee. To commit to a meal at Hangawi takes courage, for the staff confiscates your shoes, and then there is no escape. On the other hand, the polished wood floor feels really good under stocking feet.

Joining me for this meal was the vegan who fell prey to her yoga instructor. She seemed in a pleasant enough mood, particularly for a vegan, although she complained of not having had sufficient time to enjoy her usual predinner massage. She told me she'd had some really good falafel for lunch. This is how vegans normally begin a meal, by reciting the details of their previous one, a side effect of a near starvation diet. The room, appropriately serene, had polished wood tables, screens, and lots of pots and ceramics. The music was mostly that Eastern-style wailing that sounds like a soprano holding a high note.

As an aperitif, we tasted two drinks she recommended, cold pine-tree juice and hot citron-paste tea. Both were indeed delicious, and both were insanely sweet, which brings me to my fourth category of vegan cuisine: Shockingly Sweet. With no animal fat permitted in the diet and surprisingly few fried foods on menus, vegans seem to obtain almost all their pleasure from sweetness. Much of the food I sampled at Hangawi went directly to the gratification of that craving. The best dish, as it should have been, was a $29.95 plate of wild matsutaki mushrooms grilled over pine needles; the mushrooms had a clean, woodsy, earthy flavor, although I doubt they detoxified me, as promised. Vegans seem to believe that every bite they take has an immediate physiological effect on the body, while we everyday omnivores understand that it takes decades of burgers and fries to really mess us up.

My Date with a Vegan

She wore a dress with spaghetti straps, quite elegant by vegan standards, in the photo that appeared in the personals section of the *Veggie Singles News*. I wrote to her, suggesting lunch. She responded, recommending Zenith Vegetarian Cuisine, a vegan restaurant in the Hell's Kitchen section of Manhattan. Actually, any restaurant dishing up vegan food is Hell's Kitchen to me.

She looked lovely, head to toe. Well, maybe not her toes, since they were encased in vegan-sanctioned Payless nonleather shoes. She told me she had been on three previous dates with men who had answered her singles ad, and all of them had turned out to be vegetarians, not vegans. I was relieved to learn that there are not as many vegans out there as I had feared.

She told me she was twenty-nine, worked as a corporate travel agent, and lived in Queens with her eight-year-old daughter, who adores Chicken McNuggets. That's as lax a brand of family veganism as I've ever come across. She told me she didn't get along with the first vegetarian because he was too macho and insisted on paying for the meal. "We went out to shoot pool after dinner and I won," she said. "That didn't go over too well." She said she didn't get along with the second man because of his attitude. When they got to the restaurant and she asked him where he wanted to sit, he replied, "On your lap."

I agreed that was an inappropriate comment for vegans and vegetarians alike.

She said he was an Israeli.

I told her that was a pretty typical comment for an Israeli.

Her third date was the most promising, but the budding relationship stalled when he started lecturing her on the breakdown of the American family, how every household needs a man. This is not an approach recommended to anyone attempting to charm a woman who is a single parent.

I wished her the best of luck in future dating endeavors and warned her about the seductive powers of the vegan yoga instructors she was certain to meet. She promised she would ask my advice before she ever went out with a "crazy nut-job yoga instructor."

I had done my duty. If I can save even one woman from one of them, I will have left the vegan world a better place.

As long as there have been vegans, I have looked upon them as persons with whom I would not want to break bread—actually, one bite of the revoltingly dry corn bread at Angelica Kitchen should be enough to make even vegans not want to break bread with vegans.

I have now changed my mind. I had a lovely lunch with the woman who placed her advertisement in the *Veggie Single News* and would eat with her again, as long as she didn't order the "eggplant chips" at Zenith. I had a nice dinner with my friend at Hangawi, but she was my friend before turning to veganism and so we could talk about the old days, before her life centered around tofu.

I'm not even certain any longer that vegans are the worst people who have ever lived. After all, Adolf Hitler was merely a vegetarian.

GQ, APRIL 1999

SHEEP THRILLS

"Aye, I liked the old days," said John Marsh, a fifty-year-old butcher dismayed by how genteel modern haggis-making has become. He picked a fine, fat haggis out of the display case at the shop where he works and pointed to the list of ingredients.

"Nowadays," he added, "it all has to be labeled. An old butcher I worked for who started back in the thirties taught me how to make haggis. He said, 'The more crap you put in, the better it is.' In the old days anything left over at the end of the week we took out of the freezer and flung in the haggis. Making haggis then, it was a good laugh."

I had come upon Marsh at the well-regarded Lindsay Grieve Family Butchers, located on the main street of Hawick, one of those Scottish towns with a name impossible to pronounce, no matter how simple it looks. I had driven there to purchase a haggis, which I added to the growing pile on the backseat of my rental car. Some men travel alone, but I went nowhere in Scotland without a carload of haggis—canned haggis, shrink-wrapped haggis, plastic-wrapped haggis, and, whenever possible, haggis enclosed in the genuine stomach of a sheep. (One good thing about haggis: it doesn't express its unique bouquet until after it's cooked.)

My mission was to taste every haggis I could find, or at least keep trying until the haggis hangover I was developing compelled me to stop. I started in Edinburgh and made my way in an ever-widening circle around the city, traveling as far south as the Borders—the region just above England—and as far north as Pitlochry, a town known to have a butcher keen on haggis lasagna.

Haggis is heaven to a Scotsman. It is a foodstuff that resonates with the glories of days gone by, even if to outsiders it is nothing but a sack of oatmeal and innards. The primary ingredient is offal, known as "pluck" in the local vernacular, which consists of the liver, the heart, and the lungs of the chosen animal, usually a sheep. Add oatmeal, fat, and spices, wrap it in a casing made from the stomach, and you have the authentic national dish, as delectable to Scotsmen as sweetmeats served with afternoon tea. A friend of mine calls haggis the first meal in a bag.

That this food is a treasure rather than a peculiarity is almost certainly the responsibility of Robert Burns, who called it the "Great chieftain o' the puddin'-race!" in his famous ode, "To a Haggis." To be fair to Burns, the Scots might well have overestimated his passion for haggis, inasmuch as he also wrote "To a Mouse" ("Wee, sleekit, cow'rin', tim'rous beastie") and "To a Louse" ("Ha! where ya gaun, ye crowlin' ferlie!"). Regardless, the January 25 birthday of Burns is a major holiday, and on that night a lumpish haggis is piped into banquet halls with all the pomp and ceremony of a medieval banquet.

Testaments to the magnificence of this dish abound, yet nowhere in my research was I able to uncover a single utterance about the flavor—or, more materially, the smell. There are plenty of plaudits, but no tasting notes. That job, I realized, had been left to me.

Haggis isn't everywhere. It's not like it's stacked up in every petrol station, clothing store, and souvenir shop. That would be shortbread cookies. Traditionally, haggis is prepared and precooked in butcher shops, then brought home and warmed up. (These days it's mostly microwaved.) I set out to pick up samples of the most renowned, figuring I could bring them to B&Bs, where the proprietors would be happy to work up an evening meal. That last piece of business was a bit difficult to arrange—after all, B&B doesn't stand for Bed & Dinner.

My first stop was the Melville Guest House in Edinburgh, operated by Juli and Mel Jerome, who serve evening meals in their dining room, The Crock and Spurtle. (The Scots tend to name everything, not just pets.) Before dinner, I went shopping at a local supermarket for what the Jeromes assured me was the best canned haggis, Grant's Traditional Recipe. I located it in the "ready meals" section, not far from the canned pork tongue. At Marks & Spencer, the famous specialty store, I discovered a variation of haggis made entirely with pork products. Pig lungs, indeed! And I also bought a haggis from Crombie's, a stylish downtown butcher shop where it was a bit pricier than the usual $3 to $4 a pound.

Then there was Macsween, perhaps the most famous haggis-maker in all the rugged land. I drove out to the suburbs, where the plant is located, to pick up both the traditional and vegetarian versions. While there, I tried to impress Jo Macsween with the magnitude of my quest to eat more haggis in a shorter period of time than any man alive. I can't say she was impressed. "When my brother and I worked on the production side," she responded, "we ate some of each batch. We had haggis five times a day."

Back at the B&B, I learned my first lesson: haggis isn't pretty. Once the packaging is cut open, the contents spill out, looking like crumbly meat loaf. The odor, however, is complex and distinctive, with the mustiness of an old bookstore, the tang of a Turkish spice market, and the animality of a butcher shop's back room. At different times, with different haggis, I would note allspice, sage, cinnamon, and even ginger. They all had a perfume I'd call *eau d'abattoir*, the not-entirely-unpleasant smell of the inside of an animal.

Macsween's is a haggis-eater's haggis, pungent and impressive. Crombie's was much more subdued, almost to a fault. Grant's suffered from what I call the Dinty Moore effect, tasting like the can it came from. The vegetarian haggis could well have been vegan fare; it reminded me of a life-sustaining lentil-barley mash. The all-pork haggis was unapproachable; it brought to mind the body of a decaying animal lying in a meadow of wild flowers.

The Jeromes served tatties and neeps—mashed potatoes and mashed turnips—with the haggis. So would everybody else. For many Scots, tatties and neeps is the first solid food they eat as a child, which might account for the unshakable bond they have with it. As the week wore on, I became less and less appreciative of all the mashing that took place for my benefit. Haggis appears to come with no other accompaniments, even if you beg.

The next night I arrived to a greeting from curious horses at Whitehill Farm B&B, just outside Kelso, with the haggis I'd gathered up from Lindsay Grieve in Hawick, David Palmer Butcher in Jedburgh, and J.R. Mitchell & Son in Kelso, shops located just north of the border with England. I'd asked the manager of Palmer's, Allan Learmonth, if he had encountered any competition from nearby English butchers, and he said they'd indeed had the temerity to enter haggis competitions. "We wiped the floor with them," he bragged.

My welcome from Betty Smith, the proprietor of Whitehill, was somewhat restrained, and I soon realized why: I hadn't brought haggis from her favorite butcher, George Lees of Yetholm. So off I went. The Borders countryside of Scotland is a watercolor painting, and I had no reason to regret a fifteen-mile drive. My outing took me past ancient crumbling stone walls, sculpted hedges, rolling fields, and tumbling hills. Only the roadkill is disturbing, beautiful ring-necked pheasants no match for breakneck Scottish drivers.

When I walked into the shop, located in a town of six hundred, I informed Lees (a dead ringer for Patrick Stewart) that I had come to buy a haggis. He replied, "Good for you." He said his recipe was taken from a book printed in the nineteenth century, but he'd adjusted it. "Our recipe doesn't include lungs. I don't fancy eating lungs myself."

Joining David and Betty Smith and me at the four-haggis hoedown was another guest of the B&B, Susan Flack, who was born in Scotland but lives in England, where she seldom has the opportunity to enjoy haggis. "Not many there will eat it with me," she complained. I invited her to dinner after hearing this heartbreaking boarding school tale: "At St. Margaret's School in Aberdeen the dinners were unspeakably disgusting and they forced me to eat everything I didn't like. I was ten and always hungry. Once a year, on Burns Night, they served haggis, and the girls under eleven weren't given it—they got boiled eggs instead. I got desperate, wouldn't eat the eggs, and they gave haggis to me. Maybe it was made of things I wouldn't eat if they were spread out on a plate, but I loved the meatiness and the spiciness. It was heaven."

Flack looked joyfully at the long oak dining room table heaped with haggis. The Smiths remained composed. I found myself twitching a bit. The Grieve haggis won our competition handily. Everyone had a different reason for preferring it, but it seemed pleasingly beefy to me. Second was the haggis from Lees, which had an appealing liver flavor and a smooth, rich texture. For dessert Betty Smith served lemon flummery, a lemon-chiffon pudding so light I couldn't stop expressing my gratitude.

That left just two oddities on my haggis agenda, the first being venison haggis from Fletchers outside Auchtermuchty. The secret to finding the farm is to turn left after reaching the Tay Valley Cat Welfare Society, not before. When I drove up, a herd of farm-raised deer perked up at my approach, then fled across a pasture, moving as gracefully as a school of fish. I paid for my haggis in the honesty box, then brought it to Ninewells Farmhouse in Newburgh, located high on a bluff over the Tay River. The view from the porch of this B&B encompasses river, fields, hills, deer, sheep, cattle, and a tiny train that occasionally chugs past, rattling like a toy. Sir Walter Scott, it is said, looked out from this very spot and declared the view the best in Christendom.

Correctly sensing that I might be tiring of haggis unadorned, Barbara Baird stuffed it into a chicken breast. Although she cooked the dish beautifully, the chicken flavor was crushed by the omnipotent offal. The venison haggis, however, was one of my favorites—herbaceous, meaty, and rich. For dessert she prepared crannachan, a pudding that appears almost without fail at the annual Robert Burns dinners. It's prepared with cream, oatmeal, honey, raspberries, and whiskey, and is as rich as butter.

My final meal took place at Landscape, an impeccable Victorian B&B owned by Kathleen and Robbie Scott. It's located just off the main street of Pitlochry, a town that no tourist bus bypasses. I was desperately hoping that the haggis lasagna from Macdonald Brothers Butchers & Delicatessen would remind me of Italian food. Regrettably, it did not.

Kathleen Scott served clapshot, an Orkney Islands specialty of turnips and potatoes mashed together, as an accompaniment. The clapshot was worthy of applause, but I was not fond of the lasagna—the malodorous meat overwhelmed the innocent cheese and noodles. Haggis is a foodstuff with an indomitable will to win. Even worse, the béchamel had melded with the innards to produce creamed haggis. I fear years may pass before I order lasagna again.

I was done. On the return trip to New York, I put all thoughts of sheep pluck out of my head and dreamed of a nice sandwich of corned beef, chopped liver, raw onions, and chicken fat on rye bread, what I call sensible food.

Bon Appétit, MAY 2004

ARE WE HAVING FUNGUS YET?

My friends and I have arrived at the hotel-restaurant of Clément Bruno, the self-proclaimed truffle king, at 2:30 P.M., a time when the French are loath to feed the hungry. Groceries are shut down, their metal grates slammed and padlocked. Restaurateurs have stuffed menus into desk drawers, concealing them from the uncivilized who might show up after the national one-P.M. call to lunch, a kind of psychic whistle that sounds in the heads of citizens of the republic, beckoning them tableside.

The three of us have been in a car all day, driving from Italy to this tiny village of Lorgues, in southern France. So eager were we to arrive in truffle country that we have stopped for nothing but fuel (expensive) and tolls (outrageous). We walk into the restaurant, where the midday merriment has not abated, and mention to the maître d' that we are guests of the hotel who have booked fully 75 percent of Bruno's four rooms for the night. I explain that we are desperately hungry and would be grateful if he could provide us with a meager bite of cheese and bread. I sound pathetic, which is a mistake. Arrogance works so much better with the French.

He tells us, in his own way, to hit the road, mentioning a hamlet six miles down the road where we might find food. We won't. There the greeting will be the same. We will be fortunate if the villagers do not light torches and gather in a mob at the gates, determined to keep us away.

As we walk out the door, I mutter something to my friends. I cannot recall the words exactly, but I know I lost my air of hand-wringing obsequiousness. I might have cursed, and curses carry beautifully in crisp winter air. The maître d' says, "You only want cheese, yes?" I wheel around, seal the bargain. He throws in dessert.

We drop our bags in our guest rooms, which have soft, fluffy towels and cold, stone floors. Minutes later we are seated in the restaurant, at a table overlaid with heavy damask. Surrounding us are happy locals who show no inclination to return to their dwellings or fields anytime soon. The low-ceilinged restaurant is situated in a building that appears to have belonged to an eighteenth-century farmer of irreproachable refinement. The paneling is dark, the paintings are in gilded frames. Even the ceiling has frescoes. That the nymphs above us are not museum quality detracts not a bit from their charm. The fireplace is ablaze, as it should be but so rarely is in restaurants today.

On one side of us is a clearly overfed family of four. On the other is an elderly, much trimmer gathering of eight. Both groups have finished eating and commenced with the distilled spirits portion of their lunch. I am not surprised that everybody is so jolly. After all, I have shown up at the perfect moment: it is the season of the black truffle, the supreme denizen of the dark woods of France.

The restaurant Bruno is the start of a brief and glorious journey for my friends and me, a journey through the heart of culinary darkness. Technically, a truffle is nothing more than a fungus, an underevolved denizen of one of the lowest orders of the plant family, an accidental growth that springs from dampness and soil. It is, to be unmerciful, little more than a mushroom that grows in meadows, usually under oak trees, in favored regions of France from November until March. The black truffle, more properly *Tuber melanosporum*, is not even as celebrated as it once was. The decline began when *Tuber magnatum*, the white truffle of Italy, started getting excessive publicity, the same way that the clothing designers of Italy started stealing attention from the clothing designers of France a few decades ago.

Now it is the white truffle, which is actually a beige truffle, that attracts customers. The white truffle is cherished for its unbridled pungency, stronger and less sweet than that of the black truffle, and its cost is approximately five times that of the black. Yet it is the French black truffle—more versatile, more beautiful, and more delicious than the white of Italy—that I consider the more wondrous food.

Every year, about the time that the wealthy close up their Hamptons beach houses, the white truffle arrives in Manhattan and plays to packed houses in deluxe Italian restaurants. At that moment the cost of expense-account lunches rises by 50 percent as captains stand over bowls of eggy pasta and creamy risotto, shaving away. The white truffle is only eaten in one manner, raw and thinly sliced. It is not pretty, but it has an uncommon smell.

A few months later, almost unnoticed, the first black truffles reach the marketplace. Uncooked, the black truffle is a beauty. It glitters like mica, and the white veins are the equivalent of the marbling in a prime steak. When heat is applied, it turns coal black. The black truffle is part condiment, part vegetable, part indulgence. If the white truffle is a slattern with immoderate lipstick, the black truffle is a Ph.D. in a naughty dress. The black truffle is an essential component of haute French cuisine. When chopped up and put into a stew or a fricassee, the simplest of its uses, it provides nuances that elevate a dish from rustic to regal.

The aroma of the white truffle is a bombshell, bedsheets left unmade by lovers who ate garlic the night before. The black truffle intoxicates; it is an after-hours party at a formal dance. The only advice black-truffle eaters must heed is to be wary of near-fakes, either the basically useless *Tuber brumale,* the cubic zirconia of truffles, commonplace in France; or the hated *Tuber indicum,* which is harvested in China.

Our prearrranged truffle plans did not include the small lunch I have wheedled from the maître d'. We have reserved a table at Bruno for our evening meal, which will mark the start of a truffle-eating extravaganza that will take us to Monaco and throughout the south of France. For lunch, I am content to eat and drink anything. The wine list at Bruno is a disaster, an homage to off-vintages, but perhaps that is appropriate—truffles only grow well in damp seasons, precisely when grapes are at their worst. Nevertheless, I select a perfect late-afternoon cheese wine, a white Graves with a pleasing bite of Sauvignon Blanc.

Instead of cheese, the waiter brings a surprise: a green salad with shaved black truffle slivers all over it. I particularly admire the tasty ends of the truffles that have broken off accidentally and been tossed into the salad; they look like chips of black diamonds, glittery and hard-edged, and they have crunch. Those bits are like the burnt ends of barbecued ribs. Then comes the cheese, which is soft and made of goat's milk, which is no surprise, since we are in Provence, and that has black truffles over it, too. The finale is vanilla ice cream with truffled caramel sauce. Perhaps you would think, as I did, that fungus would not be a suitable complement for caramelized sugar, but the sauce is intense, earthy, and profound. Ben and Jerry take note: the ultimate mix-in has been found.

The French, as I've indicated, can be unyielding, but they can also be unpredictable and generous. The bill for each of our extravagant lunches is $17, tax and tip included. I have no reason to complain.

My room in the Hôtel de Paris looms over the legendary Monaco casino. I stand on the balcony, fantasizing, as anyone who has seen Alfred Hitchcock movies might. If I had the right mountaineering equipment, I could leap to the roof of the casino, rappel down the walls, swing through an open window, and start emptying safes. Maybe not me, but perhaps a more nimble individual who doesn't eat constantly.

It is the day after dinner at Bruno, a meal that did not live up to the uncomplicated perfection of lunch. The fault lay not with the truffles but with the uses that the chef made of them. A barge-sized block of potato topped with shaved truffles came in a truffled cream sauce; no matter how you dress up a potato, you still end up with a spud. The primary virtue of this dish was its euphonious name—*crème de truffes et truffes*. (*Truffe* is supposedly a word for potato in archaic French.) The chef inserted truffles in a savory, slow-cooked shoulder of lamb.

Although the cooking was expert, the truffles were ineffectual, over-whelmed by the intense lambiness of the meat.

Tonight I will eat at Le Louis XV, the Michelin three-star restaurant of Alain Ducasse, located on the ground floor of the hotel. In the days ahead I plan to have a dinner at La Beaugraviere, an unstarred country restaurant whose chef-owner, Guy Jullien, is famed for the simplicity and extravagance of his truffle preparations; lunch with Hervé Poron, owner of the Plantin truffle company; and dinner at the three-star Restaurant Troisgros, made dizzyingly famous by the brothers Jean and Pierre Troisgros and now run by Michel, the son of Pierre. Naturally, I will participate in a truffle hunt. To visit Provence during truffle season and not see them unearthed is like traveling to Burgundy during the harvest season and not seeing grapes being picked. The great culinary rituals cannot be ignored.

Dinner at Le Louis XV begins with an *amuse-bouche* of raw winter vegetables with a truffle sauce that incorporates Barolo wine vinegar and parmesan cheese. It takes me a moment to recall that Le Louis XV is not a French restaurant; it is a Mediterranean restaurant very near the Italian border. This dish hints at the style of the chef de cuisine, Franck Cerutti, who uses the black truffle more as a condiment than an ingredient.

Roasted scallops arrive with slivers of black truffles and sit atop a black-truffle puree made with anchovies and capers. A black-truffle risotto is prepared with a black-truffle *jus* and discs of black truffles so perfectly round I'm reminded of casino chips (or perhaps I'm still obsessing about my imaginary escapade). The next dish demonstrates this restaurant's absolute mastery of vegetables: it's merely fennel, zucchini, artichokes, baby leeks, turnips, and beans in a sauce made with balsamic vinegar, black truffles, and olive oil, but the vegetables have been uplifted. They are a source of ecstasy, not earnestness. This sequence of dishes has proved to me that the black truffle is the world's second-greatest condiment, outdone only by salt.

Like Bruno, Ducasse serves truffles with cheese. His is a Brie-style cheese with a fancy name that the chef has split open and stuffed with truffles. I can't say it's superior to the goat cheese and truffles at lunch the previous day. Like Bruno, Ducasse adds truffles to a caramel sauce, and here the three-star pedigree shows, for while Bruno's was merely delicious, this smoother, richer version makes me light-headed with pleasure, to say nothing of deeply philosophical. As the meal ends, I ask my friends why black truffles were put on this earth. The answer we arrive at is that they give small dogs something to do.

The truffle hunter, the youngest of nine children, is nearing retirement. I have driven from Monaco up into Provence to meet with him and his truffle-hunting dog, and he is not especially happy to make my acquaintance. He has made his living as a farmer, or at least he has tried to, and I am just another journalist fascinated by truffles who cares nothing of the plight of workingmen like him who can no longer make a decent living.

He harvests grapes that are sent to a cooperative and made into an inexpensive red. He grows lavender, the crop that embodies the spirit of Provence. He has a few fruit trees. He stopped growing tomatoes because prices were too low. He asks that I not use his name, since truffle hunters try not to make themselves known to revenue-collectors. Taxes and truffles don't mix. At least his truffle-hunting dog, Rita, is wildly pleased to see me. "You need a lively dog, not shy, not tentative," he says.

As we walk out onto his property, he points to a hole in the ground that Rita did not dig and says, "Yesterday, somebody stole my truffles." I am surprised when he says he knows the identity of the poacher, a local man who has not been caught in the act. "He comes at night and does not keep it a secret," he says. "He makes a hundred thousand euros [about $120,000]. If we catch him, we will take off his clothes, tie him to a tree, and leave him for four or five days. We did this to somebody already. If he is naked, he has a harder time calling for help."

I nod appreciatively at the terror this punishment must impose. Secretly, I am thinking that I would consent to being tied naked to a tree for four days if I got $120,000, tax-free.

Truffles appear in mysterious ways. They are the phantoms of the plant kingdom. They thrive in and around the roots of oak trees, although the thirty-year-old oaks that the truffle hunter planted on his property to encourage the growth of truffles do not resemble the stately oaks of American woodlands. These are gnarled and misshapen. Druids might be living in them. Black truffles of exemplary quality once grew in profusion throughout the countryside of Périgord and Provence, but now this so-called wild production is mostly gone. Nobody has learned how to cultivate first-rate truffles, but planting oak trees on land where they once thrived somehow causes truffles to return within ten years.

The harvesting is still done by animals with an extraordinary sense of smell. Traditionally, this was the pig, but now it is a dog. "I have heard of a man near Nice who still uses a pig," says the truffle hunter, "but the problem with a pig is that I cannot imagine throwing a hundred-and-fifty-kilo [330-pound] pig in the back of your truck. It is very interesting, but I have never seen a pig hunt."

Rita, who is three years old and may weigh thirty pounds, is an underweight black-and-white mutt deliberately underfed to keep her enthusiastic about digging for truffles—not that she gets to eat them. Her reward is a crust of bread. Truffle hunters who have neither pigs nor dogs have been known to hunt by the rays of the sun. They look for a telltale glint off the wings of fleas or gnats that hover above the ground where truffles grow. The truffle hunter says a man hunting by the twinkle of fleas will uncover one-third the truffles of a dog like Rita. When she smells one, or the truffle hunter follows his instincts and tells her where to dig, she becomes a miniature steam shovel. When she gets to within an inch of the prize, she stops.

Rita and the truffle hunter seem to find truffles with ease, although none are of great size. The largest weighs about three ounces and will sell for $25 at the back door of the restaurant La Beaugraviere, out of sight of the taxman. I try telling the truffle hunter that he seems to be doing well. He picks up a few hundred dollars in an afternoon while strolling through the woods with his dog, an exercise I think of as digging for dollars. He says it is not poor people like him who become rich from truffles but the middlemen and the restaurants of Paris.

He tells me a story about a widow. (These sorts of unhappy tales invariably have widows in them.) A local woman discovered a truffle weighing almost three pounds, sold it to a local *négociant* for $350, and he immediately resold it for nearly $1,200. He says to me, "I cultivate them and I sell them to people like Mr. Jullien, who sells it to you to eat. Why should there be four or five other people . . ."— he pauses in mid-sentence to gather his dislike of middlemen—"who also eat off this truffle. You are not robbed when you go to Mr. Jullien."

La Beaugraviere resembles no other French restaurant I've ever seen. It seems to have been designed by a New Mexico architect specializing in pueblos who inexplicably found work in Provence. The walls are off-orange, the fireplace oversize and rustic, the tablecloths folksy, and the paintings garish interpretations of the black truffle. The menu has a picture of a truffle hunter and his pig on it. Even the truffle hunter has warned me to expect nothing from the decor. "It does not compete with the food," he says.

The dining room is reached by walking through the kitchen, where I see federally protected game birds awaiting the roasting pan. They have been brought in by some customers, who order a jeroboam (almost a gallon) of 1989 Beaucastel Châteauneuf-du-Pape. They are dressed in sweatshirts and jeans, and they have hung their waterproof jackets over the backs of their chairs. Clearly, it is not only the dining room decor that does not compete with the food.

The glory of La Beaugraviere is truffle overload. A meal prepared by Jullien is a throwback to a long-ago time when black truffles grew everywhere and farmers tossed them into their pots along with the onions and carrots. Sea scallops are cut in two and presented with a chunk of truffle between slices, chopped truffles over the top, and more chopped truffles in a Swiss chard puree underneath. Indeed, it is truffles three ways. Black-truffle risotto has me wild with anticipation, because I prefer it to the famous risotto made with white truffles, but the chef seems overwhelmed—his dining room is packed with customers determined to eat as many black truffles as they can as quickly as possible. The boardinghouse ambience does not lend itself to refined food preparation. The risotto is overcooked. Finally, he offers his pièce de résistance: under a puff-pastry crown is foie gras and a whole truffle the size of a golf ball.

Rhapsodies are written about such indulgences, for this is the culinary equivalent of a date with a nymphomaniac. Yet, I must admit, chewing a whole black truffle is like gnawing on a radish. It is more sinful than pleasurable, like looking up the skirt of a girl you don't really like.

"My father did not organize truffles the way I do today," says Michel Troisgros of La Maison Troisgros in Roanne, where our truffle party has encamped the next day. "He was very serious about truffles, very classic, and he cooked truffles for the sake of the truffles. With the breadmaker, he would cook a whole truffle in a loaf of bread. He did not want to play with associations the way I do today."

Michel recalls being at home, in the kitchen watching preparations for a family gathering, when Pierre Troisgros did something unimaginable to a truffle. "My father julienned the truffle, cut it in sticks like matches. It had better texture, more elegance, and even the taste was different. The same product cut differently had a different taste!" From then on, he became a student of truffles. He came to understand that sheer prodigality was not their best use. He discovered that the black truffle tasted best when combined with fat.

"For me," he says, "the best friend of the truffle is foie gras and also butter, the kind with rock salt inside." He also came up with a most unlikely combination from reading an old Italian cookbook that recommended pairing the white truffle of Alba with a fresh anchovy fillet. From that he devised what he says is his finest truffle creation—slivers of raw black truffles, salted anchovy fillet, and salted butter on a thin cracker.

To me, it sounds like extra-smelly snack food. When I taste it, I'm stunned. The anchovy is no longer acting as a member of the fish family; it has become truffle-helper. It supercharges the truffles. It is a detonation of truffle flavor. Had I eaten this creation wearing a blindfold, I do not believe I would have identified the presence of an anchovy.

His truffle dinner, which follows the hors d'oeuvres, is unsurpassed. He serves fava and cocoa beans with black truffles in a light broth made from chicken stock, lemon juice, and olive oil. It is perfect, even obvious, and I can't understand why it hasn't been done before until he tells me that every one of the beautiful cocoa beans, which are ivory white with maroon veins, has to be peeled by hand. The dish is both rustic and cerebral, intellectual fare for the farmhand. There are soft langoustines with leeks, julienned truffles, and strips of raw pear, as well as a variation on chicken Kiev, which is one of the warhorses of Continental cuisine. His interpretation has pigeon breast, foie gras, and truffles in a lightly breaded crust—thankfully, no butter squirts out. He has cheese enrobed in truffles, too, but my heart is still with Bruno's goat cheese, truffles, and olive oil. At my request, he gives us one of his father's legendary truffle dishes—potatoes, shallots, and truffles in a warm vinaigrette. I find the acidity overwhelming, and when I tell him this, he shrugs and says, "It's a classic. I didn't create it." So much for truffles the old-fashioned way.

On the wall of a municipal building in the village of Richerenches is a plaque from the national council of culinary arts certifying that truffle masses are celebrated here. That is correct: each year, on the third Sunday in January, the truffle is formally revered.

I have come on a Saturday, the day of the truffle market. The streets are packed with truffle buyers and truffle sellers. There is a pizza wagon, proof that plenty of tourists are around, too. Many of them are eagerly sampling truffle liqueur, which they will buy as presents for unappreciative aunts and uncles who will leave it unopened in closets for decades. After the fair, I accompany Hervé Poron, owner of Plantin truffles, to his warehouse, and I am fortunate to be there when one of his buyers (more correctly referred to as a broker) brings in a truckload of truffles, about four hundred pounds of them.

I ask him if his prominence in the business assures him of getting the best truffles in Provence, and he replies, "I'd like to believe that, but it often happens when you buy truffles that there are not enough of the best ones. They've been sold to restaurants."

He is exceedingly practical, not prone to poetic loquacity when the subject of truffles arises. I mention the romancing of the white truffle that takes place in Italy, how restaurant owners compete to purchase the largest white truffle each season for tens of thousands of dollars so they can be photographed next to it. "With black truffles, we do not do the pictures," he says.

At his home, he suggests we sit outside in the surprisingly warm January sunshine. We are surrounded by stone walls and gnarled vines, nosed by his friendly puppy, making our own truffle *bruschetta*. His wife has brought out a plate of toasted slices of baguette and a salad bowl filled with chopped black truffles drizzled with olive oil and sprinkled with course salt. I am reminded of tales I've heard of visitors to the palace of the Shah of Iran who were dazzled by heaping bowls of beluga caviar.

I realize I will never experience another aperitif moment to match this one. Never will I possess sufficient truffles, not unless I turn to crime. I wonder if I should drive back to the little wooded cove of the truffle hunter, get down on my hands and knees, and crawl around looking for fleas.

"So," I ask Poron, "is it true that the truffle poachers, the *braconniers*, are tied naked to trees if they are caught?"

He has never heard such nonsense. He says when poachers are caught on another man's land their cars are set on fire.

This does not bother me. I have a rental car.

I continue speculating. "Say the man walking the land that is not his happens to be a simple American tourist, perhaps even a hardworking journalist who has innocently returned to gather information. Would he not be released with a friendly kiss on both cheeks?"

He shrugs.

"Perhaps," he says, "but sometimes they make mistakes."

JANUARY 2004

Dinner consisted of fourteen courses, so nobody was going hungry. There were twelve of us dining together at Les Celebrities, the restaurant of Chef Christian Delouvrier. The meal was moving along nicely, so efficiently that I briefly regretted not having sufficient time to linger over the crispy duck braised in a ginger-scented sauce *gastrique*.

I had anticipated a clumsy outing—all those courses, so many people—but I looked at my watch and happily noted that we would be on our way home by eleven P.M. Then I heard something that chilled me, a word that has become as ominous to me as a dark muttering from the pages of Poe. Over the years, all of us have come to dread certain restaurant announcements: "Does anyone here know the Heimlich maneuver?" Or, "Sorry, sir, your credit card has been confiscated." None, to me, is as unwelcome as this one:

"Cheese?" the captain asked.

I recoiled. *Please, please, please!* I silently screamed. *Please don't ask for cheese.* Cheese was not part of the menu. Cheese was not required after foie gras with figs and foie gras with grapes and lobster with truffle oil and sweet-water prawns with white truffles and codfish wrapped in prosciutto and roe deer from Scotland and, well, I think I've made my point. Unfortunately, Les Celebrities has a cheese trolley of which it is understandably proud, one with twenty-six varieties of well-ripened cheese, and I feared that somebody would say yes. Somebody did. The squeak of the wheels as the trolley approached the table was like a gurney coming for my remains.

Don't get me wrong. I love cheese, in particular the melting creaminess of the elusive French Vacherin and the teeth-rattling pungency of the dreadnought Epoisses. I serve cheese in my home, and I order cheese unfailingly whenever I'm dining in France.

I even consider myself something of a cheese expert, one of the best. Maybe I should amend that to: one of the best domestically. I am probably familiar with half the cheeses served at Les Celebrities, which would put me in the top 1 percent of all Americans. In France, I would be a disgrace. Say what you will about the French, they know their cheese. That's why the cheese trolley works in French restaurants. It comes to the table and diners absentmindedly point to the three or four they want without missing a beat in their conversation.

The cheese trolley, however, is a dining ritual that has no place in the American restaurant, where it is currently making terrifying inroads. The introduction of a cheese course to a dinner causes it to stretch on until it feels like detention hall.

The problem is not the cheese but the people eating it. While cheese is one of the staples of the American diet—according to the *New York Times*, 80 percent of all main dishes served in the United States include cheese in one form or another—Americans know nothing about the cheese course. Explaining cheese to them is like explaining baseball to a Frenchman. I used to consider a literary reading the worst form of torment, but now I believe it's sitting around a table, listening to Americans order cheese.

The captain's offer of cheese was accepted by one of the women at our table. And so the agony commenced. She settled back for a long cheese discussion. He patiently indulged her. Now, this woman knows food—she's a well-regarded *New York Times* food writer—but you'd have thought she'd never experienced cheese in any form but grilled. She pointed to the cheeses and asked for an explanation of *every single one*. Then she picked out seven or eight, and as the captain served them, she asked him to repeat his description of *every single one*.

After that, the trolley rolled on, and the cheese discourse began anew. It would have taken more than an hour for everyone who wanted cheese to get cheese, but I didn't remain to find out. I pleaded illness—*mal de fromage*—and fled.

I returned to Les Celebrities a few days later to implore chef and management to become the first important New York restaurant to disavow cheese. Chef Delouvrier not only rejected my plea for dining sanity, he said his cheese trolley would increase in size. He said on his last trip back to his native France, in every restaurant where he ate, "we see they are selling cheese to Americans like crazy."

I felt broken. I felt helpless. Fortunately, it didn't affect my appetite. I again had the duck in sauce *gastrique*. My wife had pigeon accompanied by the best vegetable I've ever tasted: *brunoise* of vegetables braised with a whole black truffle, mixed with bacon and served with foie gras on top. Now that's what I call vegetarian food.

I was feeling wonderful. And then the cheese tray screeched to a halt in front of us. I frantically waved it away, but my wife insisted. She made her selections, which squandered fourteen minutes. I got my cheese quickly because I remembered what the captain had said to her and didn't ask him to repeat everything. I don't like to brag, but I appear to be the only American who can do that.

The cheeses were magnificent, especially the Fourme d'Ambert, a sweet-tart blue cheese I'd not tasted before; a beautifully balanced Epoisses still a few days away from insanity; and an impeccable Explorateur. Afterward, I was suitably ungrateful. I told the captain that if this had been a dinner for ten and everybody had required fourteen minutes to select cheese, we would not have begun eating them until two hours and twenty minutes had passed.

He thought that sounded wonderful.

"That way they would be very hungry," he said. "Imagine how much they would have enjoyed the cheese."

GQ, JUNE 1997

DAIRY QUEENS

When New Yorkers walk into Leo's Latticini, a tiny, provolone-scented food shop in the Corona section of Queens, they no longer act like New Yorkers.

Cops stand patiently in line, caps tipped back on their heads, gobbling samples of mozzarella. The moment they taste the freshly made cheese handed over the counter by Carmela Lamorgese, Irene DeBenedittis, or Marie DeBenedittis, the three women my wife nicknamed the Mozzarella Sisters back when we lived in nearby Forest Hills, they smile and cease looking at civilians suspiciously. The Miranda warning, their favorite poetry, stops echoing in their heads.

Firemen double-park hook-and-ladders out front on 104th Street and walk in wearing their funny rubber suits. They've come straight from a Queens emergency run, having saved a family of twelve immigrants trapped in a one-bedroom apartment that burned because of faulty wiring installed by a landlord who had illegally converted a one-family home into a miniature apartment building. Their harrowing rescue behind them, they grab a Mama's Special—an Italian sub made with fresh mozzarella—and begin eating even before they're out the door.

I'm not sure I understand what happens to customers who enter Leo's—or Mama's, as it's often called. Perhaps it's the cheese, softer and sweeter than mozzarella made anywhere else, but I believe an undeniable cause of the transformation is the exceptional kindness of the sisters and their mother. Leo's Latticini (*latticini* are dairy products) is a showcase of Old World virtues and familial affection. It is magical, the kind of shop travelers hope to stumble upon in some remote Italian village, yet it's only a half-hour from Manhattan on the number 7 subway line.

Whenever I'm under the influence of the Mozzarella Sisters, I possess no free will. I always drive there clearheaded and purposeful, my mission to purchase a few supplemental groceries for the household—a pound or so of mozzarella, a jar of meaty olives from Cerignola, a liter of olive oil from Puglia, a bit of *scamorza* (a mozzarella-like cheese perfect for melting), a tub of roasted peppers marinated in garlic and olive oil, maybe a container of ravioli in Marie's fragrant tomato sauce. (It's the only pasta dish I know that's sublime when reheated the next day.)

What actually occurs on these visits is that Irene takes over and demands that I eat a complete lunch. I do so in about two minutes, while I am waiting for my purchases to be bagged. She thrusts a fistful of mozzarella at me, followed by a small plate of Marie's extra-creamy chicken salad, and finally an ingot-size hunk of provolone cut from one of the 75-to-100-pound dirigibles from Calabria that hang from the ceiling.

Sometimes Irene forces me to stuff the provolone in my mouth before I've finished the chicken salad, but I'm comforted by the presence of so many police cars and fire engines encircling the premises. They're manned by public servants trained to provide emergency resuscitation to citizens who eat too fast. I find that requesting permission to chew my food properly is counterproductive, because then Irene gets angry and accuses me of not liking the food. "When we yell at the customers, it's because we treat them like family," she explains.

I always try to make it to Leo's on Thursday, the only day Marie makes her roast pork, and thus the only time all week that her sub stuffed with pork and fresh mozzarella, then lavished with gravy, is available. I am unable to look at a calendar and see Thursday approaching without trying to find a way to take the day off so I can drive to Queens. The outrageously savory pork seems to have hints of rosemary, but Marie refuses to divulge the recipe, and the gravy is of a sort that no longer exists, dark and salty and tasting of pork drippings, gravy from a long-ago time when gravies did not come from cans.

Although I occasionally become giddy with anticipation, awaiting the arrival of Thursdays, the other days of the week have their virtues (except for Sunday and Monday, when the shop is closed). Roast beef and Virginia ham are both once-a-week items. Mama's Special, the best sub in the city, is available daily. The roast turkey with gravy is on the menu every day as well, and I have to admit it is almost as profound as the roast pork. Wednesday isn't too bad, either, since that is meatball day. Marie's have the weight of puffs of clouds.

Marie is the greatest Italian-American cook of her generation I know. Her white-meat turkey is as juicy as most people's concept of pork, and her pork is as ethereal as most people's concept of heaven. The sandwiches come on semolina rolls so fresh I have begged the sisters to tell me where the bread is from, but they refuse. The fact that I can't get this information makes me suspect that it is from Brooklyn, better known for its bakeries than Queens. I don't mind that it comes from Brooklyn, if indeed it does, but I think the sisters worry that if it becomes known in the neighborhood that their bread isn't local, they will be looked upon as snobs.

The regulars—and it doesn't take long to be accepted as one—are all treated identically. The sisters' greetings are effusive, even if you're stopping in for the second time that week. Irene or Marie comes out from behind the counter for a hug, and the questions begin: "Where have you been?" is usually the first, as though you have betrayed their trust by staying away for three days. After that, the inquiries delve into essential family matters: "How's you wife?" "How's your mom and dad?" Next they check into the in-laws. I always regret not carrying medical charts with me.

Carmela is quieter, but I have always suspected the reason for this is because she wishes to appear composed in front of her daughter, who sometimes works in the store. Carmela's daughter is still known as Little Marie, even though she is fully grown and teaches second grade down the block at PS 16. Also in the shop every day is Nancy DeBene-dittis, the mother of the three sisters and the woman who inspired the nickname Mama's. Now in her eighties, she sits in her usual place, the single small table in the corner, where she slices open the long semolina rolls that are used for sandwiches or peels the garlic used in Marie's recipes. "Write good thing," she warned me, the last time I wandered into the store. I'm certain she didn't realize she was holding a paring knife at the time.

Many years ago, because of her presence, Leo's started to be called Nancy's by the customers. Then the girls were born and started running around the shop yelling "Mama, Mama!"—so the nickname changed. Nancy keeps an eye on her daughters at all times, determined to keep them serious. This is nearly impossible.

The sisters still laugh about the time they brought a delivery to the Food Network, then located in Midtown Manhattan. Irene, who is the most easily flustered sister, despite her previous profession as a first-grade teacher, recalls that she became disconcerted when they arrived with their bags of food. "We got out of this taxi, here's this tall building, I'm nervous, we're late, I'm fighting with the taxi driver, there are all these men outside in jackets and ties. I said to Marie, 'How are we going to get all this food up to the thirty-first floor?' She said to me, 'Will you shut up! They have elevators. Do you want them to think we came from a farm?'"

In a way, they did. The first Leo's Latticini, in the Williamsburg section of Brooklyn, was started in the late 1920s by Irene and Frank Leo, immigrants from Bari, a city in southeastern Italy. Once in America, Frank got a job working for the railroad. After that, he opened a wholesale ice and coal business. When gas heaters and electric refrigerators put him out of business, he decided to start selling food. In the mid-1930s the family moved to Queens, which looked nothing like it does today. Now essentially a sprawling expanse of undersize dwellings with plastic awnings, fake-stone fronts, and microscopic yards, at that time "it was like country here, like a farm, there were so many trees," Nancy recalls. "For us, coming to Corona was like coming on vacation." And she adds, "We felt that here we could better ourselves."

Newcomers to America still find their way to Queens, although the borough today is composed not so much of immigrants from Europe as from everywhere in the world. People from more than a hundred nations live there, and Corona has as colorful a history as any place in America. To TV addicts, it is famous as the habitat of Archie Bunker, the rascally racist from *All in the Family*. To jazz aficionados, Corona is celebrated as the home of the musician Louis Armstrong, who lived in a brick fortress of a house from 1943 until his death in 1971. (Legend has it that Armstrong's fourth wife bought the house without his seeing it, and when he walked in he left his suitcases in the car, telling the driver to wait, he probably wasn't going to stay.) To art collectors, Corona is remembered as the storied headquarters of the Tiffany glass company. When Louis Comfort Tiffany decided to make glass in America even more beautiful than what he saw in France, he picked Corona as the spot to do it.

The place Frank and Irene Leo opened in the 1930s was about half the size of the current store, which itself isn't very large, merely a few strides from end to end. Back then Frank made his mozzarella in the basement. His work was continued by his son-in-law, Frank DeBenedittis, who was the husband of Nancy and father of the three sisters. DeBenedittis had started in the dairy business back in Italy, bringing a cow from door-to-door and milking it for customers. The sisters grew up in the store, none more profoundly than Marie, whose playpen sat squarely in the middle. Irene remembers her grandfather worrying that the twine holding the massive provolones that hung from the ceiling might not be strong enough and that one day his baby granddaughter would be crushed by a falling chunk of cheese.

These days Irene and Marie make the mozzarella in a back room, under a tiny photograph of their father lovingly placed in an ornate frame decorated with a tiny rose. It stands on a shelf over the vats. Carmela and her husband, Oronzo Lamorgese, are the owners of Leo's Ravioli, the pasta store next door to Leo's Latticini. With every member of the family involved in the business, Nancy says with regret that she feels her daughters are wasting their education. Irene has her master's degree, Carmela her bachelor's, and Marie is only a few credits short of graduating college. Says Nancy, "I feel very guilty. Irene had a good teaching job and made good money, and now she's here in the store." That's something of an understatement. The family is not only in the store during the day, they live above it at night—the Lamorgese family over the pasta store and the DeBenedittis family over the cheese store.

Leo's Latticini has become celebrated in recent years, at least locally. The shop supplies the food for both the home- and visiting-team clubhouses at nearby Shea Stadium, and this has brought about a change in decor. Although still cowcentric, Leo's also pays homage to the home team: during baseball season, the sisters often wear New York Mets jerseys while they work. Last season they opened a small sandwich shop in the stadium and named it Mama's of Corona. During games they sell Mama's Specials, turkey subs, and Marie's new vegetarian sub— fresh mozzarella and three kinds of roasted vegetables on a warm roll.

All manner of governmental agencies, not just the police and fire departments, are drawn to Leo's. Over the years it has evolved into an unofficial cafeteria for civil servants. Occasional customers include the United States Secret Service Countersniper Unit—proof, I'd say, that Marie's food rests easy on the stomach—as well as space-shuttle technicians from NASA, who have been known to carry subs back to Florida with them.

Al Roker, the famed TV weatherman, sent a limousine to collect a sub, and the driver firmly instructed Marie to pile on more garlic than belonged on a single sandwich. When she didn't hear a word from Roker, she stopped sleeping well. She was about to telephone him and apologize for overdoing the garlic when an autographed picture arrived.

The sisters even had a brush with glamour when Kenar, a clothing company, heard about the shop and brought in model Linda Evangelista for a fashion shoot. The whole family posed with Evangelista for an advertisement that ran in the *New York Times* and now hangs on the wall of the shop. They were delighted when a customer came into the

Ten Reasons Why White Wine Is Better than Red Wine

1. White wine does not stain clothing, which is important to those of us who dine with enthusiasm.

2. White wine does not cause debilitating headaches, whereas red wine contains chemicals identical to those hidden from United Nations inspectors.

3. White wine includes Champagne.

4. No decanting required. Watching sommeliers light candles and stare at red wine sediment is like attending a bad seance.

5. White wine goes with cheese the way red wine only wishes it did.

6. Making white wine keeps the Germans distracted.

7. Ever notice that the winos hanging around vacant lots strewn with broken bottles and dead cats are always drinking red wine?

8. Sure, red wine lowers cholesterol, but is that any way to decide on a beverage?

9. Bad red wine is always worse than bad white wine.

10. Red wine drinkers talk constantly about *terroir* and barnyard aromas. They're best brought to their senses by throwing a glass of cold white wine in their faces.

WINE

NOSE JOB

My feet hurt, my shoulders ached, and my neck was as stiff as my wing-tip collar. Even worse, my pockets were empty.

A few hours into the first of my two evenings working as a sommelier at Maurice, the acclaimed restaurant at the Hotel Parker-Meridien in Manhattan, I had learned quite a bit about the duties of the professional wine steward, including how physically tiring it is to be unerringly polite. I had also learned why there are so few sommeliers left in America—only about sixty at last count. The rest probably starved to death, penniless and gnawing on corks.

The real wine steward at Maurice is Roger Dagorn, thirty-nine, a native of France, a past president of the Sommelier Society of America, and the father of three children he must never see, considering the hours he works. Dagorn is one of the best wine stewards in the country. He'd have to be to allow me in his dining room. I've never worked in the food-service industry, and as for my mastery of the art of serving fine wine, I only know to pour larger amounts in my glass than in those of my friends.

To most people, sommeliers are dour men with slicked-back hair and patent-leather shoes. At one time, this was a fairly accurate appraisal, although almost all the wine stewards I've encountered recently have been reasonable and unintimidating fellows. (These days, it's the salesmen in good wine shops that I find haughty and patronizing.) Unlike wine stewards of old—men as leathery as a tannic Cabernet—Dagorn is more like young Champagne: bright, effervescent, and correct with every course. Dressed in the classic black-and-burgundy sommelier's suit (with an apron to hold pen, pad, corkscrew, napkin, and more), he is a comfortably approachable figure. Unlike me—and most professional wine stewards I know—he does not worry about tips. "You have to remember that the customer has to think of the waiter, the captain, and the maître d' before he thinks of the sommelier," Dagorn said. "You wonder if he should even bother."

A wine steward at one of Boston's most famous restaurants once told me he felt he deserved a 10 percent tip on every bottle he sold, and other wine stewards have confirmed this figure. They suggest that the customer break down the check, tipping the waiter and the captain for the food and the wine steward for the wine. (When paying by credit card, this would necessitate inking in a separate line on the receipt.) The wine steward from Boston is now out of the business, which suggests that things rarely worked out to his satisfaction.

When I signed on with Dagorn for my two-night stint, I charitably informed him that I would pass on to him the hundreds of dollars in tips I expected to receive for the thousands of dollars' worth of wine I expected to sell. He didn't seem concerned. He was more worried about my inexperience in dealing with customers, and he gave me a crash course in service that included placement of wine lists and ice buckets in strategic parts of the room, opening the wine correctly ("Turn the corkscrew, not the bottle") and proper presentation of the cork ("I don't see any purpose in smelling it; I've had too many bad corks when the wine was superb"). I remember a story told by the ex–wine steward from Boston of a customer who sent back a perfectly sound bottle of Montrachet after smelling the cork. The man, who was showing off for his friends, had sniffed the wrong end.

As the gate separating the restaurant from the hotel lobby slid up at five-thirty on a Wednesday evening, I was as ready as I could be in my rented tuxedo. Around my neck hung a *taste-vin*, the small silver tasting cup that has come to signify the office of the sommelier. In truth, I felt self-conscious and overly accessorized, like the Reverend Al Sharpton out for a night on the town. I fervently hoped that nobody would order

Champagne, for I imagined the cork exploding out of my hands, leaving a trail of lawsuits as it ricocheted off the heads of customers. And, I prayed, let nobody speak French. I understand little, and my vocabulary is limited to *omelette au fromage*.

So there I stood, as perfectly trained as Dagorn could get me in a few hours.

"Hands out of your pockets," he said.

"Button your coat," he said.

At the first table I served, I leaned over too far while presenting the bottle, and my *taste-vin* banged against it, clanging like a cowbell. Dagorn understood. "It happens to me, too," he said. "It's not so bad. It lets them know you're there." My second table consisted of a group of Californians ordering French wine for the first time and wishing to share the experience with me. They requested the 1981 Château L'Angelus, a St.-Emilion, and asked how it differed from the Cabernet Sauvignons they were used to drinking back home. All St.-Emilions are blends, usually with Merlot dominating and the rest Cabernet Franc and Cabernet Sauvignon. Ordinarily, I love to talk that Merlot talk.

I froze. I nervously started to speak at length about the Pomerol grape. (There is no such thing, although there is a Pomerol region in Bordeaux.) Fortunately, they didn't know enough about French wine to realize how idiotic I sounded. Following my discourse on Bordeaux, the Californians ordered their second bottle—a Robert Mondavi Cabernet Sauvignon. They did not leave a tip.

At 8:10 P.M., I broke my first cork while extracting it from the bottle. That wasn't as bad as what I did next. When I started to pour, tiny bits of cork floated into *madame*'s glass. Resisting the impulse to plunge my pinkie into her wine and scoop out the debris, I ran for Dagorn. He said I should have taken the glass away and brought another. As we hurried back, we saw that *madame* had already plunged her pinkie in and removed the cork. (No tip.)

I then served a gentleman who insisted on testing me to see if I could correctly pronounce "Montrachet." Meanwhile, Dagorn took charge of a party of Japanese tourists. I pronounced Montrachet impeccably—

both *t*'s are silent. My inquisitor was impressed, but not enough to leave a tip. The Japanese left $11 for Dagorn. We could not figure out how they had arrived at such an odd amount, but Dagorn was pleased. The Japanese may be inscrutable, but at least they reward a hardworking wine steward.

Dagorn pointed to a table of three men who looked like the cast of *Cheers* out for a boisterous, free-spending evening. Hoping to improve my self-esteem, he sent me their way. "There's your first tip," he predicted. They ordered mineral water. "To expect tips is to leave yourself open to disappointment," Dagorn said.

By ten P.M., I was hungry and starting to dislike all the privileged people eating the wonderful food denied to me. I had dined, if you could call it that, with the rest of the staff in the in-house cafeteria before starting work. We'd eaten Salisbury steak and gravy, not chef Christian Delouvrier's medallions of veal with juniper sauce. Out of the kitchen came a fragrant chocolate soufflé; once pierced, it filled the room with the bouquet of dark chocolate. "Not so good for the wine," Dagorn mumbled. Even worse for my morale, I thought. I cheered up when Dagorn told me that leftovers were served to the staff after the restaurant closed. Since the wine steward is usually finished before the waiters and captains, he gets first crack at the food. I had rack of lamb.

My second night started with the Champagne challenge. I was terrified, but the Mumm's Cordon Rouge opened with an ethereal "poof." I poured the way I had seen Dagorn do it: I placed the thumb of my right hand in the punt (the indentation in the bottle's bottom) and cradled the bottle with the fingers of that hand. By pouring this way, a technique that requires the lower-arm strength of a power-lifter and the hand-eye coordination of a fighter pilot, I managed to dribble wine down the side of the host's glass. (No tip, and none deserved.)

Dagorn advised me that in such cases, when sheer ineptitude prevails, the only recourse is a joke. I tried this the next time I crumbled a cork into fine powder. I told the astonished customers that my performance was the theater that went with their pre-theater menu. They chuckled (but did not tip).

An Englishman was seated at one of my tables. The English are per-haps the most predictable wine drinkers in the world. "He'll order the Château Talbot," whispered a captain. He did. "He'll say it's too cold," whispered Dagorn. He did. After tasting the wine, the Englishman said to me, "This is a fourth growth, isn't it?" I replied in a deferential tone, "I believe so, sir." Actually, I had no idea. I would rather memorize the periodic table of elements than the 1855 Bordeaux classifications. I pressed on, obsequiously adding, "And I believe it deserves a much higher rating." He replied, "Indeed."

I was certain my first tip would be forthcoming. It was not. He was probably saving his money to buy a third growth.

A likable fellow from the Southwest started asking so many per-sonal questions I decided to confess that I was a wine writer, not a wine steward. He was amused. A guest at his table, a rude young man of the sort who flourishes when the stock market is going up, decided I should be the beneficiary of his bad manners. He had already whined to the maître d' that none of the waiters or captains would go to the lobby and make telephone calls to arrange his personal transportation. As I walked around the table pouring wine, he grabbed my *taste-vin* and yanked hard on it, saying, "What's this, buddy, an ashtray?" I was reminded of Harrison Ford in *Witness,* living among the gentle Amish but unable to resist smashing the face of a bully. I pictured a staff of grateful waiters carrying me from the restaurant on their shoulders after I had performed a similar act of retaliation. I did nothing.

"Patience," said Dagorn, who saw everything, including my finger-ing the knife blade on my corkscrew.

Soon afterward, I got my only tip. A woman ordered a glass of white wine, and she so enjoyed it that her husband asked what it was. I scrib-bled "Trimbach Pinot Gris" on a slip of paper, and he pressed two one-dollar bills into my hand. I was exceedingly proud. While I am not quite ready to give up my day job as a writer, I have on many occasions been paid far less per word.

GQ, MARCH 1989

GREAT EXPECTORATIONS

A comprehensive new wine book, *The New Frank Schoonmaker Encyclopedia of Wine*, contains a surprising omission between the entries for *spiritueux* (French for "spirits") and *spitzen* (German for "peak"). The missing word is *spitting* (English for "not getting drunk at wine tastings").

I attribute the exclusion of this topic not to error but to modesty, because the man who recently revised the encyclopedia, Alexis Bespaloff, is without question the greatest wine spitter in America today. Because he is humble by nature, he is loath to agree. "I'm not a spit-meister," Bespaloff protests. "I'm just a wine taster, and spitting is a method of self-preservation. If you don't spit, you'll be pickled before lunchtime."

I am of a different opinion, for I recognize greatness. Bespaloff may not be quite the equal of the venerable John Smithes of Portugal, who is described by Ben Howkins of the port firm of Taylor Fladgate as a man who can "hit the ear of a dog at twenty paces," but he is a national treasure. Being rated the greatest domestic spitter is nothing to purse one's lips at.

Spitting is a mandatory activity practiced by oenophiles, yet it is seldom given its due. Christian Moueix, the co-owner of Château Petrus, says, "Sometimes I must tell people tasting my wine that it is all right to spit. They are not comfortable. They think the wine is too good or too expensive." The word *spitting* has odious connotations—other than wine tasting, I cannot think of a single activity associated with it that one should do in the company of friends. It also requires certain skills that have never received the attention they deserve. Those who excel at it, like Olympic kayaking champions, are seldom rewarded. Yet, as Howkins points out, "If people have never seen great spitting before, it's quite an impressive thing."

Bespaloff claims to possess merely "an ability to spit out of my mouth and not get any on my shoes," but he is being unduly self-deprecating. I watched him not long ago at a Bordeaux tasting, and I thought he performed with uncommon grace, a veritable Baryshnikov around the spit bucket.

When tasting, he first aerated the wine in his glass with three or four economical flicks of the wrist, then he threw back his head and drained about a half-inch of the liquid. There was none of the ostentation of the novice, no gurgling or hissing or obvious intake of air. With closed mouth, he appeared to chew. He paused, scribbled a few notes, chewed another dozen or so times, reflected briefly, then spit.

Around him, tasters were hunched over buckets in unseemly positions, allowing wine to dribble out of their mouth. Others were attempting to spit from significant distances but going about it so sloppily that the results were reminiscent of a bomb going off in a paint factory. When Bespaloff spit, out came a discreet stream that hit the bucket dead center, achieving what in rifle competition would be known as a tight shot group. When he saw me watching him, he stepped back and fired another masterful blast, this one from about three feet away. "I'm pretty accurate," he explained, "but I'm not what you'd call a great distance spitter. It's not like I stand ten feet back and spit in magnificent parabolas over people's heads."

Bespaloff says there was nothing in his upbringing or training to indicate that he would become a world-class spitter, but nobody in the wine world really knows what makes one person a maestro and another a mess. There are as many theories on spitting as there are wines to be spit. It is thought by some that a gap between the two front teeth is an anatomical advantage, but, Bespaloff points out, "If that were the secret, then Lauren Hutton would be the best." Mike Grgich, owner of Grgich

Hills Cellars in California, says all great spitters must be tall. He is five-six. Author Hugh Johnson attributes whatever small status he has achieved as a spitter to the trumpet lessons he took as a child. "A good embouchure, the lip muscles, contributes," he says. Louis Latour, the famed Burgundy vineyard owner and *négociant*, says the key to precision spitting is sobriety.

Alas, there are no definitive answers, even from Bespaloff. This is a gentleman with consummate knowledge of the wine business, a man with more than a quarter-century of experience as a wine writer, a professional taster who can identify the most obscure varietals from the most inaccessible regions, yet when I asked him for the secret of spitting, he claimed to know nothing he could pass on. "The secret is years of self-denial and low wages," he said, reverting to the standard excuse given by every wine writer to explain every shortcoming. Come to think of it, none of us is particularly well paid.

Bespaloff has more than 1.5 million copies of his books in print and is one of the largest-selling authors of wine books in the world. As his reputation as a wine writer grew, so too did his reputation as a wine spitter, although he never paid it much heed. There came a time about ten years ago when a small magazine acknowledged his preeminence by featuring him in an article on spitting. He showed it to his mother, pointing out the professional recognition that had come his way thanks to the top-notch university education she had provided her son. "She gave me a funny look," he says.

It is unfortunate that spitting is such a spurned science that even a mother cannot take pride in her son's accomplishments. Within the wine community, this is not the case, particularly in Portugal and Australia, where fine spitters achieve legendary status. Peter Cobb, a director of the Cockburn's firm in Portugal, says of the aforementioned Smithes, "He's around eighty now, hasn't got a tooth in his head, and still spits prodigious distances." Adds Bruce Guimaraens, the winemaker at Fonseca, "He's the best we've had in the past fifty years in the port trade. He can drown a fly on the wing at fifty feet." John Burnett, the managing director at Croft and the likely successor to Smithes as Portugal's top spitter, calls himself "probably one of the best living [spitters] today," but he concedes that he doesn't ring the spittoon with quite the same authority as Smithes.

In Australia, the hot spitters are Len Evans, a writer and wine producer, and Greg Clayfield, the winemaker at Lindemans. Clayfield, a good two decades younger than Bespaloff, bows to the American's experience and ranks himself as merely a first-rate regional spitter—"the best in the cooler climates of Australia." Interestingly, Clayfield predicts the day will come when the top spitter in the world will be a woman, which surprises me. Women tend to spit discreetly and world-class spitting requires presumptuousness. "I believe women can be more accurate spitters than men if they work at it," Clayfield says, "but they are incredibly bad novices."

Eunice Fried, an experienced wine writer, concedes that men are superior spitters, but she blames it on upbringing, not on physical limitations. "The problem is that girls were brought up to be young ladies and young ladies never spit. I wrote back in the mid-seventies that women should start practicing to catch up." The British wine writer . Jancis Robinson, a Master of Wine, says, "I've seen quite a few ace spitters and they've all been male. That's because men are more into sports and ace spitting is a sport. It's speed and accuracy and power. All we women want to do is not make disgusting exhibitions of ourselves. We do it neatly. We are not so competitive."

Distance alone does not make one a great spitter. I would never speak ill of the late Alexis Lichine, one of the major figures in the wine community, but in truth his presence was feared in tasting rooms. The wine writer Anthony Dias Blue recalls Lichine spitting "a laser-thin stream six feet into a bucket," but others remember a man of considerably less accuracy. Bespaloff, otherwise a great admirer of Lichine's, tells of attending a stand-up tasting with Lichine and Peter Sichel, a vineyard owner and wine importer. "Peter was telling us proudly about his new slacks. A moment later, Lichine leaned over without looking and spit red wine toward the bucket. The stream went over the top and hit Peter in the pants." Thomas Matthews of *The Wine Spectator* says the spitter he most fears is Edmund Penning-Rowsell, the dean of British wine writers. "He's long but insouciant," says Matthews. "He takes a sip and if there is a spit bucket in the vicinity, there it goes. At a tasting, he's a menace. There's a huge circle around him of empty space and stained carpet."

Not all spitting stories are sad sagas of soggy socks and soiled shoes. Jean-Louis Brillet, a producer of Cognac, says the most precise spitter he has seen is the legendary French oenologist Emile Peynaud but he adds, "The greatest thing is that we see Mr. Peynaud take in very large quantities of wine and spit out very small quantities. Where is the rest?" The famous Italian winemaker Piero Antinori says that as a child he was in awe of his family firm's seventy-five-year-old oenologist, who would taste and spit with a lit cigarette in his mouth. Jean-Michel Cazes of Château Lynch-Bages in Bordeaux has seen an equally wondrous sight: "My grandfather and [Bordeaux wine-merchant] Emmanuel Cruse had the same technique. They would sit there, tasting and spitting with pipes in their mouths."

Alan Stillman, a Manhattan restaurateur, recalls that nearly twenty years ago he and his wife stopped for a picnic in Burgundy just outside the fence surrounding the vineyards of the famed Domaine de la Romanee-Conti. "A man wandered up. We didn't know it then, but he was the cellarmaster of DRC, and we were sitting on DRC property. I introduced myself, offered him a glass of red wine. He took a mouthful and must have spit it thirty feet. He said, sneering, 'Bordeaux!'" Michael Aaron, the owner of the Sherry-Lehmann wine shop in Manhattan, was working in Bordeaux in 1959 when he attended a wine tasting at Château Cos d'Estournel and observed the spitting equivalent of a rear-end collision. Taster number one learned over the spit bucket at the precise moment that taster number two swung toward the same bucket. Number one was a balding fellow, and number two's stream hit him precisely on the crown, causing him to take offense. "They had to be separated. There was almost a fistfight," Aaron says.

Bespaloff recalls that it was 1963 when he spit in a wine cellar for the very first time. He was tasting Beaujolais and, he says, "I understood that it was all right to spit on the ground in a cellar, but to avoid embarrassment, I tasted a little more slowly than the proprietor. When he spit, I spit." Since then, Bespaloff has grown in stature and prowess to become an icon of this arcane art, a virtual spitting savant, yet he still reacts uneasily when his greatness is recognized.

"I modestly lower my head," he says.

Is it modesty? Or is he checking to see if he got any on his shoes?

GQ, MARCH 1990

$25,000 WINE WEEK: A TALE OF EXCESS

I have friends who regularly travel to Europe on wine-drinking pilgrim-ages, excursions into decadence that leave me gasping with envy. After hearing their stories, I find myself imagining I'm one of them. I see myself picking up a wine list at a magnificent restaurant such as Monaco's Le Louis XV and ordering a *grand cru* white Burgundy with a rim as golden as the Limoges china—there I am, leaning back and gazing upward, as the bouquet of my perfumed Corton-Charlemagne soars toward the nymphs and angels gamboling on the twenty-five-foot ceiling.

This past January, I gathered up my courage and my bankroll and announced that I would be joining them on their upcoming trip to France and Monaco. The itinerary included La Beaugraviere in Provence, a restaurant that is unstarred in the Michelin guide but has an enthu-siastic following among wine drinkers, as well as four of the most esteemed establishments in Europe, all with three-star Michelin rat-ings: Le Louis XV; Troisgros, in Roanne; Paul Bocuse, outside Lyons; and Guy Savoy, in Paris.

My fantasy was not just to accompany these wine connoisseurs but to be one of them. It was not long into the trip, at the distressingly appointed La Beaugraviere, which looks as though it was transported intact from Guadalajara, that I learned how deluded I was. We were sitting around, gulping complimentary hors d'oeuvres and perusing wine lists, a predinner ritual of ours, when I spotted a treasure, an old-vines Châteauneuf-du-Pape from a fabulous vintage. I couldn't wait to tell them about it. I was certain they would carry me to the dinner table on their shoulders. I gulped my gougere and tried to get their attention.

The man I'll call Sommelier No. 1 was asking the man I'll call Wine Merchant No. 1, in a wine-weary sort of way, "Do you like Clape's wines?" Auguste Clape is a renowned producer of Cornas. To the group of connoisseurs I was with, Cornas is just a simple, heat-soaked Syrah of little consequence.

Excitedly, I interrupted. "Look, the 1989 Domaine de la Janesse Vielles Vigne, only a hundred twenty dollars."

Nobody looked up. The merchant turned to the sommelier and replied, "I find them rustic, never really appealing."

I was beginning to understand my place. I was a noncollector, a nobody. The sounds I made were as insignificant as those of a small forest animal rustling the underbrush. That evening we did not quaff my wonderful wine discovery. It did not rate consideration. I was among my betters, as far as selecting wine was concerned.

After nearly a week of frustrating meals with these men, I still call them my friends, which demonstrates my forgiving nature. Our dinners typically lasted five hours, including the time we spent studying wine lists while sipping glasses of simple, $100-per-bottle Chablis. On the single occasion when one of my friends knocked over a glass, the sort of accident one might expect when men drink long into the night, the person soaked from neck to waist was me. I told these men I would protect their identities, describe them only by their professions or hobbies, and it was Wine Collector No. 1 who marinated my Giorgio Armani Collezioni shirt ($175, on sale) in 1990 Beaucastel Hommage à Jacques Perrin Châteauneuf-du-Pape ($710, in magnum).

I can only demonstrate so much journalistic integrity: Thanks a lot, Alan Belzer.

The group included two wine directors from top New York restaurants, two principals in one of Manhattan's most prestigious wine shops, and two wine collectors. Five of the six characterize themselves as bargain hunters. The sixth, Wine Merchant No. 2, says he refuses to spend excessively but is mostly interested in finding once-in-a-lifetime rarities. To them, seeking out well-priced wines means paying less for a bottle on a list in France than they would pay for it in a shop in America. For the most part, that meant drinking cult wines from Coche-Dury (white Burgundies), Henri Jayer (red Burgundies), Guigal (single-vineyard Côte-Rotie) and, to a lesser extent, Jaboulet (Hermitage).

They also admire the unrivaled wine service they encounter in France, because it encompasses discreet attention, appropriate glassware, and formidable knowledge. I anticipated exquisite service, even though we were American tourists, and for the most part we received it. French restaurant owners, like all restaurateurs, are very polite to customers who spend $3,000 to $4,000 each night on wine. I've always believed that rational persons should not consume magnificent wines in high-priced restaurants, because of excessive markups, which only proves that I've spent too much time dining in New York. At Alain Ducasse's Le Louis XV, the 1992 Coche-Dury Corton-Charlemagne, a mineral-laced bombshell of a white, cost $400. Wine Merchant No. 2 said, "Anytime you see Coche for four hundred dollars, you should drink it for breakfast, lunch, and dinner. This bottle is about a thousand dollars below the retail price in New York."

At Troisgros, we paid $825 for 1990 Jayer Cros Parantoux, a stunning (although youthful) red Burgundy. I had recently seen it on the list of a reasonably priced restaurant in New York for $3,750. None of these men, no matter what they already had in their cellars at home, was able to resist a bargain, much as a woman with a dozen pair of $800 Manolo Blahnik shoes in her closet at home cannot stop herself when she sees another pair on sale for $400. To them, Henri Jayer is the Manolo Blahnik of wine.

Almost every wine we ordered came from a memorable vintage, although we did have a 1991 Comte de Vogue Musigny ($620, in magnum) at Le Louis XV because my friends knew the estate had produced a long, sweet, beautifully colored Burgundy in that difficult year. They know years the way rabbis know the Ten Commandments, the way Roman Catholic priests know the Stations of the Cross. They know when hail fell in the Côte de Nuits (most famously in 1983) and when labor shortages caused difficulties with the harvest in Germany (most infamously in 1945). On impulse, we sent a glass of the 1991 Musigny to a man dining alone, and he sent back a charming note wishing us luck and thanking us for making him feel a part of such a fortunate group. "Doing something like that makes me feel like a god," said Wine Merchant No. 2, an unintentionally perceptive remark, because wine collectors often see themselves that way.

Their weakness where wine is concerned is a disinclination to experiment. At Le Louis XV, I spotted a bottle of 1982 Cotnari Grasa Selection de Grains Nobles in the La Moldavie section of the list. It was a sweet wine none of us had ever heard of, and for all we knew, 1982 was as great a year in Moldavia as it was in Bordeaux. I could not have resisted the call of an authentic Marxist-Leninist wine produced in Romania during the dictatorship of Nicolae Ceausescu, but my friends refused to try it. Wine Collector No. 2 said, "We seek out opportunities we will remember for the rest of our lives. We are not here to rough it."

Only once did they drink a wine of my choosing, and that was because I arrived before they did at Guy Savoy—they took taxis, I rode the Metro. I selected a 2000 Ostertag Pinot Gris, overpriced at $140, but I feared these connoisseurs would have sneered at something less expensive. The sommelier agreed to serve it blind.

They guessed the grape. I never said they weren't good.

Wine collectors are not like stamp collectors. They are not passive or diffident, and they do not hoard. They are aggressively social, and their labels are their calling cards. They arrive accompanied by Baron Rothschild of Bordeaux and Rene Dauvissat of Chablis. They do not serve their wines; they trumpet them. When a half-dozen wine collectors of equal stature get together, not one will entirely agree with another man's choice. They want to drink what they like. They are type A–plus, one and all, correctly perceiving themselves as winners in the wine world.

The three words you will never hear one wine collector say to another are these: "You know best."

My friends frequently argued over who was getting to pick the wines and who was being ignored, but these discussions always took place at lunch, when the wine was not too serious—a modest vertical of young, $200 J.L. Chave Hermitages, for example. Dinners were amiable. No matter how much wine was consumed, the men became more mellow the more they drank, as though the wines passed along their harmonious qualities.

Wine collectors are seldom, if ever, aware of their shortcomings, because they are rarely pointed out. They always assume they will be admired wherever they go, and the fact that they arrive with their wines makes it so. They are certain their ability to drink well and converse articulately about what is in their glasses makes them desirable companions. So self-assured are they that they believe people in less fortunate wine circumstances are pleased to have them around. Generally speaking, they are correct.

I have sat spellbound, listening to their tales of excess. A few years back the two merchants and the two collectors lunched at Alain Chapel and noticed a 1929 DRC Romanee-Conti on the list, although without a price. They inquired and thought they heard the sommelier say 14,000 francs (just over $2,000). When the bill came, the price was 40,000 francs. Even after paying just under $7,000, they reveled in their good luck. The wine was that wonderful. It is probably unnecessary to add that these gentlemen are willing to spend fortunes on wine but nothing on French lessons.

So it was on this trip when the connoisseur of rarities saw a 1929 Jaboulet Hermitage La Chapelle on the list at La Beaugraviere for $1,300. By reputation, this is a wine of majesty, produced in a region beloved by Thomas Jefferson and the Russian imperial court. The owner of La Beaugraviere announced that it was the last of a full case of twelve bottles that had been topped off and recorked at the winery in the 1990s. Knowing something is the last of anything makes my friends want it all the more.

A bottle that old is not a guarantee of pleasure but a venture into high-stakes poker. If it is as magnificent as the 1929 Romanee-Conti consumed at Alain Chapel, the experience can be existential. If not, it is merely expensive.

Sommelier No. 2 accepted the responsibility of tasting the '29 Hermitage.

Merchant No. 1 whispered to me, "I wouldn't order it, because I don't want to take the responsibility."

Sommelier No. 1 disagreed. "It's worth having so we don't regret not having it for the rest of our lives."

The cork came out, perhaps too easily. The wine burbled into the glass. The designated taster sniffed, then breathed deeply. I looked at his face and did not see rapture. I saw $1,300 worth of perplexity. I saw costly indecision. He chewed. He stared. The table hushed. He spoke the three words I would soon learn to loathe.

He said, "Tastes like wine."

I felt as though I had opened the door to greet my mail-order bride and the best I could utter was, "Well, it's a woman." (Did I mention the testosterone level of wine collectors?)

He tasted again and added, "Wine's been cooped up a long time. A slight Madeira and chocolate to it."

To that I'd add tea. We had a $1,300 bottle of Lipton's. La Beaugraviere's owner tasted and pronounced it fine, one of the best bottles from the case. Added La Beaugraviere's sommelier, "Very good." I felt these were not disinterested opinions.

We drank it in silence, and silence is a bad thing at dinner, particularly the silence of despair.

In the course of our trip, we sent back just one bottle, a 1989 La Mouline from Guigal that was indisputably corked. We accepted many that I would have sent back had I any influence with my friends. Their attitude seemed to be that if it was still recognizable as wine, we were obligated to pay for it. Their most charitable act, in my opinion, was accepting a 1967 Beaucastel Châteauneuf-du-Pape that cost $380 at La Beaugraviere.

It came to the table with such a low fill that I immediately would have said *non*, had I spoken French. As the bottle was being opened, the glass collar that holds the cork, in essence the entire top, snapped off. To me, this constitutes defective goods, since I'm the kind of picky fellow who doesn't like drinking beverages containing shards of glass. The wine was accepted and it was surprisingly good, with a lovely, complex nose and fast-fading, dark berry flavors, more Burgundian than Rhône-like. Nevertheless, drinking it gave me the willies.

The worst bottle we accepted was at Paul Bocuse, the gaudy shrine to the most famous chef in the world. For sentimental reasons, Sommelier No. 1 wanted to have 1976 Guigal La Mouline ($770). He told us he was working as a waiter in 1983 when he bought this wine in a shop for $30. It convinced him that he wanted to spend the rest of his life in the wine business.

Although the wine was still full of fruit, it was also cloudy and murky, so dark and ugly that it could be studied only by somebody wearing a miner's hat. The Paul Bocuse sommelier insisted it had been stored impeccably. We decided the only way it could have looked the way it did was if the waiter assigned to bring it up from the cellar had tripped on the steps and shaken up the sediment. I found it entirely without pleasure and left almost all of my share in the glass.

If the finest white wine (and possibly the best value) of the trip was the '92 Coche-Dury Corton-Charlemagne at Le Louis XV, the two best red wines came from the cellars of Troisgros, a restaurant of unparalleled finesse. Unrivaled was the 1971 Romanee-Saint Vivant Marey-Monge ($700), a profoundly rich, impeccably aged Burgundy with a hint of pleasing gaminess. The moment I tasted, I blurted, "This is it." Almost as impressive was the 1985 La Turque ($820). The release of this celebrated wine in the late eighties incited a stampede among collectors, but since then it has been largely ignored. I tried it young and thought it was good. This bottle was magnificent. It had hints of smoke and licorice, and the structure was unusually elegant for a Rhône.

.   .   .

Finally, my time came. Weary of my complaints, my friends announced that I could select all the wines at Guy Savoy, a small, austere establishment down the street from the Arc de Triomphe. I went to the restaurant early. I grabbed a wine list. A kindly captain served me slivers of foie gras while I made my choices. My budget was $3,000.

By now I knew what everybody liked, and I was certain I could come through. The Ostertag Pinot Gris served blind to begin the meal was just a tease. I planned to follow it with 1995 Gagnard Batard-Montrachet in magnum, several 1985 Domaine de Montile Pommards and a magnum of 1985 Dujac Clos de la Roche. If they wanted to go for the jackpot, I would suggest 1947 Gaunoux Pommard Rugiens ($1,470).

I announced my selections, and praise came showering down upon me. I was declared a man of perception, taste, and thoughtfulness.

Then they picked up their wine lists, chatted with the sommelier and overrode everything. They didn't order a single bottle I wanted. When I requested an explanation, Wine Collector No. 2 said, "I have to say we didn't find the wines we really wanted until the professionals got here. By "the professionals," he primarily meant himself.

Later, I asked the group what I had done wrong. One friend told me I hadn't spoken loudly or authoritatively enough. Another said I had lost confidence in my own selections. I was about to protest, but then I remembered something.

It would do me no good to complain. Wine collectors never admit they're wrong.

Food & Wine, JULY 2003

GRATUITY

"PLEASE, PLEASE, MORE!" GASPED SHARON STONE

She canceled three times while she was in California, offering explanations a gentleman would have to accept: the rescheduling of a movie opening, a debilitating case of food poisoning, the tragic death of a friend. When she came to New York, she had ingenious new excuses for not dining with me. I always lied and said I understood.

What I was never certain of during the long months of eager invitations from me and effortless cancellations by her was whether Sharon Stone was acting like a woman or like a movie star. I have dined with both, and neither satisfies my fantasy of an ideal table companion. Dining with stars tends to be rushed, simplistic, and humorless, although Oprah Winfrey was a magnificent exception during her chubby, all-you-can-eat years. Friends reporting to me from the Coast suggested that Stone was another glorious anomaly. They said she appeared to possess the two most precious dining attributes, curiosity and capacity. In other words, she was a woman who knew how to eat like a man.

When it comes to dining with women, I have become skeptical. I simply don't bounce back from those experiences the way I used to. Once I was wonderfully resilient, but these days I question the fundamental concept of men and women going to a restaurant together. I even wonder where it all began, when the dinner table became the preferred venue for men and women to get better acquainted. It is now one of the burdens that men bear.

I have been dining with women for well over a quarter-century, and I feel as exhausted as a war-weary veteran approaching retirement. I understand that younger men, those about the age of the Bordeaux I enjoy, might feel otherwise, that they still look upon a meal as the setting for a seduction, but I am beyond such expectations. All I desire after a long, languid dinner is a long, languid night's sleep.

Young men, for the most part, are blessed. They can look forward to the companionship of callow, indulgent females who have not yet metamorphosed into dinner-table dominatrices. All the women I know start snarling instructions the moment they are seated: Don't touch the rolls! Hands off the butter! (My wife is so irrationally against bread that I now think of her as the Anticrust.) They glare when men order foie gras, the health food of southwest France, and they believe a creamy mille-feuille followed by a plate of petits fours is the same as having two desserts. They fail to understand that the tiny cookies and candies served after a four-course meal are not an indulgence but a tasty transition between the richness of the dinner experience and the emptiness of the long journey home.

For men, food is a well-earned indulgence. For women, it inspires ambivalence. They sit down with the general presumption that the best meal has the least food. Men are gastronomically guided by an inner glutton, but women almost never feel comfortable enough about themselves to eat what they desire. It's a miracle they ingest enough to survive. Ultimately, most women become perverse portion-control technicians who look upon delicious food as the enemy of health. They resent men who refuse to join in their obsession.

I believed Sharon Stone would be different somehow, more like a man, but as the months and then the seasons passed and still our dinner date failed to materialize, I felt increasingly hopeless. Her evasive tactics suggested she cared little for food, yet my sources in California reported seeing her in restaurants all the time. What concerned me was whether I had tried too hard, made myself too available. As a movie star, she would expect anyone like me, a meek supplicant, to have total disregard for his own needs and make myself eternally available.

However, this is precisely the wrong way to treat women, who respond to excessive tolerance with disdain.

Finally, after months of waiting, I got the call. Battle stations. This was not a drill.

Her person was on the line. I picked up the phone. Dinner was imminent, I was informed. "What is the cuisine?" her person asked.

(A note of clarification here: At no time in the course of any of the calls and cancellations did I speak with Stone herself. Throughout the negotiations, she relied on subordinates—seconds, if you will—to speak for her. I tried looking at this in a positive manner, imagining it a form of Old World formality. Instead of an arranged marriage, we were to have an arranged meal.)

I told her person I had selected the Manhattan restaurant March, a fine and thoughtful establishment. The chef, Wayne Nish, approaches the dining experience with restrained originality. I wanted the food to be correct enough that she would not think me careless, but creative enough that she would have little opportunity to be bored.

The cuisine, I said, was "eclectic."

"How should she dress?" her person asked stiffly.

"Appropriately," I replied formally. I realized we were assuming the roles of characters on *Masterpiece Theatre*.

I was astounded how in control I felt. For the briefest moment, I was a partner, not just a pawn, in the life of Sharon Stone. I was her future companion, not the social equivalent of the guy who drives the catering truck to the set.

That phase of our relationship ended immediately. Her person told me that Stone would be available for dinner from eight P.M. until ten P.M. With that pronouncement, I felt the star had ducked back into her darkened limousine, leaving me gaping on the sidewalk. How like a woman, I thought, to insist on ending an evening at the very hour when civilized persons are ordering port.

She was allotting me two hours. What are two hours at a dinner table with a woman? A gathering of men could eat a great deal in such a meager allotment of time, but women do not believe in relentless consumption. Women waste minutes fussing over the fat content of dishes. They spend enormous amounts of time doing whatever it is that women do when they leave their seats and disappear in the direction of the restrooms.

I asked Nish if he could feed us satisfactorily in such a brief period. He said he had envisioned a tasting menu of seven courses and seven wines and could get the food to us in the specified time. He explained that he, too, had endured the heartbreak of dining with women.

He told me this story: Many years ago, he and his ex-wife-to-be set out to eat the meal of their lives. They had saved for it. He ordered a stellar Bordeaux, one so expensive he was certain they could never have it again. When the captain took their order, she requested scallops, a disastrous pairing with a Cabernet Sauvignon–based wine. Horrified, Nish asked her what she planned to do about the Bordeaux, the wine they had waited so long to enjoy together. She replied, "Oh, you go ahead and have the wine."

Yes, Nish understood.

Sharon Stone arrived almost on time. She was escorted from her black limousine to the foyer of the restaurant by a bulky but cordial gentleman who waited by her side until I came forward and acknowledged receipt of the valuable property. I felt as though I were being handed classified documents.

I told Stone how nice she looked. She smiled genially but did not reciprocate. She looked much as I thought she would, only better. She wore a black crêpe Vera Wang cocktail dress, and I was flattered, since Vera Wang is what everybody is wearing to the right places with the right people these days. Hers was low cut, but modest. She wore no jewelry. She needed none.

The maître d' seated us at a corner table tucked away in the back. Stone stirred her Bollinger Champagne with a spoon to dissipate the bubbles, a French custom she must have picked up at some banquet in Paris, while telling me of the sacrifice she had made in order to be with me. She was supposed to have gone to a reading, but she had canceled. I was tempted to make a little joke, ask if it wasn't a little late in her career to have to read for a part. I kept my mouth shut.

She asked me about the restaurant. I told her it was underappreciated, and she replied, "I know the feeling." She told me one of the difficulties she encounters whenever she dines out: "I go to the ladies' room, everybody goes." She was perfect—understated, self-deprecating, endearing. When a woman that beautiful is that well mannered, it's hard not to appreciate her. I reminded myself that she had yet to show any interest in food.

Our first course, the *amuse-gueule,* consisted of twin beggar's purses, which are tiny crêpes filled with pricey ingredients, gathered up and tied at the top like little sacks. One contained caviar and sour cream, the other lobster and black truffles. Her admiration for Nish's lobster-truffle creation was precisely the sort of restrained admiration I admire in a food critic. "I have to say, 'great,'" she said.

Her evaluation of our second dish, a carpaccio of lobster, essentially raw lobster, was harsh. She found it "a little sad, droopy." This was accurate enough but a bit unfair, inasmuch as virtually any dead fish will droop. The entire world of sashimi sags, for that matter.

The third course transfixed her, and Stone enraptured is a welcome sight. She liked (and I loved) the jumbo lump crabmeat with corn juice and black truffles, the juice accenting the sweetness of the crab, the truffles its faint earthiness. Yet it was her enthusiasm for the wine that made her irresistible.

The wine director of March, Joseph Scalice, had paired the crab with Château de Beaucastel white Châteauneuf-du-Pape, not the ordinary bottling but the rare 100 percent Rousanne from old vines. After sipping, she changed from a remote figure into an eager, open, giving, vulnerable one. This is what wine is supposed to do to a woman, but I'm saddened by how infrequently the transformation takes place. I believe this is because women now understand the power of alcohol and struggle against it.

She gazed at the nectar—let's assume a wine with no apparent resid-
ual sugar qualifies as nectar. Her eyes appeared unfocused, apparently
in pleasure. She was looking at this beverage the way a woman is supposed to look at the man treating her to dinner. Still, I was pleased. She
said, "The wine reminds me of the gowns of Catherine the Great—
gold with traces of pink." I rocked backward, staggered by an arche-
typal example of earth-twentieth-century winespeak. This woman was
truly a gifted wine amateur.

She leaned toward me, and Sharon Stone leaning forward, drawing
you into whatever drama is being played out in her mind, is a positive
dining experience. "Please, please, more meals, if only we have wine like
this," she gasped. "I have sex stories. I'll tell you everyone in Hollywood
I slept with. Please, more. I'll be a gourmet tramp."

Alas, I took her at her word.

I told her I wished to be discreet, not prurient. I only wanted to learn
the motivation for her affairs, not the intimate details of them. I had
been cautious throughout the first hour of our meal, saying nothing
about her choices of roles (bad) or men (worse). I posed this question:
Why would a woman like her, the most fascinating movie star I'd dined
with since cooking for Claudette Colbert in her hotel suite some years
ago (nice name-drop, wouldn't you agree?), consort with the kind of
men any sensible woman would shoot on sight?

"What do you mean?" she asked, leaning away, the Roussanne-
induced twinkling of vulnerability gone.

"Dweezil Zappa," I replied, equally cold.

She crossed her arms. "Dweezil," she said, "was my friend for many
years. And then he made enormous pleas to date me, and then I went
out with him three times after knowing him for four years. And then
he went on television and said he was dating me. I was disappointed
by his lack of decorum and integrity, and therefore he is not in my
life."

She stared.

Was I so wrong to have asked? Doesn't everybody want to know why

Sharon Stone is dating Dweezil Zappa? Doesn't everybody want to know why anybody dates Dweezil Zappa?

"I'd like to point something out to you," she said.

I waited. It was that or flee.

"You dated the wrong people, too. We both fucked up."

I nodded slightly, conceding the point. Everyone makes mistakes. I attempted a rebuttal. I explained to her that were we to stand side by side, most people would select her as the individual more likely to meet a congenial partner.

"Where do I go to meet people?" she said. "The 7-Eleven? The mall? A club? I can't go to those places to meet people. I can't meet people at work. That's considered bad taste. And everybody who meets me has a preconceived notion of me. So if it's not a friend, I start off on the wrong tangent."

As the courses progressed, we seemed to recover from our little contretemps. At least that's what I thought. I reacted sincerely and sympathetically when she described her life as "little, a small life." I managed to elicit a chuckle when she asked me to explain the physics of a shooting star and I replied, "It's about friction. You understand friction, don't you?"

She ate every bite of every dish except the wild-mushroom ravioli, which incorporated calves' brain as a binder. Like all women, she has an infallible knack for detecting the presence of invisible ingredients capable of triggering culinary apprehensions. She said to me, "Have you ever noticed that at every long dinner, the fifth course, the one before the meat and potatoes, is the icky-poo-poo course." I could only agree.

She was polite. I was mannerly. The meal ended well. More important, I had come to understand her palate, which is about all a man can hope to understand about a woman. When she departed, handed back over to that bulky, decidedly undroopy gentleman, I felt there was every likelihood that we would dine together again.

I didn't know when or where it would be, but I prepared for the eventuality by purchasing all the wines she admired. An old friend in the

New York retail wine business coerced two bottles of Beaucastel Rousanne out of the distributor—that amounts to about 3 percent of the entire allocation of this wine to the New York market. Because she had taken pleasure in the 1991 Diamond Creek Cabernet Sauvignon that accompanied our rack of lamb, I obtained a magnum of the 1986 vintage from a shop in Missouri. I also had them throw in a few vintages of Chapoutier's Ermitage de l'Oree in case she wanted to taste a white Rhône even lusher than the Beaucastel.

These wines, which I have come to call the Sharon Stone Collection, remain untouched. I never saw her again.

I had thought, naïvely, that the Dweezil Zappa query had not been a fatal error. We had moved to a higher conversational plane, talking physics and all that. I had forgotten that women rarely remember what has been eaten but always recall what has been said.

I never spoke to her person again. Her person and the editor-in-chief of *GQ* magazine, who is not my person, spoke on the telephone. This is his re-creation of that conversation:

"How did it go?" he asked.

Long silence.

"He was asking a lot of questions," her person finally relied.

"About what?" he asked.

"Dweezil Zappa."

Shortly afterward, the editor-in-chief called me into his office to get my side of the story. I admitted using the Z word.

To this day, I do not know where I went so wrong. Sure, I asked about Zappa, but he's hardly the bottom of the barrel where her relationships are concerned. In another interview a few years ago, she happily talked about dating Dwight Yoakam. I find it almost impossible to differentiate between those two emaciated musicians, although I suppose Zappa's unemployable and Yoakam's unendurable. It's not as if I had exposed the single blemish in an otherwise model dating life.

I did, in fact, hear from her again. She sent me a charming little note thanking me for "the food, the wine and your odd perspective on my naive dating patterns."

It's a shame about women. They always say that dinner isn't about food, it's about conversation. I gave her conversation. They claim it isn't about wine, it's about relationships. I discussed little but relationships. My meal with Sharon Stone proved what I've always known. No matter how hard a man tries, meals with women don't work out.

GQ, FEBRUARY 1999

Acknowledgments

Like Costco, I do business in bulk. I have people to thank going back to Mrs. Decker, my fifth-grade teacher at Aronimink Elementary School. That includes the kids from class 7J2 at Upper Darby Junior High School, even if they were cool enough to get into Dick Clark's *American Bandstand* and I was not. When you assemble a collection of stories that covers as wide a topic as these, a lot of people come to mind.

I appreciate the sacrifice of everybody who ever went out to eat with me when I was reviewing a restaurant. I know it wasn't fun. I am indebted to every chef who ever cooked food I wrote about, because I know they didn't get into their line of work thinking I was going to walk into their place of business and criticize them. I owe much to photographers, designers, and the guys who work the linotype machines. (Even if these stories don't go back that far, I do.)

Few writers are willing to acknowledge a terrible truth: writing requires editing. Marty Beiser babied most of the stories in this book when he was managing editor of *GQ*. What I cherish about Marty, in addition to our yearly dinners at Fabio Picchi's Cibrèo in Florence, is that he always did just enough. Before him, my editor was Eliot Kaplan, and working with them were three copy chiefs who personally toiled over my words. They are Maura Fritz, Nancy Negovetich, and the particularly long-suffering Laura Vitale. I owe her so many dinners I don't know when I'll finish paying off.

Everything trickles down, and I am indebted to the editors in chief who have valued my work, especially Dana Cowin, Barbara Fairchild, Jim Nelson, and Tom Wallace. I add to the list one CEO, Dorothy Cann Hamilton. In quite another category are the editors who have put up with me mostly out of friendship: Pam (The Genius) Kaufman, Mary Ellen Ward, and the incredibly patient Michael Hainey, who is my confidant, therapist, and provider. He owes me so many meals I don't know when he'll finish paying off.

Time now to drop a few names. I have been enriched by associations with Oprah Winfrey, Robert M. Parker Jr., Daniel Boulud, and Jean-Georges Vongerichten. In this category I also put Eric Ripert, who telephones regularly to tell me I should have a more positive attitude, like a Frenchman.

Providing comfort after calls like his were two Condé Nast assistants who behaved more like my mother: Katherine Kane and Courtney Kemp. I also leaned on Paul Forrester and Tim Sultan, responsible for thousands of corrections to my copy, and to the legendary Baronness Sheri De Borchgrave, researcher extraordinaire. No woman has ever been better at telling a man he's wrong.

Always present in my life is Julian Niccolini of the Four Seasons, although in truth I've always preferred his partners, Alex von Bidder and Trideep Bose. Though Maguy Le Coze insists I loved her late brother, Gilbert, more than her, I adore the woman who taught me to appreciate sea urchins. Is it possible to thank entire restaurants? The staffs of the Four Seasons and Le Bernardin have always been astoundingly kind. To that category I add Montrachet, plus its wine director, Daniel Johnnes, who will hunt me down if I don't single him out.

Knowing restaurateurs Drew Nieporent, Costas Spiliadis, Tony May, Gennaro Picone, Tommaso Verdillo, Danny Meyer, Sirio Macchione, Alan Stillman, and the entire DeBenedittis family of Corona have done wonders for my life and my work. In special categories all their own are John Cuneo, for immortalizing me in cartoons, and Nina Griscom, once my television partner. When people remind me of our Food Network show, they always ask about her.

I have friends everywhere, which comes from being a wandering journalist. Glen and Marshall Simpkins in Boston bring peace of mind, while Alison Arnett has been both a colleague in criticism and an unfailing pal. I'll always be grateful to Bob Phelps, who taught me how to talk about writing, a great gift. In Philly, I've been close to Ray Didinger and Maria Gallagher forever, and to Dan and Barbara Rottenberg longer. My Canadian connections are Mike Boone in Montreal, Bob and Nancy Dunn out west, living proof that you don't have to see people to remain close. In Los Angeles, Merril Shindler remains my restaurant guru, while Ron and Flori Wormser astonish me with their unselfishness. As a non-fiction writer I try to avoid novelists, but I've made an exception for the bard of Cleveland, Michael Jaffe.

Never failing me, no matter how often I forget to call, are Alexis Bespaloff and Cecelia Lewis. Unsurpassed in understanding are Gerri Hirshey and Mark Zwonitzer. Terribly missed is Steve DePietro; I was planning to hang out with him in my old age. Writers are supposed to avoid enduring relationships with public-relations people, but I've failed now and then, most profoundly with Margaret Stern, Ruth Hirshey, Karen Murphy, Pam Hunter, Melanie Young, Sally Fischer, and the man who cut the ribbon at Ratner's, Joe Goldstein.

Just plain best-of-friends, and often showing up in pairs, are Kathy Levy and Michael Pecht; Robyn and Peter Travers; Willie Norkin; Susan Squire; Suzanne Ausnit and John Salak; Victoria and Stephen Worth.

Thank you, Ed and Pat Teague, the perfect in-laws. They even praise my cooking, which shows how great in-laws can be. I'm only a little envious that my sister, Lynn, inherited our mother's skill at the stove, and that she lavishes her talents on my brother-in-law, Dick Adelman. I have yet to thank my mother and father, Ida and Norman, because I don't exactly know how to do justice to them. My father didn't live to see this book, and my mother won't understand what it is when I show it to her, but my love for them has diminished not a whit. Their nobility in old age taught me as much as their guidance when I was young.

My wine buddies have played a considerable role in my life. I bow to the generosity of Fred Shaw, Robert Groblewski, Glenn Vogt, Alan Belzer, and Jeff Joseph. Although Belzer and Joseph have both traveled long and far with me, even Belzer must admit that nobody surpasses

Joseph as the man to have along when you have to eat a lot. His wife, Pat Jones, is nearly the perfect woman, and not only because she must live with her husband's culinary demands. Larger than life is Carl Doumani. In a category all his own is Park Smith, a magnificent wine collector and a magnificent man. I just wish we didn't always have to drink Châteauneuf-du-Pape.

Thank you, Amy Cooper, the most understanding woman alive. There is nobody like you.

I couldn't do anything without Jenny Ciardullo, who looks after Sophie, our corgi. And I could not have written anything had Sophie not been upstairs with me in the cathode-ray gloom of my office, looking on.

I am indebted to everyone behind this book, starting with Kathy Robbins, my agent; and her deputy, David Halpern, whose soothing calls were of immeasurable help. My thanks to Susan Weinberg, the publisher of HarperCollins; Susan Friedland, my buddy at HarperCollins; and Michael Solomon, for his day-to-day sanity and editorial acumen.

And now we come to David Hirshey, the man behind this book and, perhaps, my career. He was the first person to tell me that I was born to be a food writer. Inasmuch as I was trying to be a news columnist at the time, I didn't take it well.

Always, Dave was there for me, although he was never with me. My phone would ring and it would be him, calling from Michael's restaurant in Manhattan, where he'd be having lunch with a bestselling author. Me, he'd urge to work harder. "Just give me an hour," he'd say, before demanding revisions that kept me up for a week. Without David Hirshey, this book wouldn't exist. I might not even exist, at least in my present form. Thank you, Dave. Some things mean even more to me than a meal.